————◦•◦————

In memory of my father, Sam,
who died too soon at ninety-one,
who stood on a soapbox at age fifteen
and railed against oppression,
who gave me my career
as well as my ideals.

————◦•◦————

FREE

★★★★★★★ FOR *★★★★★★★*

ALL

DEFENDING LIBERTY
IN AMERICA TODAY

W ★ E ★ N ★ D ★ Y
KAMINER

BEACON PRESS   BOSTON

Beacon Press
25 Beacon Street
Boston, Massachusetts
02108-2892
www.beacon.org

Beacon Press books are published under the auspices of
the Unitarian Universalist Association of Congregations.

Printed in the United States of America

05 04 03 02   5 4 3 2

This book is printed on acid-free paper that meets the uncoated paper
ANSI/NISO specifications for permanence as revised in 1992.

Text design by George Restrepo

Library of Congress Cataloging-in-Publication Data

Kaminer, Wendy.
Free for all : defending liberty in America today / Wendy Kaminer.
p. cm.
ISBN 0-8070-4411-3 (pbk. : alk. paper)
1. Civil rights—United States. I. Title.
KF4750.K36 2002
323'.0973—dc21   2002006200

CONTENTS

8.

9.

10.

INTRODUCTION

Love of liberty is supposed to come naturally to Americans. It's supposed to be transmitted through our culture—like love of shopping; it's supposed to be instilled in us in childhood. When I was in grade school, we started our days by singing to our "sweet land of liberty" and pledging allegiance to the flag that stands for liberty, and justice, for all. We learned about the American Revolution, the Declaration of Independence, and the Emancipation Proclamation. A child of the Cold War, I felt lucky to be an American, because, unlike "Red" Chinese or Soviet children, I was free.

I'm still pleased to be an American and still feel relatively free, but I've discovered freedom's fragility; I've learned much of what I wasn't taught in grade school. While I was saluting liberty, African Americans were systematically denied the right to vote (or eat at "white" lunch counters); McCarthyism raged and the House Un-American Activities Committee was persecuting people who held unpopular political views or were associated with unpopular organizations. Our lessons in America's love of liberty were incomplete; we weren't told that Americans sometimes loathed liberty, or feared it, and fell prey to the temptations of political repression. Our lessons in liberty were also self-defeating: When you force children to salute the flag and recite the "Pledge of Allegiance" you don't teach them to exercise freedom so much as you accustom them to the imposition of political orthodoxies.

America's disloyalty to liberty is disheartening but predictable. Liberty leashes power and, right and left, people who find themselves in possession of power tend to resist restraints upon its use. Cynics don't care if they abuse power to advance their own interests; people who take pride in their own virtue generally manage to convince themselves that they exercise power virtuously (even when they exercise it harshly) to serve the public good. Powerful people convinced of their own goodness are as dangerous to individual liberty as powerful people for whom goodness is irrelevant.

So concern for liberty often has a disproportionate relationship to proximity to power. The more protected you feel by your own power or the power of your friends, the less threatened you imagine your own rights. But if you're concerned about the rights of other people, including those you disdain or whose views you abhor, you're apt to be wary of power, even when you or your friends possess it.

You're likely to put less faith in power as a means of forging a just society and more faith in fairness.

Of course, many people claim to value fairness over power, but in practice, few of us do. Few people are willing to extend the same rights to their enemies that they extend to their friends; indeed, you can usually rely on people across the political spectrum to use whatever power they possess to defeat their enemies, partly by denying them rights; most would probably consider it politically naive to do otherwise. Liberals lambaste civil libertarians when they defend the rights of Skinheads or Klansmen. (In 1978, the ACLU lost considerable support for defending the right of a neo-Nazi group to march in a community of Holocaust survivors in Skokie, Illinois.) Conservatives attack the civil libertarian defense of religious minorities who are expected to adopt the majority's religious practices in public schools. (Insisting on their right to pray, proponents of official school prayer also insist upon the power to impose their prayers on others.) Liberals and conservatives alike favor restricting the rights of criminal suspects or members of religious sects denounced as cults. Liberals and conservatives alike will use their power to censor speech they consider dangerous or hateful, although they rarely admit that the restriction of pornography, racist speech, or violent entertainment is censorship; they're more likely to call it common sense.

Civil libertarianism is a nonpartisan virtue, just as repression is a nonpartisan vice. During the 1920s and 1950s, when the government conducted witch-hunts against the left, a commitment to political freedom was associated with liberalism. During the 1990s, when some left-wing college administrators promulgated repressive speech and sexual misconduct codes and, with little due process, prosecuted students for political incorrectness, conservatives laid claim to liberty's torch. Now, their commitment to liberty will be tested, on and off campus, by left-wing protests of the Bush Administration's military campaigns. I suspect that most conservatives will fail freedom's test, as liberals failed when they turned on sexist, racist, or otherwise "offensive" speech. It's worth noting that in the aftermath of September 11, students and professors of various political persuasions were disciplined for making statements for or against the war effort, and for allegedly offending or defending Muslims. Their liberty to speak depended on their conformity to views that prevailed on their campuses. Power trumped fairness, as usual.

What distinguishes a civil libertarian is a focus on preserving fair processes rather than obtaining particular results. A commitment to civil liberty simply requires fealty to the golden rule: extend the same rights to both your friends and foes—the rights you hope to enjoy yourself. This is, in part, a political strategy: Power shifts between your allies and opponents, often unpredictably. Your rights are most secure if they derive from established constitutional principles, not patronage. But the equal allocation of rights is also a moral imperative. I oppose censorship not simply because I fear that the power to censor might be turned against the speech I like but in the belief that people have a moral right to indulge in speech I hate. The right to view Nazi porn or tune in to Jerry Springer or Bill O'Reilly may seem ignoble compared to the right to read Montaigne, but it includes the individual's essential right to entertain moral preferences. Restrict it and you substitute the authority of the state for the individual conscience.

That, of course, is precisely the aim of censors who don't trust individuals to make moral choices or withstand the corrupting effect of "bad" speech to which they may be exposed inadvertently. This assumption that government knows best suggests that we're a nation of children (while the government is staffed by adults), and it's no coincidence that censorship campaigns often begin with the stated intent of protecting minors. Censorship in the name of child welfare usually garners popular support, although it treats child rearing as the collective responsibility of government officials and not individual parents. In any case, if individuals can't be trusted to choose "good" speech over bad (or "good" religions over "cults"), then neither can their government, which is, after all, composed of individuals, with all their vices; it's not as if being elected or appointed to office magically cleanses them of sin.

Civil libertarianism doesn't rely on assumptions about our moral character. The belief that we should all enjoy the same rights doesn't reflect faith in everyone's ability or inclination to exercise rights virtuously. Instead, it's based on a conviction that we don't have to earn inalienable rights or win them in a national popularity contest: Stupid, nasty people have the same right to vote as their intelligent, compassionate neighbors.

This belief in equality of rights is hardly controversial; at least it evokes rhetorical acclaim. But, for most of our history, equality has been greatly qualified by the usual forms of discrimination. Sex, race, ethnicity, religion, and sexual orientation (if not intelligence or kindliness) have all been used as criteria for distributing rights. Historically, Americans have had a "yes, but" belief in equality: We believe in equal rights, but only for people considered deserving, or capable, of exercising them. For over a century, women were denied the vote because they weren't trusted with it; for nearly two centuries they were legally excluded from male professions, because they were presumed incompetent to engage in them, or because female doctors or firefighters were considered unnatural, like female soldiers today. Sometimes, rights are denied in God's name. In the nineteenth century, the women's rights movement was apt to be considered ungodly. Today, some consider homosexuality a sin, and gay people are denied the right to marry because same-sex marriages are deemed unnatural, or a violation of God's plan. Interracial marriages were barred for similar reasons only thirty-five years ago.

Is the right to marry fundamental, like the right to pray or speak freely? What are the boundaries of our right to privacy? What rights should people enjoy when they're arrested? What rights should survive imprisonment? (The right to live freely in society may be forfeited when you commit a crime, but what about the right not to be raped in state custody?) Are we endowed with a fundamental right to end our lives? Does democracy depend upon the right to own a gun?

Civil libertarianism begins with a roster of inalienable human rights—like rights of speech, religion, privacy, and due process—which are often contested. Does the right to privacy include the right to obtain an abortion, use contraception, or marry the person or persons of your choice? Are violent video games protected forms of speech? Does the right to be free of "cruel and unusual punishment" preclude the death penalty or the torture of suspected terrorists? But reaching general consensus on a list of fundamental rights is only the prelude to battles that occur when rights conflict. Does the First Amendment right to conduct an aggressive protest outside an abortion clinic unduly interfere with women's privacy rights to obtain abortions?

Civil liberties often conflict with civil rights, as liberty inevitably conflicts with equality, dividing liberal and conservative libertarians. The 1964 Civil Rights Act that prohibited discrimination in public accommodation and transit systems (as well as in the workplace) subordinated the associational freedom of white supremacists to the equality rights of African Americans. The conflict between the freedom to discriminate and the right to equal treatment in public places was properly resolved about one hundred years too late, most Americans would probably agree. But it's worth noting that the conflict existed. Bigots have civil liberties, too. Today, while laws against official segregation are no longer controversial, workplace regulations aimed at benefiting women, racial minorities, or other historically disadvantaged groups, like disabled people, raise similar questions about balancing employers' liberties with employees' rights. Conservative libertarians generally value economic liberties, like the liberty to hire, fire, and promote without government intervention, over civil rights against discrimination.

The conflict over rights and freedoms in the workplace reflects the conflict for left-of-center libertarians between their attachment to liberty and their notions of justice. In the liberal view, an unregulated marketplace inevitably exploits the most powerless members of society and produces gross inequalities of wealth that effectively prevent many people from enjoying the rights to which they're entitled. In our society, your ability to exercise rights usually depends on your income: You have no practical right to obtain an abortion if you can't afford to pay for one and there are no free clinics within your reach. The extent of your due process rights is often determined by your ability to hire a lawyer. Conservative libertarians disagree about the effect of free markets, arguing that they would benefit everyone; but the history of maximum hour, minimum wage, child labor, and occupational safety laws shows that many businesses and industries treat workers decently only when they're legally required to do so.

I share liberal faith in a regulated marketplace (despite my opposition to particular regulations, like workplace speech codes intended to prevent harassment), but I regard the state as an occasional ally, never a friend. I'm wary of liberalism's anti-libertarian tendencies. Because liberals often depend upon government to fulfill their vision of social justice through welfare programs and antidiscrimination laws, they risk losing the mistrust of government that is essential to maintaining liberty. They risk becoming statists.

Of course, liberals are not alone in embracing statism. Virtually all of us rely on the state and want to dedicate it to our vision of the public good. Sometimes only the government can protect individuals from excesses of corporate power. Only the government can administer penal laws to protect individuals from each other. Only the government can conduct foreign policy and provide for the national defense, virtually everyone agrees. Liberals and conservatives have different visions of a just and virtuous state, but they all want to harness its power. Even practically pure libertarians might agree on a short list of essential governmental functions, although they always regard government suspiciously. (In their view, it's always a necessary evil, never an ally.) Only libertarians resist efforts to direct government power to moral reforms. Social conservatives want government to rid us of promiscuity, among other disputed vices; liberals expect the government to rid us of prejudice.

The temptation to restrict freedoms that are popularly linked with injustice or vice has always been strong. Often people fear the freedom of others as much as they desire their own. In fact, mistrust of liberty may be as hardy an American tradition as mistrust of big government. Left and right, people expect government to keep them safe, and to make their neighbors more virtuous.

State power has become particularly seductive after September 11; it promises more protection than liberty. Ask people to choose between freedom and security and almost all will choose security. Freedom depends on peace and some measure of order, after all. People in high-crime neighborhoods are not at liberty to walk the streets, civil libertarians are often reminded when they fight for the rights of criminal suspects. (Not all criminal suspects are criminals, they respond.) People in the Middle East, Israelis and Palestinians, are prisoners of violence, like Protestants and Catholics in Northern Ireland before their truce. So I don't champion liberty in the belief that it matters more than safety. But I believe it matters almost as much, and I'm skeptical when government officials tell me that sacrificing freedom will make me more secure. Left and right, most of them always want me to have less freedom just so they can have more power, regardless of security.

I shiver a little when I hear the familiar post–September 11 debate about balancing liberty and security. "Are freedom and security a zero-sum game?" people ask, and the answer is predetermined by the question. If politicians and law enforcement agents want us to surrender liberty reflexively, they have only to suggest that it lessens our security. They don't have to demonstrate precisely how the destruction of particular liberties will lessen particular threats—unless we ask a different question. Since September 11, it has been clear that freedom is apt to be protected best by a pragmatic focus on security. Thus, the first question to ask of a counter-terrorism proposal is "How will this make us safe?" It turns out, not coincidentally, that the laws and policies that are most effective in eroding our freedoms are often among the least effective in maintaining security, as the history of political repression in America points out. (Consider the internment of Japanese Americans during World War II.)

By destroying our sense of security, the September 11 attack greatly weakened our commitment to liberty. Among its secondary tragedies was the death of a nascent movement to reform the criminal justice system and curb law enforcement abuses; by the beginning of 2001, the public had begun paying attention to racial profiling, police brutality, and the likelihood of wrongful convictions (revealed partly by DNA testing). Support for capital punishment; long, mandatory minimum sentences; and the harsh, ineffective war on drugs was slowly beginning to decline. But if people were beginning to question the government's exercise of its prosecutorial powers on September 10, they stopped abruptly on September 11. Their abandonment of reform was inevitable. The more we fear overwhelming external threats, the more likely we will blindly trust the government. A few survivalists may retreat off-grid to wilderness cabins or fallout shelters stocked with gas masks, antibiotics, and a year's supply of Spam, but most of us prefer to continue our pre-9/11 lives and vest our survival in the wisdom and wiliness of government officials, notably the president. What else but the government, who else but the president, could protect us from terrorists?

George Bush's high approval ratings probably measure public fear of terrorism more than reasoned faith in his abilities. The irony in the post-9/11 embrace of big government, often dangerously overlooked, is that public trust in government rose just when government failed us most dramatically. The September 11 attack and our lack of preparedness for future attacks reflect colossal failures of intelligence, airport security, and attention to public health. Why are we so ill prepared for an anthrax attack or other acts of bioterrorism? Why are some nuclear power plants in abysmal condition? In mid-2002, why is it still relatively easy to smuggle weapons aboard an airplane? The first response of the administration and the public to September 11 was a law enforcement crackdown and a demand for new restrictions on liberty, although there was no evidence that the attacks resulted from too much liberty or too little law enforcement power. There was reason to believe that it was facilitated by law enforcement and intelligence blunders.

But for months criticism of government incompetence or negligence in protecting us was rare. At first, Congress made noises about investigating intelligence failures, but most of the noise and willingness to criticize the intelligence apparatus quickly dissipated. Even the appalling blunders of the Immigration and Naturalization Service—notably the issuance of visa approvals for two dead hijackers after the attack—did not evoke much second-guessing of the administration's capabilities. It was not until May 2002, when leaked CIA and FBI documents revealed that federal agents had some forewarning of the attack, that the administration was forced to defend its actions and inactions before September 11. Still, the initial round of questioning was quelled by predictable assaults on the patriotism of the question-ers and by a series of terrifying predictions of what Vice President Cheney called "near-certain" future attacks, probably involving weapons of mass destruction. (In June 2002 the administration changed tack; having been forced to acknowledge FBI and CIA blun-ders, the president proposed a bureaucratic reorganization and the establishment of a cabinet department for homeland defense. Con-gressional investigations into U.S. counter-terrorism efforts in the months and years preceding the attack have commenced, but who knows how vigorously they will be pursued or where they will lead?)

It's not surprising that doomsday warnings by the vice-president and other high-ranking officials initially succeeded in deflecting the critics who surfaced in the spring of 2002. Fear is a powerful distrac-tion. But it is instructive that while general faith in government and federal workers was declining, people seemed willing to continue supporting the president and his appointees, even as they advertised their impotence. With its warnings, the administration implicitly ac-knowledged that the assault on Afghanistan had accomplished little: Al Qaeda operatives were still chattering away, and future devastation was inevitable. The officials in charge of waging America's war on ter-rorism seemed resigned to losing it. But the public seemed too frightened to notice, and soon the administration was asserting its competence once again, publicizing the arrest of an American citizen allegedly associated with Al Qaeda and suspected of having an interest in detonating a dirty bomb in Washington, D.C. Americans will not readily lose trust in the Bush Administration's ability to protect them; it's difficult for people to admit that their leaders are failing when failure is too terrifying to contemplate.

But blind faith in government, or the executive branch, at least, is nearly as dangerous as terrorism: It facilitates domestic repression and a disinclination to question the administration's diplomatic and military strategies. This public passivity poses foreign as well as do-mestic dangers. The problem presented by a decades-old worldwide network of anonymous terrorists isn't simple. The administration isn't infallible and would likely benefit from the challenge of oppos-ing views. So, while John Ashcroft and others denounce criticism of the government as dangerous and treasonous, I suspect that a compliant public poses greater dangers than public engagement and dissent. Patriotism requires speech, not silence (or mere applause). I wouldn't call the failure to scrutinize the actions of government officials treason—a hanging offense—but it could someday prove fatal. Follow the government blindly and it will lead you into the sea.

AUTHOR'S NOTE

Civil liberties are always in jeopardy and always require attention. The essays in this collection discuss particular threats to due process, criminal justice, and freedom of speech, religion, and privacy that prevailed in the late 1990s through the beginning of 2002. They include critiques of anti-libertarianism on the right and left. Most of these essays appeared first in *The American Prospect*. All were updated in the spring of 2002 and with the exception of the last two essays ("Games Prosecutors Play" and "Taking Liberties") all were recast in the past rather than present tense.

Attentive readers will notice some recurrent references and themes, which I find unavoidable. Repeated abuses by the government demand repeated responses, and some initiatives, like the disastrous war on drugs, cannot be condemned too often. Besides, liberties are intertwined; pull one skein of freedom's fabric, and it eventually unravels.

1

HOMELAND OFFENSE, POST-9/11

PATRIOTIC DISSENT

I don't imagine that he welcomed it, but September 11 was not a bad day politically for George Bush. It marked his transformation from a relatively unpopular, arguably unelected, and widely unrespected president to a "leader" with practically unanimous support. Gone were Republican fears of a recession (that could not be blamed on a terrorist attack). Gone were the problems of a disappearing surplus, a shortage of funds for the military, or the need to raid social security. At least for the short term, Bush's overshadowing political vulnerability was gone. Suddenly, on September 12, he was no longer an acceptable punch line.

The mainstream press and entertainment industry—never paragons of courage—immediately stopped mocking George W. Instead, they praised his newfound "gravitas." It seemed that the frat boy had been "seasoned" by tragedy. Comedy Central had little choice but to cancel reruns of *That's My Bush,* the half-hour comedy that mocked the president as a helpless buffoon. Making fun of politicians is an exemplary American tradition (and one indication of political freedom). But to find anyone lampooning the president or his foreign policy after September 11, you had to read the comics—mainly Garry Trudeau's *Doonesbury* or Aaron McGruder's *Boondocks*—if you could find them in your local paper: several strips of *Boondocks* were pulled from newspapers after September 11.

It's not that Bush gave people new reasons to trust his judgment or abilities (other than the fact that he didn't nuke the Taliban or stumble badly through his speeches). Unlike former New York City mayor Rudolph Giuliani, he did not respond to the attack with instinctive fortitude and grace. It's just that Americans became too frightened to continue viewing the president as an inexperienced, shallow, spoiled man of average intelligence.

Public fear immunized the president from criticism, or even muted disapproval, as well as satire. White House press secretary Ari Fleischer famously lambasted *Politically Incorrect* host Bill Maher for criticizing U.S. military policy, ominously observing, "Americans need to watch what they say." (Maher, anxious to remain on the air, took his advice.) Massachusetts congressman Marty Meehan was assailed for questioning the administration's claim that on September 11, Air Force One had been targeted for attack. Later we learned that

A version of this piece appeared in The American Prospect, *November 5, 2001*

reports of a threat to Air Force One reflected "a misunderstanding." But that was probably small comfort to Tom Gutting, city editor of the *Texas City Sun*, who was fired for his September 22 column criticizing Bush's behavior on the eleventh. Dan Guthrie, a columnist for the *Oregon Daily Courier*, was also fired after he criticized the president for "hiding in a Nebraska hole" after the attacks.

The desperate belief in Bush's newfound wisdom naturally extended to a belief in the wisdom of his antiterrorism strategies. Dissenters were lucky to be patronized (*Newsweek* described antiwar protesters as "the Birkenstock and beads set"). They were more often threatened and demonized. In the *Washington Post*, Michael Kelly equated pacifism with pro-terrorism. Conservative columnist Andrew Sullivan warned about the formation of a Fifth Column on the "decadent left." *New Republic* editor Peter Beinart ruled, "Domestic political dissent is immoral without a prior statement of national solidarity."

Of course, everyone is entitled to express an opinion, however injudicious—everyone except for critics of the president and his policies, it seemed: "Criticism of our chief executive and those around him needs to be responsible and appropriate," newspaper columnist Dan Guthrie's publisher explained before firing him. "Labeling [Bush] and other top leaders as cowards as the United States tries to unite after its bloodiest terrorist attack ever isn't responsible or appropriate."

Responsible speech, in the prevailing post–September 11 view, did not include speech that questioned, much less mocked, the administration and unsettled the public by suggesting that the president's policies might not provide the best protection against terrorism. The denigration of dissent implied that we didn't need to entertain debates about the causes of terrorism or strategies for combating it, at home as well as abroad: In this complex and unpredictable war, which put the nation at unprecedented risk, we needed only to cheer on the president.

The taboo on dissent in the months following September 11 promoted a debased vision of patriotism as a promise to root for your team; it imagined the citizen as merely a fan. This undemocratic notion of citizenship has perennial appeal; it demands very little of us. We had only to obey and applaud the administration, wait patiently on airport security lines, and populate the malls. Our job was to shop, the president said in the fall of 2001; he also urged us to take vacations. Drowned out by all the cheerleading was the notion of patriotism as fidelity to the nation's democratic values and respect for the obligations of citizenship—a concern for public as well as private interests and a commitment to monitor and evaluate the actions of our government. Patriotism requires us to judge our leaders coolly and criticize or even satirize them freely.

This is not to suggest that we should automatically oppose the administration's military actions (which I supported in the fall of 2001, worriedly and skeptically) or that we should oppose all new domestic security measures, without question. But we shouldn't reflexively support them either. When the administration seeks to expand its power to spy on us, for example, it should be required to show how the loss of anonymity and freedom would gain us more security. Before September 11, for example, the FBI already enjoyed broad power to eavesdrop and intercepted some two million innocent telephone and Internet conversations every year (according to government reports). Indeed, while the administration successfully pressured Congress into greatly expanding the unilateral powers of federal law enforcement, it didn't bother presenting any evidence that restrictions on federal power contributed to the September 11 attack or that expansions of power would deter similar attacks in the future.

But it was hardly surprising that the administration was granted most of the broad, unaccountable police power it sought (and what Congress didn't give, the Justice Department subsequently took). People were terrified: According to a survey conducted in the fall of 2001, one-third of New Yorkers favored the internment of people suspected of being "sympathetic to terrorists." The attorney general kept fear alive by reminding us that terrorists were lurking and planning more attacks: "Terrorism is a clear and present danger to America today," John Ashcroft told the Senate, carefully using the legal catchphrase that justifies the suspension of constitutional safeguards on government power.

I'm not disputing Ashcroft's assessment of terrorism's threat; I'm merely pointing out his use of it to stave off Congressional inquiries into the practical value of any or all of the administration's counter-terrorism initiatives. We've good reason to fear terrorism, of course, and most people probably find the prospect of additional attacks more frightening than the nature of our response to them domestically. Still, we shouldn't underestimate the dangers of sacrificing freedom to fear. During the 2000 campaign, George Bush said that he opposed the use of secret evidence in federal prosecutions of noncitizens; one year later, he advocated imprisoning immigrants on the basis of no evidence at all. But Americans should not assume that only immigrants and people who appear to be Middle Eastern are at risk. Soon we will all be under surveillance. We are all suspects now.

Patriotism does not oblige us to acquiesce in the destruction of liberty. Patriotism obliges us to question it, at least. In Iraq, you can't quarrel with the president. But this is still America, I hope.

SAFETY AND FREEDOM

Of all the lame excuses offered for the failures of U.S. intelligence and security that facilitated the World Trade Center attack, the most disingenuous was the repeated claim that antiterrorism efforts have been restrained by respect for America's freedoms. Tell that to the victims of harsh counter-terrorism and immigration laws passed in the aftermath of the Oklahoma City bombing: the Arab Americans who were wrongfully imprisoned for several years on the basis of secret evidence; the asylum seekers who have been turned away from our borders by low-level bureaucrats without ever receiving a hearing; the thousands of lawful immigrants imprisoned and threatened with deportation for minor offenses committed years ago. Tell it to the victims of racial profiling on the nation's highways as well as in our airports.

I don't doubt that some federal law enforcement agents are honorable and respectful of individual freedom, but in general the law enforcement bureaucracy respects our freedoms grudgingly, only when it must, under court order or the pressure of bad publicity. Congress is often just as bad. While both the House and Senate include some staunch civil libertarians, they haven't had nearly enough influence to stop the anti-libertarian but highly ineffective counter-terrorism and crime-control laws that recent democratic and republican administrations embraced. Often, law enforcement agents violate our rights because they've been authorized to do so by law.

Lawmakers have, in turn, been authorized by voters to sacrifice rights to promises of public safety. Sixty-five percent of people surveyed in 1995, after Oklahoma City, favored giving the FBI power to infiltrate and spy on suspected terrorist groups, without evidence of a crime. Fifty-eight percent wanted to give the government power to deport any noncitizen suspected of planning terrorism. Fifty-four percent agreed that in the fight against terrorism, the government should not be hampered by concern for individual rights. Support for restrictions on liberty are at least as strong today. A November 2001 *Washington Post* poll found that a majority of Americans supported the president's controversial order establishing military tribunals for any noncitizen he suspected of supporting or engaging in terrorism. Nearly 90 percent of people surveyed supported the secret detentions of some six hundred immigrants after the September 11 attacks. (The number of detainees was soon over one thousand.)

This piece appeared in The American Prospect, *October 22, 2001*

When people agree to cede liberty for the sake of order, they usually imagine ceding other people's liberties, not their own. Most survey respondents who supported the administration's post-9/11 detentions were probably not Middle Eastern immigrants. But if most Americans would not volunteer to be rounded up and interned for weeks or months in the fight against terrorism, many are willing to tolerate minor bureaucratic intrusions for the sake of feeling safer, even when the feeling is illusory.

Consider our submissive behavior in airports before September 11. I understand why we lined up at security gates and submitted bags to an X ray; it was a minor inconvenience that seemed to have a rational relation to safety. But why did we docilely hand over our government-issued picture IDs? The ID requirement didn't deter terrorists, who easily falsify IDs (and lie about their intentions and the contents of their bags), but it did discourage people from transferring their discount tickets. It probably increased revenue for the airlines more than security for passengers.

This is a small point, but the now passé notion that a picture ID requirement coupled with a stupid-question routine was a meaningful security measure epitomized our sloppy, thoughtless approach to airline safety. Security lapses had nothing to do with the preservation of freedom, as post-9/11 reports on inadequate security at Boston's Logan Airport showed. As the *Boston Globe* reported soon after the attack, low wages, poor benefits, high turnover, and inadequate background checks by the private companies hired to handle airport security contributed to the unsafe conditions at Logan—which had not gone unnoticed. According to the *Wall Street Journal,* in 1998, the FAA investigated a private cleaning service employed by the Massachusetts Port Authority (which runs Logan and was itself run by grossly unqualified political appointees). It fined Massport and major airlines $178,000 after a teenager successfully stowed away on a plane in 1999. The airlines themselves successfully resisted stronger federal oversight of security and mandates that would have affected their bottom lines. The usual suspects—incompetence and venality, and not respect for liberty—are what hampered the fight against terrorism.

Imagine if federal law enforcement devoted all the time, money, and attention it now devotes to an ineffective, repressive war on drugs to the understanding and deterring of terrorism. Consider the corrosive effect of the drug war on both Fourth Amendment freedoms and foreign policy: In the spring of 2001, the Bush Administration announced a $40 million gift to the Taliban in consideration of its promise to ban opium production. If the administration wants to prosecute people who aid and abet terrorists, it should turn itself in immediately. There are evils to blame for the Trade Center attack, as the president observed, but many of them are domestic.

FEAR ITSELF

Terrorists enjoyed a symbolic victory when Congress shut down on October 18, 2001, to check the premises for anthrax, but both the House and Senate have seemed increasingly irrelevant anyway since the September 11 attack. The administration, not Congress, is responsible for new counter-terrorism legislation, which includes breathtaking expansions of federal law enforcement power (like the authority to conduct secret searches of your home or office in any criminal investigation). The USA Act of 2001 passed the Senate 96 to 1 with little debate (after Wisconsin Democrat Russ Feingold embarrassed and infuriated some of his liberal colleagues by attempting to introduce privacy protections to the bill). A very similar bill, dubbed the Patriot Act, was passed by the House after a coup by the administration and House Republican leaders, who managed a middle-of-the-night substitution of their bill for a compromise that had been crafted by the Judiciary Committee. The administration's bill was passed by the House (by a vote of 337 to 79) before many members had the opportunity even to read it.

Episodes like this could relieve some Democrats from the burden of worrying about controlling Congress. If Congress is going to act like an auxiliary of the executive branch, when freedom and safety are at stake, it doesn't matter much whether Democrats or Republicans are nominally in charge. These days, only bipartisanship, not dissent, is considered patriotic; and bipartisanship has come to mean obeisance to Republican rule.

I'm not denigrating patriotism; I just wish we'd reconsider its requirements. Legislators who abdicate their legislative power are no more patriotic than apathetic voters who stay home on Election Day. Dissent, not self-censorship, is patriotic. If, for example, you believed that the war against Afghanistan was immoral, or dangerously counterproductive, you were obliged to say so. Conservatives known for excoriating the Clinton Administration or loudly lamenting the tawdriness of American culture should be among the first to agree that we have both a right and an obligation to dissent from prevailing opinion when we think it's dead wrong. (You have to wonder why criticism of government is unpatriotic when offered by the left and a public service when issued from the right.) If I were to draw up a list of great citizens and patriots, it would include a number of dissent-

This piece appeared in The American Prospect, *December 3, 2001*

ers, like Martin Luther King, Elizabeth Cady Stanton, and Eugene Debs, who was imprisoned in the early years of the twentieth century for criticizing U.S. entry into World War I. Debs was much more of a patriot than the bureaucrats who imprisoned him for airing his opinions.

Today's beleaguered antiwar protesters may be mistaken in their analysis of terrorism, but they're better Americans than people who reacted to the fall 2001 anthrax attack by hoarding antibiotics that their fellow citizens may have needed. Dissenters pose no threat to the nation (and, rightly or wrongly, they believe the nation's interests are served by their ideas), but people who stockpiled Cipro or stupidly self-medicated in the belief that an antibiotic is like a vaccine endangered everyone's health—and acted only out of self-interest. If patriotism requires a sense of community and a willingness to make some sacrifices for the public good, it is undermined by the survivalism that takes hold when people feel besieged. In the 1960s, some fantasized about fallout shelters, stocked with canned goods and ammunition, but the image of an armed man defending his fortified basement from the neighbors never seemed appealing or even slightly patriotic to me.

Panic isn't exactly unpatriotic, but it is more likely to engender selfishness than the extraordinary altruism of those firefighters who ran up the stairs of the World Trade Center while everyone else ran down. So it's fair to say that we have a patriotic duty to each other to stave off panic and the survivalist behaviors it encourages. (Stoicism has rarely seemed more virtuous.) During the anthrax scare, I became impatient with ordinary people who feared opening their mail (although I had a good deal of sympathy for postal workers). And I wasn't persuaded by people who rationalized their panic by pointing to the unprecedented nature of bioterrorism. What do they imagine the plague felt like to people in the Middle Ages? What must AIDS feel like to people in Africa today?

Some say we can't live with fear, but few people have ever lived without it. (You don't have to imagine a holocaust; just think of life in a high-crime housing project.) There's probably no period in history that hasn't been shaped by fear of war or disease and arbitrary death. From that perspective, there's nothing particularly new about what Americans are enduring today, except for the fact that it's Americans who are enduring it. And at least we don't have to believe that the threat of anthrax or smallpox comes from a wrathful omnipotent God or nature; we know it's posed by other human beings and can at least imagine stopping them.

So it was discouraging to hear the president describe Bin Laden as "the evil one," as if he were Satan himself, or a demon on *Buffy the Vampire Slayer*. We need to acknowledge that he's a murderous human being, however much we want to exclude him from the species. There's nothing supernatural about terrorism; human barbarism requires no help from the devil. People who believe that confronting terrorism requires God's help will disagree. But I suspect that what we mostly need now is self-control.

AN IMPERIAL PRESIDENCY

Terrorism was expected to bring back big government, but lately it seems federal power isn't growing so much as it is coalescing in the White House. Some in Congress have reacted to recent power grabs by the administration with appropriate outrage. But the tendency of Congress to guard its own power shouldn't obscure its now historic role in stripping power from the federal courts. Attacks on the judiciary intensified after September 11, but, like terrorist cells, they have been growing for years.

This has been an ominous development. The twentieth-century rights revolution, which helped liberate racial minorities, women, and gay people and increased the fairness of criminal prosecutions, was largely occasioned by the willingness of the federal judiciary to begin enforcing the Bill of Rights. That, of course, is why many social conservatives hate the courts.

Since they came to power in the 1980s, conservatives have been working to deprive the federal courts of their authority. In the 1990s, they were joined by Clinton Democrats, gravitating right. Relying partly on fear generated by the Oklahoma City bombing, Congress enacted laws that greatly limited the power of federal courts to review state convictions, to remedy unsafe, unconstitutional prison conditions, and to review determinations by immigration officials deporting people or denying them asylum.

As the bombing of the Murrah Building demonstrated, the tragedy of terrorism is an opportunity for officials impatient with the constitutional checks and balances that help protect democracy. In the fall of 2001, as many critics of the administration observed, we witnessed the birth of an imperial presidency, shaped by the new unilateral powers of federal law enforcement officials. The hastily enacted USA-Patriot Act strips the courts of much of their power to review and monitor electronic surveillance by law enforcement as well as intelligence agencies; it also allows access to private student records, disclosure of information obtained through grand jury proceedings, and even long-term and possibly indefinite detention of noncitizens without any meaningful judicial review. Of course, Congress bears considerable responsibility for the inaptly named Patriot Act (what's more unpatriotic than autocracy?) even though many members may never have gotten around to actually reading or comprehending the

A version of this piece appeared in The American Prospect, *December 17, 2001*

bill. But the executive branch also assumed formidable new judicial powers without congressional authorization, most notably in the president's order establishing military tribunals.

Before the president gave himself sole authority to try any noncitizens he suspects of terrorism before vaguely defined military tribunals, they were entitled to trials in open court, conducted according to constitutionally mandated safeguards regarding the right to counsel, admission of evidence, and burden of proof on the government. Of course, there are legitimate questions about the wisdom of airing some evidence in open court, but judges are used to limiting exposure of sensitive information in extraordinary cases involving terrorism, or sadly ordinary cases of rape. People who scoff at the prospect of applying constitutional safeguards to terrorism cases should remember that they do not only benefit the accused; they benefit all of us by increasing the reliability and credibility of trials.

Predictable, but surprisingly productive, controversies erupted over the establishment of military tribunals; in March 2002, several months after the president's initial order, the administration issued procedures for the tribunals that reflected some concerns about condemning suspected terrorists to death without any due process. Civil libertarians reacted with equal outrage, but less effect, to the Justice Department regulation providing the attorney general with sole discretion to monitor conversations between federal prisoners and their lawyers. This regulation was not necessary to prevent criminal conspiracies between lawyers and clients: Before it was promulgated, federal agents could seek a court order authorizing a wiretap on an attorney/client conversation. The regulation's primary effect was to increase the power of the attorney general, at the expense of an already weakened judiciary.

The unilateral power of the president and his law enforcement appointees will also be greatly enhanced by the breakdown of boundaries between intelligence operations and domestic crime control, which Congress approved. It should be stressed repeatedly that many new powers enjoyed by the executive branch under the USA-Patriot Act are not limited to cases involving terrorism; they extend to ordinary criminal investigations. For example, the act allows federal agents to obtain wiretap authorization from special secret courts under the loose standards of the 1978 Foreign Intelligence Surveillance Act, when intelligence gathering is not the primary purpose of their investigation.

Proposals to continue expanding law enforcement's power are

more unsettling. "If federal agents have someone in custody whom they know has vital information about a pending attack, should they have the power to torture him?" That question about torture is becoming familiar; not surprisingly, it usually elicits a "yes." But it might be more accurate to pose a hypothetical involving multiple detainees, some of whom are suspected of having information about a pending attack. Should all of them be tortured, under law? Torture occurs whether or not it's authorized, in cases involving ordinary criminal suspects as well as suspected terrorists. (The constitutional prohibition on the use of coerced confessions reflects an acknowledgment that they exist: Statements are sometimes beaten out of people.) But legalizing torture would validate it morally and increase its occurrence. If you condone the use of torture, or kangaroo courts, you have to accept their arbitrary use against the innocent.

The suggestion that we are in the process of becoming at home what we have been battling abroad—an autocracy with little regard for human rights—is hyperbolic, or, at least, premature. But the Bush Administration's autocratic behavior, buttressed by public hunger for a strongman, does raise the question of how to battle evil without being entirely corrupted by it (some taint is probably inevitable).

We could simply focus pragmatically on enhancing security, instead of reflexively enhancing executive power. What's striking about most repressive measures passed during wartime is their irrelevance to security. Americans were not safer during World War I and its aftermath because immigrants and dissenters were imprisoned or deported; they were not safer during World War II when Japanese Americans were interned, or during the 1990s when Arab Americans were detained on the basis of secret evidence. We may not be any safer today, early in 2002, because of the secret detention of over one thousand immigrants after September 11.

Attorney General Ashcroft claims the detentions have protected us, but if they did little to enhance our security, he'd be the last to say and we'd be the last to know. In fact, documents reluctantly released by the administration in response to Freedom of Information Act requests, lawsuits, and public criticism indicated that only a very small number of detainees were suspected of having any connection to terrorism: Out of the 1,200 people arrested, only 10 were believed to be connected directly to Al Qaeda or the hijackers; about 18 people were suspected of having distant connections either to the hijackers or the other 10 suspicious detainees. In other words, the government seemed to have imprisoned about 1,170 people who were innocent of any connection to terrorism and posed no evident threat to public safety. Some were kept for weeks without being charged and without being given access to lawyers in violation even of the repressive Patriot Act. Many were charged with minor, or technical, immigration violations. Six months after the attack and detentions, information about the people detained is still sketchy because the government still resists releasing information about them. But based on what we know so far, it's fair to say that the great majority of these arrests did not make America safer, although they did make our country less free.

The post–September 11 sweeps by law enforcement were understandable, at first; it was the prolonged detention of so many people, in violation of so many due process rights, that raised concerns about safety and freedom. (Some administration critics worried about the consequences of alienating the Muslim community at a time when the government greatly needed its cooperation.) Respecting the very loose restrictions imposed by Congress on the Justice Department's power to detain people and providing detainees with access to the courts would have lessened the potential for their abuse, without threatening our security. In general, we are not made safer by eliminating congressional oversight of the executive or judicial review of federal law enforcement activities. Members of Congress and judges are not generally cavalier about national security, and considering the FBI's abysmal record during the last decade, our safety would probably increase if the bureau were carefully monitored.

If the president, attorney general, and their army of agents trust themselves with unbridled discretion, we should mistrust them for their arrogance. If they continue appropriating power from Congress and the courts, we should condemn them for political profiteering. People rightfully want decisive leadership during times of great crisis, but decisiveness needn't preclude a measure of simple modesty. We need leaders prone to wonder whether God endorses them, leaders with no delusions about their fallibilities. An administration intent on ignoring or dismantling constitutional checks on its power is seeking to rule, not to lead.

IGNORANT BLISS

In the locker room, two women are discussing the war against terrorism; they agree that Attorney General Ashcroft is right not to reveal information about the one-thousand-plus people detained since September II. The trouble is "We're too soft" on the detainees, one opines. "No, the trouble is that a lot of people detained are innocent," I interject unwisely, explaining that only a handful of people summarily imprisoned are reported to have any connection to terrorism. The women are unimpressed. One suggests that being imprisoned for a few months is not so terrible, even if you're innocent. Immigrants should expect as much in times like these she says, stressing that she's not anti-immigrant. Her own family emigrated from Ireland a few generations ago.

I don't imagine that either of these women would march off to prison in a spurt of misplaced patriotism, if the attorney general came breaking down her door. But they're clearly willing to sacrifice the rights of others not to be unfairly and unnecessarily detained. "Think about the widows," one said, with more passion than logic. When I asked how the widows might be helped by imprisoning innocent people or people guilty only of minor offenses who pose no threat to society, she scowled and left the room.

Conversations like these obviously reflect prevailing anger and fear, but public disdain for other people's liberties is neither a new phenomenon nor one associated primarily with wartime. A survey of Americans conducted in the early 1980s found only minority support for free speech. Seventy-one percent of people surveyed would have denied atheists the right to air their views in a public auditorium; nearly 60 percent would have denied the same right to gay rights activists and people intent on denouncing the government. A mere plurality, 41 percent, believed that people advocating "unpopular causes" should have the right to conduct mass protests.

So civil libertarians should not have been surprised by recent evidence of overwhelming public support for a repressive domestic war against terrorism. In a November 2001 NPR/Kaiser/Kennedy School poll, over 60 percent of people surveyed favored the use of military tribunals for noncitizens suspected of terrorism, and 68 percent favored government eavesdropping on conversations between terrorist suspects and their lawyers. Concern about abuse of

This piece appeared in The American Prospect, *January 1, 2002*

new law enforcement powers was strong but abstract, and confused: Sixty-five percent of respondents believed that broad new powers of law enforcement would be used against the innocent, and 58 percent expected to give up some of their own rights to fight terrorism; but only 32 percent felt personally threatened by new antiterrorism legislation.

The rights of citizens suspected of nothing worse than disagreeing with their government were also regarded with hostility: Over 60 percent agreed that someone who attributes terrorist activity to American behavior abroad should not be allowed to work in the government or teach in the public schools. (Can loyalty oaths be far behind?) Forty percent of people surveyed favored censorship of stories about antiwar protests, and over one-third favored censorship of stories criticizing the president's conduct of the war (if the war is wrongly conceived or badly conducted, they apparently don't want to know about it).

In part, responses like these reflect some understandable public ignorance about administration policies. It's doubtful that many people realized that, in assuming unilateral power to monitor conversations between prisoners and their lawyers, the attorney general usurped power previously exercised by the courts. It's doubtful that many people comprehended the broad scope of the order establishing military tribunals, especially since the administration was extremely disingenuous in describing it. As Anthony Lewis observed in the *New York Times,* the president's counsel, Alberto Gonzales, wrongly suggested that the order allowed for civilian review of tribunal proceedings; that only active members and supporters of terrorist groups could be subjected to the tribunals; and that they would operate like court-martials, under the Uniform Code of Military Justice. (In fact, court-martials afford more rights to the accused than the tribunals as originally conceived.)

But the NPR/Kaiser/Kennedy School poll also reflects the public's willingness to embrace ignorance. The desire to repress criticism of the president, the war effort, and American policies abroad expresses people's impulse only to hear what they need to believe. "Why do they hate us," we asked after September 11, but it's clear that there are some answers the majority simply isn't willing to hear. There are some illusions of presidential infallibility that many can't bear to see shattered.

Unfortunately, presidents and their appointees do make mistakes, which we ignore at our peril: Some former FBI officials expressed concern that the widespread detention of immigrants after September II hampered intelligence efforts, leaving us more vulnerable to future attacks. Presidents, and attorney generals, need desperately to be second-guessed, as conservative critics of the Clinton Administration might agree. After all, if political leaders were always right, honorable, responsible, and highly competent, we would have had better airport security, better intelligence, and a better public health system long before September II exposed our own internal weaknesses. So you don't have to care about civil liberties to worry about suppression of unpopular views during an extremely complicated, volatile, and unpredictable war. You only have to care about security and success in the fight against terrorism.

2

NO PLACE TO HIDE

SOMEONE TO WATCH OVER ME

American culture thrives on contradictions. It exalts individualism and is rife with the conformity so essential to consumerism. It preaches self-reliance and personal accountability while enriching pop therapists who provide reassurances and excuses to the anxious middle class. It nurtures feminism and encourages face-lifts.

So in late-twentieth-century America, we should not have been entirely surprised by the paradoxical convergence of an exhibitionist, voyeuristic culture and a growing demand for law enforcement surveillance with pervasive concern about privacy. By 2000, the intensity of these opposing trends was particularly dramatic. While "reality TV" shows debuted and security cameras in public places proliferated, Democratic and Republican pollsters were attesting to a "groundswell" of concern about privacy, which politicians rushed to address. During the 2000 campaign, George Bush declared himself a "privacy rights person." Al Gore speechified about privacy on the Internet. Congress considered hundreds of privacy protection bills.

Privacy became a familiar, pervasive concern in the 1990s, as technology and the continued expansion of the prosecutorial state threatened our ability to keep secrets. Raising the alarm about government or private industry invading our personal lives, civil libertarians tended to assume that practically everyone valued privacy. According to a 1995 Harris Poll, 82 percent of respondents were concerned about personal privacy (compared to 64 percent in 1978.)

But we routinely traded privacy for the promise of security, welcoming cameras that monitored parking garages, elevators, or banks and meekly tolerating the senseless demands of airlines for easily falsified photo IDs. After September 11, we quickly became accustomed to exhibiting IDs to office-building security guards—who would have admitted Osama Bin Laden if he shaved his beard, changed his clothes, and showed them a picture ID. Fear of crime or terrorism and the comfort of illusory security measures usually prevails over privacy.

With equal enthusiasm, we traded privacy for fame, or the hope of it. If notoriety is a threat, sometimes it is also a promise. Americans have long been attracted and revolted by exposure, at least since Louis Brandeis and Samuel Warren published their landmark treatise

Excerpts from this piece were published in The American Prospect, *August 2000; on IntellectualCapital.com, March 1999; and included in a talk delivered at the University of Illinois, Chicago, October 2001*

on privacy in the *Harvard Law Review* over a century ago. Today, with the digital revolution making privacy as obsolete as the rotary phone, it's worth stressing that their nineteenth-century plea for the right to be let alone was inspired by new technology, mainly photography. Brandeis and Warren were concerned with the "unauthorized circulation of portraits of private persons" in the press and with the rise of gossip. They wanted to create a remedy for involuntary, "unwarranted" invasions of privacy. (They recognized that privacy rights should not always protect public figures engaged in matters of public interest, recognizing as well the difficulties of distinguishing between public and private concerns.)

Brandeis and Warren treasured privacy as essential to human dignity, and they lived at a time when exhibitionism was not respectable, much less a sign of mental health. It would have been hard for them to imagine that dignity would one day seem a small price to pay for a moment of fame. "The general object in view is to protect the privacy of private life," they wrote. What happens when private life loses allure, when, like trees falling in the forest, people want someone watching to make sure they exist? Gossip becomes a preeminent form of information. Over one hundred years ago, Brandeis and Warren worried that gossip was no longer an idle pastime. It was becoming "a trade," they warned, presciently describing the dangers it posed: Gossip appeals to our baser instincts, the "weak side of human nature" that takes pleasure in the "misfortunes and frailties" of others. It was dignified by print and "crowds space available" for discussion of public issues. The trouble with gossip, they eloquently observed, was that "it usurps the place of interest in brains capable of other things."

We surely saw proof of that during the 1990s, with the rise of tabloid TV. As many critics have noted, we were collectively obsessed with trivialities, which generally involved the details of other people's private lives. There was some self-consciousness about the elevation of gossip to news: Pundits were forever telling us why someone's private conduct qualified as a public issue. But the explanations were perfunctory; everyone knew that gossip was news, regardless.

By the time the scandals of the 1990s broke, we already inhabited a talk-show culture that provided forums for the exhibitionists among us and entertainment for the voyeurs. It was spawned by popular therapies that taught us to fear repression or denial more than exposure. The therapeutic culture pathologized privacy, silence, and stoicism and promoted the belief that healthy people talk about themselves—sometimes incessantly and often in public—at least in support groups. Discretion about your private life was often facilely equated with repression.

Late-twentieth-century liberation movements, notably feminism and the gay rights movement, contributed to conflicts and confusion over privacy. In the gay community, where discretion had been forced upon people (where it could fairly be called repressive) exposure became a political act, not simply a therapeutic one. Unfortunately, it also became a controversial political mandate, as a few closeted homosexuals were outed. Some people who once had secrecy forced upon them felt entitled to force exposure on others. Feminists also fought simultaneously for privacy and publicity. They defended personal and familial privacy when it protected reproductive rights and condemned privacy when it protected men who abused their wives and children, or merely enjoyed pornography.

So in the mid-1990s, a report that over 80 percent of Americans were concerned with privacy didn't tell us very much. Did over 80 percent of Americans believe that police shouldn't have the power to take DNA samples from suspected criminals or that sex offenders shouldn't be identified to their neighbors? Did they want to limit the power of police to conduct warrantless searches? In recent years, the courts expanded it, with no outcry from the public. Long before September 11, people gave government broad powers to wiretap. They supported a war on drugs that eviscerated the Fourth Amendment and the privacy rights it was intended to protect. Did 80 percent of all Americans believe that welfare recipients have privacy rights against social workers or that employers have no right to demand drug tests of employees? Would over 80 percent of all Americans have turned down the chance to appear on the *Today Show* or *Oprah*? How many Americans were ready to throw out their credit cards?

It has always been difficult to talk about privacy in general. On September 10, 2001, you would not have found majority support for the privacy rights of criminal suspects or welfare recipients. You would have found considerable public support for maintaining the privacy of medical records, except perhaps when the government claims a need to investigate Medicaid fraud—someone else's fraud, of course. People tend to regard privacy the way they regard other civil liberties or tax breaks: they support the ones they use.

Civil libertarians often say that you shouldn't support any new restriction on liberty unless you're willing to be subjected to it. But many people take the opposite approach, supporting repressive laws and policies that they expect will only be applied to others—criminals, terrorists, or recent immigrants. Shortly after September 11, one man identified as a libertarian told the *New York Times* that he understood the need for racial profiling, so long as it wasn't used against "ordinary people." Of course, ordinary people constitute profiling's primary victims. If law enforcement agents were psychic and could intuit the presence of terrorists and other criminals, they'd have no need for profiling.

The value of surveillance to a fearful, insecure, and intrusive society is its ubiquity. Governmental and corporate authorities cast their surveillance nets over all of us, hoping to deter high crimes and low misdemeanors (like shopping on the Internet at work) and promising to snare only the guilty few. How do you escape surveillance? Maintaining privacy has long required the constant vigilance of ordinary people—vigilance that few of us have exercised. For years, people gave up their privacy inadvertently, as they gave up their social security numbers to department store clerks in order to establish charge accounts. People claimed they cared about privacy, but God forbid they didn't have a Macy's charge card.

Sometimes people were simply unaware of the threats to their privacy. A 1998 survey by the New York Civil Liberties Union found at least 2,380 surveillance cameras monitoring public spaces; an estimated 2,000 of them were private. Sometimes people had little choice but to forfeit their privacy rights. Millions of employees have been monitored in the workplace: Employers read their E-mails, monitor their computer use, and review personal computer files, or they demand drug tests.

But while many people resent being spied upon, some have begun to feel entitled to spy upon others: New computer programs allow people to monitor their spouse's E-mails or on-line reading habits. Cameras in day-care centers allow parents to keep children, and day-care workers, under constant watch. Armed with video cameras, people tape their children incessantly; the middle class has probably reared a generation of performers. It's not surprising when young denizens of the cyber-culture install cameras in their own homes and exhibit themselves 24/7 on the Net.

Of course, many of their parents didn't exactly shy away from exhibiting themselves. Before the pop therapies of the 1980s encouraged people to spill the toxic secrets of family life, the baby boom generation was supposedly letting it all hang out. The counterculture was always self-consciously attention grabbing. It was trumped by talk shows, which, in turn, were trumped by reality programming, which, oddly enough, came into prominence at about the same time that polls were showing strong public concern about protecting privacy. While media stories on protecting privacy abounded, media encroachments on privacy astounded. Over 20 million people tuned in to watch *Survivor*, which was soon followed by *Big Brother*, the show that confined ten strangers to a house for one hundred days and subjected them to constant surveillance. Soon, reality-based shows were commonplace. Reporters polled experts to find out what this phenomenon said about our psyche. If you didn't watch reality TV, you could always read about it—while you worried about your anonymity if you were reading on-line. The press loved the story of reality TV but covered the privacy debate as well, mirroring the culture's cognitive dissonance.

But the contradictions in our relationship to privacy are not all that difficult to resolve: People exhibit in the belief that they can choose what to reveal and what to conceal. Even exhibitionists have many things to hide. Think of Bill Clinton. Exhibitionists plan on exposing only what they choose to expose. They exhibit in the belief that they're in control of their public presentation. But their control is most tenuous. Think again of Clinton. Even the president can't control a hostile or prurient press.

Once you enter the public sphere, you put yourself at the mercy of public curiosity and its handmaiden—the media. That's why celebrities have press agents. That's why people who have actively sought celebrity—rock stars, models, or movie stars—find themselves in the anomalous position of demanding privacy. Nicole Kidman once appeared half nude on the cover of *Newsweek* next to a tag line promising she would discuss her marriage to Tom Cruise and their fight for privacy. Only in a culture that values secrecy but craves celebrity could you make a straight-faced plea for privacy by posing barely clothed on the cover of a national news magazine and talking about your marriage with millions of strangers. When J. D. Salinger says he values his privacy I believe him. Nicole Kidman's desire for privacy is apparently a bit more equivocal.

But Kidman's appearance on *Newsweek*'s cover only proved the point: People who voluntarily surrender their privacy may not want it wrested from them. It's not privacy that people value so much as the power to control what is revealed and concealed. We want both public and private lives, and we want the power to police the boundaries between them. But in a surveillance state, that power is surrendered by individuals and wielded by the government.

In a democracy, the creation of a surveillance state has to be predicated on consent, and consent is obtained by popularizing an avuncular image of a government that monitors us benignly. In Great Britain, surveillance cameras routinely monitor public spaces, with relatively little opposition. Privacy expert Jeffrey Rosen has observed (in the *New York Times Magazine*) that the British public tends to regard its intrusive government not as a Big Brother but as a kindly uncle or aunt.

Paternalistic government inevitably gains popularity during crises, when people need to view the president as a father figure. The day after Bush's address to Congress on September 20, 2001, one self-identified Democrat interviewed on National Public Radio referred to the president approvingly as our "daddy in chief." This suggests that we're a nation of children, and children are used to being monitored by their parents; in fact, they take comfort in it. Having Mommy and Daddy watching, even from a distance, makes children feel safe. People feel threatened or at least unsettled by surveillance when an apparently hostile or indifferent authority conducts it. They find surveillance comforting when they believe it's offered in a spirit of loving protectiveness. So, the more politicians and law enforcement agents scare us about crime or terrorism, the more we need to trust in their good faith and abilities; the more we trust them, the more we welcome or at least accept surveillance.

The craving for community, as well as security, can also undermine privacy. There are some crude, obvious ways in which communal life and codes of behavior threaten individual liberty. One conservative pundit has opined that less privacy would probably lead to more virtue. We would have less adultery, he suggested, if people monitored each other's private lives. Evidence of this assertion is scarce; the public has been monitoring the private lives of celebrities for some years without discouraging any of them from fooling around. In any case, my own vision of a virtuous society is not one that's built on a network of neighborhood spies.

But even the most benevolent communities pose subtle threats to privacy. Religion has always been an obvious and important source of community. (Even atheists or agnostics sometimes go to church for the sake of their social lives.) But the more we focus on religion as a public function, the less respect we may have for it as a private prerogative.

This was evident in the 2000 presidential campaign, when former senator Bill Bradley refused to answer questions about his religious beliefs, asserting that religion was a private matter and notappropriate fodder for a political campaign. That was, or should have been, an unremarkable observation; yet it garnered attention because other candidates were flaunting their religiosity, the way they flaunted their happy marriages. A desire not to talk publicly about a personal belief in God was considered suspicious or, at least, noteworthy; respect for religious privacy had surely declined.

Or, consider the role of public religious rituals and displays when people came together to mourn the September 11 attack. It engendered an understandable urge to pray and grieve collectively, which partly reflected the sense that the nation had suffered a collective blow. But when communities in crisis exaggerate and exalt religion's public function, public life can expand at the expense of the private realm. The ideology of mourning that prevailed immediately after September 11 reflected the influence of pop therapies as well as religion. A familiar therapeutic ethic prevailed: Exhibitionism was encouraged. (Remember the Cantor Fitzgerald executive who cried to Larry King?) Stoicism and self-containment were suspect.

What defenses do we have against communal, cultural, or governmental incursions on our privacy? Perhaps technology can help us subvert surveillance, as well as establish it. Perhaps America's libertarian streak (evident in the digital culture) will encourage the individualism that evaluates cultural and communal norms instead of simply obeying them. But the best defense of privacy may be anonymity. People can best tolerate surveillance that doesn't threaten anonymity—and plays no role in monitoring virtue. New Yorkers in high-rise apartments have long felt free to spy on each other, so long as both watcher and watchee remained anonymous. I frequent a nude beach in the summer; I'm perfectly comfortable there, so long as I don't encounter anyone I know.

It is, therefore, important to distinguish privacy from anonymity. The more anonymous you feel, the less privacy you need. Consider the plight of homeless people. They have virtually no privacy living on the street, but they also have no public identities. They're practically invisible to many of us. The curse of their anonymity perversely affords them a modicum of privacy. The more uncomfortable you make people, the more invisible you may become. But social neglect is a high price to pay for anonymity.

And anonymity is a high price to pay for privacy. I'm happy on the nude beach not encountering friends or colleagues, but off the beach, I'd be lost without them. What's the lesson of this? What do we lose when we lose control of privacy and must resort to anonymity? We lose both liberty—the freedom to be ourselves in public—and the ability to form community. And if we can't form community, we can't act collectively, or politically. The loss of privacy could deter the formation of political movements—including movements against surveillance. It's not just that surveillance will chill dissent—as it is intended to do. It's that our willingness to gather together and act collectively may be predicated on the confidence that we can still exist and thrive as private individuals.

Secrecy is essential to civil society and social relations. Some applaud the "openness" (or shamelessness) of the new exhibitionism, in the belief that it will bring us together. But social life would be intolerable for many of us without the possibility of solitude. Without it, community, as well as individualism, is at risk. The more public space expands, the more it threatens public life. We need not know everything about each other, so that we don't have to feel exposed by every encounter. Privacy makes public life possible.

PUBLIC LIVES

Public surveillance cameras, facial-recognition systems, secret FBI searches of library records, and other invasions of privacy proposed in the name of security pose no threat to law-abiding citizens, according to the snoops who support them. They suggest that if you're not engaged in illegal activities, you have nothing to hide from the government, implying that only criminals will oppose being systematically monitored by bureaucrats. Some Americans will find this argument convincing: It's easier to quantify the threat of terrorism —sudden death—than the promise of privacy—an inchoate sense of freedom and autonomy. I never could explain to my mother why I liked closing the door of my room when I was a kid. I wasn't doing anything behind closed doors that I couldn't have done out in the open—but I was doing it unwatched and alone.

Those days are gone; these days the desire to be let alone can't be expected to prevail against the desire to feel safe. So opposing surveillance because it violates privacy is probably futile. We can more effectively oppose it for failing to improve security.

Consider the false promise of facial-recognition systems. A 2002 report by the American Civil Liberties Union revealed that the widely publicized facial-recognition system used by police on the streets of Tampa, Florida, "never identified even a single individual contained in the department's database of photographs." Instead, "The system made many false positives, including such errors as confusing what were to a human easily identifiable male and female images." (The ACLU report was based on a review of police logs, obtained through Florida's open-records law.)

Technological inaccuracies like these were coupled with human errors, or abuses of discretion. A facial recognition system can only be as good as its database in identifying terrorists or other violent criminals, and, in Tampa, the photographic database was not limited to known criminals: it included people whom the police were interested in questioning, in the belief that they might have "valuable intelligence." Under guidelines like this, ordinary, law-abiding citizens who venture out in public might find themselves setting off alarms in facial-recognition systems (should they ever work properly).

But whether or not your photograph is in the database your privacy is likely to be invaded by a facial-recognition system. "So what,

A portion of this piece appeared in Free Inquiry, *spring 2002*

you have no expectation of privacy in a public street," advocates of surveillance respond. But that's not entirely true; you do expect not to be singled out in a crowd and examined by official voyeurs. Cameras scan crowds and often zoom in on individuals; and, as the ACLU observed, in Britain, where electronic surveillance is becoming routine, camera operators are apt to focus disproportionately on racial minorities, or they wile away the hours peering up women's skirts. In Michigan, according to a report by the *Detroit Free Press*, police used a database to stalk women and intimidate other citizens.

Given the ways in which facial-recognition systems have been used and abused so far, it's fair to say that they constitute a threat—to privacy, liberty, and even physical safety—not a promise of security. But we are beginning to use them more, not less. Several cities have decided to deploy the kind of system that failed so miserably in Tampa. By early 2002, Washington, D.C., was building a surveillance infrastructure to coordinate cameras on subways, in retail establishments, and in parking lots—to ensure that no one will be able to walk around in public in Washington without being watched and photographed. Facial recognition is also billed as an important airport security tool. Airports in several cities, including Boston, Providence, and Palm Beach, are setting up facial recognition systems. Meanwhile, precautions that might actually enhance security, like reliable screening of all checked bags and carry-ons, are far from ever being implemented.

We may have national ID cards before we ever have a reasonable assurance of safe air travel. In fact, national IDs are touted as air-travel security and efficiency measures. ID cards with biometric identifiers can't be falsified, advocates say; they guarantee that identification cards correctly identify the people displaying them. Not exactly. How will we ensure that the ID itself is not based on false information? Terrorists can obtain driver's licenses and other legal documents, with which they could, in turn, obtain national IDs, encoded with their fingerprints. (The September 11 hijackers had IDs, and some were in this country legally.)

But if national IDs would afford relatively little protection against terror, they would help the government and private sector track the movements of law-abiding people who obtain IDs truthfully. Creating national ID cards would entail the creation of a national database, including what was once private information about all of us. Advocates of IDs promise that the data won't be shared, but sharing (and snooping) are inevitable. IRS employees sometimes browse illegally through our tax returns; similarly, unscrupulous workers would entertain or enrich themselves reading data generated by national IDs. Law enforcement agencies (and their employees) would share information legally, and soon the national ID would be used as routinely as social security numbers—which were originally intended for use only by the government, only for taxpayer identification.

The evolution of the social security number into a national identifier is instructive; it demonstrates the likely future for national ID cards. Once the government promised us that social security numbers would not be used for unrelated, unofficial purposes; now we can't get charge cards or cable TV service without revealing them. If, or when, we have national IDs, police officers will eventually ask for them at every traffic stop, or they'll stop us for the purpose of inspecting our IDs; private security guards will demand that we produce them as we enter high-rise office buildings or shopping malls; landlords will insist on ID checks before signing any leases. Without gaining much security, what will we lose? We'll lose any vestige of anonymity and any right not to be stopped and questioned by public or private security personnel, for no good reason. We'll lose the right to say, "Leave me alone," or "It's none of your business."

Our business is the government's business under the 2001 counter-terrorism law. The Patriot Act gives federal law enforcement agents the authority to conduct secret searches, subject to very little judicial review. Targets of these searches (who are not given a chance to oppose them) may include libraries and bookstores. FBI agents are empowered to demand that a librarian or bookstore owner produce the borrowing or purchasing records of any user or customer; or they might simply demand a list of all the people who had borrowed or purchased a particular book. They may also put a library computer under surveillance, if they declare that a suspected criminal might have used it. So, when you go to the public library to use the Internet or borrow a book, you may be under federal surveillance, but you'll probably never know it. A librarian or bookstore owner who is ordered to give up records to the FBI may be subject to a gag order and legally prohibited from challenging or even talking about the search.

Many Americans probably trust the FBI and other law enforcement agencies to use their power only against terrorists—although if government agents could instinctively identify terrorists they wouldn't need to monitor and investigate the rest of us clandestinely. In any case, if the targets of investigations are prevented from revealing, much less challenging, law enforcement actions, we'll never know when the government is acting abusively. This is surely a perversion of democracy. As a general rule, the actions of government officials are supposed to be public, so that we can hold them accountable and the actions of private citizens are supposed to be, well, private—absent good reason to believe that they pose a public threat. Government snoops have it backward. We're the ones entitled to keep secrets from them.

3

CAN WE TALK?

TOXIC MEDIA

Like Claude Rains in *Casablanca*, Al Gore was shocked—shocked!—that the entertainment industry was marketing violent material to minors. Countering Hollywood's macho entertainments with some macho rhetoric of his own, 2000 presidential candidate Gore gave the industry six months to "clean up its act" and declare a "cease-fire" in what he apparently saw as the media's war against America's children.

No one should have been surprised by this threat to impose government regulations on the marketing of popular entertainments (which immediately followed issuance of a Federal Trade Commission [FTC] report on marketing violent media). As his choice of an ostentatiously virtuous running mate made clear in 2000, Al Gore positioned himself as the moral voice of the Democratic Party—replete with godliness and a desire to cleanse the culture. With a concomitant promise to protect ordinary Americans from rapacious corporations, Gore was an early twenty-first—century version of a nineteenth-century female Progressive—a God-loving social purist with a soft spot for working families and, not so incidentally, women's rights.

Many Victorian women's rights activists, like Frances Willard, of the Women's Christian Temperance Union, and Julia Ward Howe, enthusiastically supported the suppression of "impure" or "vicious" literature, which was blamed for corrupting the nation's youth. "Books are feeders for brothels" according to the notorious nineteenth-century anti-vice crusader Anthony Comstock, for whom the nation's first obscenity law was named. Violent media provides ammunition for violent acts, many people today would agree. President Clinton commissioned the FTC report on violent media immediately after the 1999 shootings at Columbine High. That was when centrist politicians and commentators were touting the new "commonsense" view of youth violence: It was caused by both the prevalence of firearms and the availability of violent media. Gun control would be complemented by culture control.

So, in June 1999, two Democratic senators, Joe Lieberman and the usually thoughtful Kent Conrad, joined with Republicans Trent Lott and John McCain in proposing federal legislation requiring the labeling of violent audio and visual media. These requirements, which were to be enforced by the FTC, were amendments to the cigarette labeling act.

This piece appeared in The American Prospect, *October 23, 2000*

Advocates of censorship often charge that media can be "toxic" (as well as "addictive"), like tobacco and other drugs. By describing whatever film or CD they disdain as a defective product, they undermine the view of it as speech. (We should regulate pornography the way we regulate exploding Ford Pintos, one feminist antiporn activist used to say; she seemed to consider *Playboy* an incendiary device.) In endorsing Internet-filtering programs, Al Gore has remarked that minors should be protected from "dangerous places" on the Internet—in other words, "dangerous" speech. Some web sites should effectively be locked up, just as medicine cabinets are locked up, to protect children from poisons, the then vice president asserted at a 1997 Internet summit.

Once you define violent or sexually explicit media as toxic products, it is not terribly difficult to justify regulating their advertising at least, if not their distribution and production. Commercial speech generally enjoys constitutional protection, but as advocates of marketing restrictions assert, the First Amendment does not protect false or misleading advertising or ads promoting illegal activities. That's true but not necessarily relevant here. Campaigns marketing violent media to children may be sleazy, but they don't promote an illegal activity (the sale of violent media to minors is not generally criminal); and they may not qualify as deceptive or unfair. (Many popular entertainments are just as bad as their ad campaigns suggest.) Ratings are not determined or mandated by the government (yet), so why should it be a federal offense for industry executives to violate the spirit of their own voluntary codes?

Effective regulation of media-marketing campaigns will require new federal legislation that will entangle the government in the production of popular entertainments. What might this legislation entail? Ratings and labeling would be mandatory, supervised by the FTC (or some other federal agency), and any efforts to subvert the ratings system would be a federal offense. Testifying before the Senate Commerce Committee on September 12, 2000, Joe Lieberman promised that federal regulation of the entertainment industry would focus on "how they market, not what they produce," but that promise ignored the effect of marketing considerations on content.

Many would be pleased if labeling and marketing regulations indirectly deterred production of some violent entertainments, imagining perhaps that slasher movies and violent video games would be the primary victims of a new regulatory regime. But it's not hard to imagine a docudrama about domestic abuse or abortion, or a coming-of-age story about a gay teen receiving the same restrictive rating as a sleazy movie about a serial murderer. In any case, a stringent, federally mandated and monitored ratings and labeling system will not enhance parental control; it will instead provide a vehicle for bureaucratic control. Federal officials, not parents, will determine what media will be available to children when they devise and enforce the ratings.

Some have claimed that federal action is justified, nonetheless, by an overriding need to save lives. At the September 2000 hearing inspired by the FTC report, several senators and other witnesses vigorously decried not just the marketing of films, CDs, and video games, but also their content (clarifying their agenda). Charging the entertainment industry with "literally making a killing off of marketing to kids," Kansas Republican Sam Brownback called upon the industry to stop producing the entertainments he abhors. Joe Lieberman charged that media violence was "part of a toxic mix that has turned some of our children into killers." Lynne Cheney (current second lady and former head of the National Endowment for the Humanities) declared that "there is a problem with the product they market, no matter how they market it." Congressman Henry Hyde proposed prohibiting sales of "harmful" media to minors.

What all this hyperbolic rhetoric obscured (or ignored) was the dearth of hard evidence that violent media actually turns "children into killers." In fact, the recent FTC study, on which would-be censors relied, found no clear causal connection between violent media and violent behavior. "Exposure to violent materials probably is not even the most important factor" in determining whether a child will turn violent, FTC chair Robert Pitofsky observed. The most he would say was that exposure to violent media "does seem to correlate with aggressive attitudes, insensitivity toward violence, and an exaggerated view of how much violence occurs in the world."

This is not exactly a defense of media violence, but it does present a fairly balanced view of its effects, which do not justify limitations on speech. Living in a free society entails a commitment not to prohibit speech unless it clearly, directly, and intentionally causes violence. If the federal government can regulate violent media because it allegedly causes violence, it can also regulate inflammatory political rhetoric, like assertions that abortion providers kill babies. Antiabortion rhetoric probably has even a clearer connection to violence than any violent movie, but both must be protected. If Disney can be brought under the thumb of federal regulators, so can any American cleric who denounces abortion as murder.

It's unfortunate and ironic that amoral corporations, like Disney or Time/Warner, stand as champions and beneficiaries of First Amendment rights. As gatekeepers of the culture, they're not exactly committed to maintaining an open, diverse marketplace of ideas. Indeed, de facto censorship engineered by media conglomerates may threaten public discourse nearly as much as federal regulation. And, gratuitously violent media enriches neither our discourse nor our culture.

But speech doesn't have to provide cultural enrichment to enjoy constitutional protection. We don't need a First Amendment to protect popular, inoffensive speech or speech that a majority of people believe has social value. We need it to protect speech that Lynn Cheney or Joe Lieberman considers demeaning and degrading. Censorship campaigns often begin with a drive to protect children (or women), but they rarely end there.

TOXIC MEDIA VS. TOXIC CENSORSHIP

IN THE OCTOBER 23, 2000, ISSUE OF *THE AMERICAN PROSPECT*, WENDY
KAMINER ARGUED THAT POLITICAL CALLS FOR REGULATING "TOXIC ME-
DIA"—LIKE VIOLENT MOVIES OR PROFANE RAP ALBUMS—CAN LEAD TO
DANGEROUS CENSORSHIP AND REPRESSION. BUT WHAT IF THERE'S A LE-
GITIMATE PUBLIC INTEREST IN MONITORING THE CULTURAL PRODUCTS
KIDS CONSUME? MICHAEL MASSING SAYS THAT KAMINER'S ARGUMENT IS
TYPICAL OF LIBERALS' "REFLEXIVE DISDAIN" TOWARD THE EXPRESSED
CONCERNS OF PARENTS ON THIS ISSUE. THE TWO WRITERS ELABORATE IN
THE EXCHANGE THAT FOLLOWS.

Michael Massing writes:

Anytime a public official issues a peep of protest about the violent fare
on television, a chorus of liberal voices rises in denunciation. The
most recent instance came in September, when the Federal Trade
Commission (FTC) issued a report criticizing the marketing of movies and music with violent content to young people. Citing the report,
both Al Gore and Joe Lieberman blasted Hollywood. And the response
from liberal commentators was furious.

Gore's "frenzied and often self-contradictory posturing about
Hollywood," Frank Rich wrote in the *New York Times,* provided "a
creepy, if G-rated, preview of coming attractions depicting what his
administration may be like at its opportunistic and pandering
worst." Richard Rhodes, on the *Times*'s op-ed page, derided "moral
entrepreneurs" who were "at it again, pounding the entertainment
industry for advertising its Grand Guignolesque confections to children." *The Nation* accused the two Democratic candidates of making "a
deft feint to the right, enlisting the Federal Trade Commission for
blatantly partisan purposes."

And in her *American Prospect* piece "Toxic Media," Wendy Kaminer
sneeringly dismissed Gore as a "God-loving social purist" with "a
desire to cleanse the culture." Gore and others who share his concern
about violent programming, she argued, are nothing less than "advocates of censorship."

Kaminer and company seem to see themselves as brave uphold-
ers of free speech in the face of vote-hungry politicians. In fact, they
represent a new orthodoxy among liberals, who, wrapping themselves

This exchange appeared in The American Prospect, *January 1, 2001.*

© *2000 Michael Massing. Reproduced with permission.*

in the First Amendment, airily dismiss an issue of genuine concern to millions of American parents.

Needless to say, any talk of restricting what can or cannot appear on television does raise free-speech concerns. But it also involves what we as a society think is appropriate for young people to see and listen to. Any serious consideration of the issue must attempt to balance these competing interests. Yet Kaminer and the rest refuse even to acknowledge the conflict.

Kaminer grudgingly admits that "neither our discourse nor our culture is exactly enriched by gratuitously violent media." Nonetheless, she will brook no restriction of any sort on what appears on television. No limits on the hours during which violent programs can be shown. No ratings system to help parents decide what their children should watch. No restrictions (even voluntary ones) on the marketing practices of entertainment companies. She rejects mere criticism of the movie industry as a form of censorship. No matter how many slasher films Hollywood turns out, and no matter how often they are advertised on TV, Kaminer contends, we must grin and bear it. Let's examine her arguments.

"Living in a free society," Kaminer writes, "entails a commitment not to prohibit speech unless it clearly, directly, and intentionally causes violence. If violent entertainment can be regulated by the federal government because it allegedly causes violence, so can inflammatory political rhetoric, like assertions that abortion providers kill babies. Antiabortion rhetoric probably has even a clearer connection to violence than any violent movie, but both must be protected. If Disney can be brought under the thumb of federal regulators, so can Cardinal [Bernard] Law when he denounces abortion as murder."

This seems absurd. Nobody in the current debate is even remotely talking about imposing restrictions on political speech; anyone who did would be tarred and feathered. To make such an argument shows how far the new orthodox will overreach to make their point.

"Some may consider the decline of violent entertainment no great loss," Kaminer writes, "imagining perhaps that slasher movies and violent video games will be the primary victims of a new federal-labeling regime. But it's not hard to imagine a docudrama about domestic abuse or abortion or a coming-of-age story about a gay teen receiving the same restricted rating as a sleazy movie about a serial murderer. In any case, a stringent, federally mandated and monitored rating and labeling system will not enhance parental control; it's a vehicle for bureaucratic control. Federal officials, not parents, will determine what entertainment will be available to children when they devise and enforce the ratings." While any rating system must necessarily reflect subjective judgments, the type of abuses Kaminer here warns of seems farfetched. And while government bureaucrats may be involved in devising a ratings system, it is parents who ultimately decide what their kids will watch. Certainly many parents are grateful for whatever help they can get in determining what is appropriate fare for their children.

Like many other liberal critics, Kaminer questions the very idea that exposure to violent media negatively affects young people. The FTC study on which "would-be censors rely," she writes, "found no clear causal connection between violent media and violent behavior. 'Exposure to violent materials probably is not even the most important factor' in determining whether a child will turn violent, FTC chairman Robert Pitofsky observed. The most he would say was that exposure to violent media 'does seem to correlate with aggressive attitudes, insensitivity to violence, and an exaggerated view of how much violence occurs in the world.' "

It is undoubtedly true that exposure to media violence is not the most important factor in determining whether a child becomes violent. Most young people who watch shoot-'em-ups on TV are not going to go out and reenact them in real life. Nonetheless, one would think that the correlations Pitofsky cited—to aggressive attitudes and insensitivity to violence—would seem serious enough to warrant concern. Indeed, for more than thirty years now, the data about those effects have been accumulating. In 1972 the U.S. surgeon general's office conducted a comprehensive review of the existing research and found that televised violence contributes to antisocial behavior. Ten years later, the National Institute of Mental Health conducted another review and came to a similar conclusion. Between 1990 and 1996, the American Medical Association, the American Psychological Association, the American Academy of Pediatrics, and the American Academy of Child and Adolescent Psychiatry all concluded that TV violence fosters aggressive behavior in the real world. Clearly, millions of parents believe this, as evidenced by their fitful struggles to exercise some control over what their kids watch.

In light of this, it's hard to understand the zeal with which Kaminer and her colleagues dismiss criticism of the entertainment industry—until one considers the broader context in which it is occurring.

Traditionally, the fight against media violence has been led by Conservatives—William Bennett and Bob Dole, Jerry Falwell and the Christian Coalition. In the process, they have pushed an agenda that goes well beyond concern for the mental health of young people; rather, they seem to be trying to impose on society their own narrow moral vision. If the Christian Coalition got its way, we would find not only bludgeonings and beheadings barred from the airwaves but also sexual couplings, off-color jokes, family dysfunction, and everything else deemed unwholesome by right-wing standards. Anxiety over this seems to underlie Kaminer's concerns about the slippery slope. Such worries, however, should not lead to a blithe rejection of the research showing the potential negative consequences of violent programming.

So what is to be done? I agree with Kaminer that ratings systems are flawed—not, however, because they are instruments of bureaucratic control, but because they're not very effective. With the sleaze of contemporary culture so pervasive, it's hard for even the most determined parents to shield their kids, especially when so many Americans with children are forced to work long hours.

Nor are tightened controls over marketing the answer. The debate over the recent FTC report misses the real point. It's not the commercials that are the problem but the movies themselves. It's the endless flood of gratuitously violent films and misogynistic music lyrics that pose the real threat to young kids, and until something is done to restrict the flow, the harmful fallout will continue.

Certainly one does not want to encourage direct government intervention. The prospect of new laws or executive orders declaring what can and cannot appear on TV or in movie theaters and record stores does pose a threat to free speech. But speaking out against violent media does not. As First Amendment advocates themselves are quick to assert, the best antidote to bad speech is more speech. Public figures should continue to criticize and pressure Hollywood to stop producing such noxious fare. If enough voices are raised in protest, the movie studios might finally respond. Kaminer regards this as censorship, but aren't politicians who speak up on such matters exercising their own First Amendment rights? Well, it might be argued, if there's a market for this type of programming, shouldn't entertainment companies be free to provide it? To a degree, yes. But at the same time, society has a right to demand a certain level of responsible behavior by the entertainment industry, especially where young people are concerned.

Tobacco provides a good analogy. Cigarettes are legal but also lethal. At one point, they were widely advertised on TV. But in the late 1960s, as evidence of their toxicity mounted, public-interest groups began demanding more controls. The Federal Communications Commission reacted by calling for more counteradvertising, in the form of commercials dramatizing the health risks associated with smoking. In response, the tobacco companies—realizing the threat such commercials posed to their profits—agreed not to advertise their products on TV. And cigarette commercials have remained off the air ever since.

If Kaminer were writing back then, she would probably criticize such actions as infringing on the free-speech rights of the tobacco companies. Most Americans, though, would applaud such measures as helping to safeguard the nation's health.

No one, of course, would argue that violent movies pose as much of a threat to the nation's health as tobacco does. But the research studies that have accumulated over the years—together with the commonsense concerns of many parents—more than justify the calls on the entertainment industry to exercise greater restraint. And it would help if liberal critics joined in the campaign. If matters are left to the Bennetts and Falwells, the effort to clean up the media could take a troubling direction. At the very least, it's time for liberals to give up their reflexive disdain and recognize that the issue is a serious one requiring vigorous debate.

Kaminer responds:

Michael Massing sure is mad at me. It's probably anger, not bad faith, that leads him to misrepresent my views so grossly. I did not and would not foolishly condemn mere criticism of media content as censorship (I began my own writing career as a book critic and generally believe that nothing and no one should be protected from critics). I condemned Al Gore, Joe Lieberman, and other politicians for threatening to impose governmental controls on the entertainment industry, if it continues producing films, video games, or CDs that they don't like. Massing may disagree that proposed federal restrictions on how entertainments are marketed will affect what entertainments are produced, but he can hardly equate demands for legal restrictions on marketing campaigns with mere criticisms of marketing techniques or content.

Massing dismisses recent attacks on the media by politicians from both parties as mere "peeps of protests." That's not how I'd characterize a series of Senate hearings and legislative proposals aimed at curbing media violence. (It's not just marketing techniques that are being targeted, as testimony at the recent Senate commerce committee hearing made clear.) Or, consider the 1996 Communications Decency Act, prohibiting "indecency" on the Internet, signed into law by President Clinton and invalidated by the Supreme Court not long after. Was that merely another "peep"? After the CDA was struck down, Congress and the president tried again to criminalize speech in cyberspace with the Child Online Protection Act, recently struck down by a federal appeals court. It would prohibit commercial dissemination of Internet speech deemed "harmful to minors."

Who decides precisely what speech is harmful to minors? Massing ignores this troubling question at the heart of all censorship debates. He says that restrictions on media involve what "we as a society think is appropriate for young people to see and listen to," and I can only respond, "Who's 'we'?" Our diverse society is deeply divided over questions about sexual morality, race discrimination, militarism, vengeance, and gun ownership. Are minors morally corrupted or energized and informed by rap? We, "as a society," disagree. I doubt that even Massing and I, let alone "society," could reach consensus on the ideal media diet for America's youth.

To some extent, this does leave us at the mercy of industry executives. A sophisticated critique of my position would have likened the power of media conglomerates to the power of government and elaborated on the problem of de facto censorship. As I noted in my column, a marketplace controlled by a few media giants is not exactly free and receptive to diverse or unsettling ideas. So, my own opposition to government control of the media doesn't reflect any illusions about the quality of discourse that a laissez-faire approach produces. I do think that media critiques are important (and protected by the First Amendment, of course), and I did not oppose voluntary controls by the entertainment industry. How could I? Media executives are in the business of controlling content and marketing, as are editors of magazines like *The American Prospect*. But I do question the voluntary nature of ratings systems instituted under threats of government control.

Advocates of regulation argue that restrictions on content are justified because the proliferation of violent entertainment constitutes a national emergency. In their view, violent images are direct causes of violent behavior. Pornography causes rape, according to some feminists; sex education causes teenage pregnancy, Jerry Falwell and Phyllis Schlafly have suggested; violent video games, CDs, and films cause high school shootings and other horrors, Michael Massing, and many others, believe. Indeed, it has become conventional wisdom that violent entertainment causes violent behavior.

Massing and I will not resolve the debate about the relationship between images and behavior in this brief exchange. (Interested readers can find a critique of the literature on violence in "Blaming the Media," by Marjorie Heins, in the fall 2000 issue of the *Media Studies Journal*.) But I do want to stress, again, that even the Federal Trade Commission found only a correlation, not a causal relationship, between imaginary and actual violence. Massing observes reasonably that this correlation is cause for concern, but he's wrong to assume that "concern" about the effects of violent entertainment justifies regulation of the entertainment industry. The preservation of free speech requires much more than "concern"; it requires evidence that speech presents actual and more or less immediate dangers, not mere speculation, or even educated guesses about its consequences. Violent entertainment may be a problem for society, but it is not a problem that law can solve, so long as we value free speech. If the government could regulate any speech that provoked "concern," it could regulate any unsettling or offensive speech; it could, and undoubtedly would, regulate dissent.

Massing dismisses as absurd my suggestion that government regulation of popular entertainment could affect political speech. Either he has an exceedingly narrow definition of "political," or he knows nothing of past and present censorship campaigns. Put aside the view of many people that rap music (which so offends many members of Congress) is political, and consider less controversial examples. Efforts to protect children (and women) from sex and violence in the media routinely target political speech. Blocking software installed or proposed for use in public schools and libraries across the country is notorious for blocking discussions of homosexuality, abortion, and AIDS prevention, among other political subjects. Censorship crusades in public schools have targeted writers like Maya Angelou, John Steinbeck, Margaret Atwood, E. M. Forster, and other authors whose works can fairly be called "political." In Colorado in the mid 1990s, a public-school teacher was fired for showing Bernardo Bertolucci's antifascist film *1900* to his senior class; the Colorado Supreme Court upheld his firing.

People who dare to suggest restricting political speech risk being "tarred and feathered," Massing confidently asserts. Not quite.

Some ascend to the nation's highest courts; others are elected to Congress and state legislatures. Is it unrealistic to believe that anti-abortion rhetoric might be restricted? State laws prohibiting protests outside abortion clinics, establishing no-speech "buffer zones," have been passed and upheld by the Supreme Court. It's also worth noting that Congress has very nearly passed a constitutional amendment criminalizing flag burning. The amendment, which was passed several times by the House and very narrowly defeated in the Senate, remains a serious threat. It's hard to imagine a clearer effort to censor political speech, but advocates of a flag burning amendment are usually re-elected to Congress, not run out of town on a rail.

Massing may regard these efforts as irrelevant to crusades against violent entertainment, but that's a bit like suggesting that discrimination against one stigmatized group of people has nothing to do with discrimination against another. What threatens First Amendment freedoms more than any isolated instance of censorship is the unifying rationale of all censorship campaigns—the presumption that "bad" speech directly causes "bad" behavior and that government officials should be empowered to distinguish good speech from bad. It's not the slippery slope I fear (that has always seemed like an inapt metaphor to me). It's the specter of bureaucrats and politicians armed with scythes, hacking through an open field.

SCREEN SAVIORS

Protecting civil liberties is an exercise in déjà vu. On March 20, 2001, for the third time in five years, the American Civil Liberties Union filed suit in the Third Circuit Court of Appeals in Philadelphia seeking to enjoin a federal law aimed at protecting children from the ravages of the Internet. First, the ACLU successfully challenged the 1996 Communications Decency Act (CDA), which prohibited "indecency" in cyberspace, and was struck down by a nearly unanimous Supreme Court. Then Congress enacted the Child Online Protection Act (COPA), criminalizing the commercial dissemination of speech deemed "harmful to minors"; the ACLU went back to the Third Circuit, which invalidated COPA. (In May 2002, the Supreme Court upheld the law in part but continued to enjoin its enforcement and sent it back to the lower courts for further review.) In the meantime, the ACLU, along with the American Library Association, challenged the Children's Internet Protection Act (CIPA), which conditions federal support for the nation's public schools and libraries on the installation of blocking software on computers. The ACLU suit focused on application of the law to public libraries. On May 31, 2002, a federal district court in Philadelphia struck down CIPA. After an extensive trial, the court found that filtering programs were both under- and over-inclusive: that is, they did not block "substantial amounts of content" that libraries intended to block but did block "large quantities" of constitutionally protected material that libraries did not intend to block. (It's unclear at this time if the government will appeal this decision to the Supreme Court.)

Supporters of CIPA sometimes argue that the use of censor-ware represents an ordinary exercise of discretion by librarians and school administrators who regularly edit material available to kids (devising a curriculum is partly a process of elimination). But in fact the use of blocking software represents a delegation of discretion to the anonymous employees of publicly unaccountable companies, like Cyberpatrol and NetNanny, who decide which sites will be blocked. Parents who take comfort from these programs might as well randomly select a group of people from the subway to monitor their children's reading habits.

The problems with CIPA are as obvious as the limitations of

This piece appeared in The American Prospect, *June 4, 2001* blocking software, which have been frequently chronicled. As the district court stressed, filtering programs are blunt instruments that censor a range of web sites unquestionably protected by the First Amendment—web sites of organizations ranging from Planned Parenthood (a plaintiff in the ACLU suit) to the U.S. Army Corp of Engineers; even a map of Disney World has fallen prey to the whims of cyber-censors. (The March 2001 issue of *Consumer Reports* confirmed the software's unreliability.)

Almost everyone's ox is likely to be gored. Recent conservative converts to the cause of free speech on the Internet include state chapters of the Eagle Forum and the American Family Association, which has been informed by Cyberpatrol that its web site is subject to being censored because of its opposition to "homosexual activism." One former Republican candidate for Congress joined the challenge to CIPA because Cyberpatrol blocked his campaign web site, which broadcast his positions on numerous issues, including the use of blocking software (he was for it).

Congress engages in self-parody when it passes legislation like CIPA, which was even opposed by the commission Congress established to study on-line protections for kids, but the consequences of this stupid law will not be funny. Critics have charged that it will widen the digital divide: If CIPA were resurrected and effectively enforced, it would arbitrarily limit access to the information and ideas available to children from low-income homes who depend on school and library computers.

But fear of the Internet and other media are stronger than appreciation of their benefits, especially with regard to kids. Anxiety, even paranoia, about the dangers faced by children today is intense. It's reflected partly in the dramatic increase in child-rearing manuals, which responsible parents are expected to read; in the popular view, parenting is not for amateurs. But even the manuals recognize that parents have limited control outside the home (although they are encouraged to intervene at school). Parents who are appalled by popular culture can retreat from it entirely into insular communities (consider the Amish), or they can retreat in part by home schooling their kids. But exile is an option for only a few, and many people who oppose popular culture don't want to retreat from it anyway; they want to reform it.

You can't control popular culture without controlling speech, which many are hungry to do, in the belief that they would be regulating behavior or harm, not expression. People often assume that whatever speech they deem offensive actually causes serious harm. ("It's not about censorship; it's about harassment" or "discrimination," the politically correct are apt to say.) "Bad" speech is viewed, at best, as a form of reckless endangerment, especially when minors are involved. The dearth of empirical evidence demonstrating that sexual explicitness poses psychological harm to minors is irrelevant to people for whom the harm of offensive material is an article of faith. Many are equally convinced that violent material endangers minors and society in general, although evidence of its actual harm remains speculative. The belief that video games, for example, cause school shootings and other horrors is merely a belief, which does not justify prohibiting them.

There is little question that the Constitution (and a regard for free speech in general) requires proof that speech causes actual, and immediate, harm before it can be prohibited. That principle was recently affirmed by the estimable Judge Richard Posner of the Seventh Circuit Court of Appeals, in an opinion enjoining enforcement of an Indianapolis ordinance that would limit a minor's access to violent video games. In *American Amusement Machine Association v. Kendrick,* Posner stressed that the government's claim that violent video games incited violence was entirely unsubstantiated. The few studies cited by the city did not show that "video games have ever caused anyone to commit a violent act, as opposed to feeling aggressive, or have caused the average level of violence to increase anywhere." (In addition, there was no indication that the games affected by the Indianapolis law were similar to the games that were studied.)

Conventional wisdom about the harm of violent video games (and other media) often persuades legislators to prohibit unpopular speech, but it is not evidence in a court of law. "The grounds (for suppressing speech) must be compelling, not merely plausible," Judge Posner observed. Besides, he suggested, the harm of censorship is as plausible as the harm of violent speech:

"People are unlikely to become well-functioning, independent-minded adults and responsible citizens if they are raised in an intellectual bubble. No doubt the city would concede this point if the question were whether to forbid children to read without the presence of an adult the *Odyssey*, with its graphic descriptions of Odysseus's grinding out the eye of Polyphemus with a heated sharpened stake, killing the suitors, and hanging the treacherous maidservants . . ."

I wish I had this much faith in government officials. School administrators regularly censor respected works of literature (like *Huck-*

leberry Finn) to mollify angry parents (sometimes all it takes to ban a book is one or two complaints). "It's not about censorship, it's about protecting children," the censors will say. But depriving kids of access to information, ideas, and their choice of literary pleasures seems more like punishment than protection to me. Once the juvenile courts deprived children of due process rights in order to protect them. I'm often suspicious of child-savers.

COURTING UNSAFE SPEECH

It is possible, of course, that computer-simulated images of virtual children having virtual sex may encourage pedophiles to act on their impulses or assist them in seducing children. There is, however, little or no empirical evidence that these images have such dire effects. Congress criminalized virtual child porn anyway.

The Child Pornography Prevention Act of 1996 (CPPA) prohibited computer images that "appear" to show actual children engaged in sex; it also banned advertising, promoting, or describing any sexually explicit images "in such a manner that conveys the impression" that actual children are depicted. Antiporn activists insisted that this ban on virtual porn was essential to protecting children and enforcing laws against actual child pornography, since prosecutors may not be able to distinguish the actual from the virtual variety. Free speech advocates charged that the CPPA allowed for the prosecution of thought crimes, by criminalizing nonobscene images of imaginary children engaged in imaginary sex. The Supreme Court agreed: On April 16, 2002, in *Ashcroft v. Free Speech Coalition*, it struck down the virtual porn provisions of the CPPA, in a 6 to 3 decision. The Court left intact parts of the law that banned using or manipulating images of actual children to produce pornography; but it found the ban on virtual porn clearly unconstitutional because it "proscribe(d) the visual depiction of an idea." Writing for the majority, Justice Kennedy eloquently pointed out the obvious: "The right to think is the beginning of freedom, and speech must be protected from the government because speech is the beginning of thought."

Speech is the beginning of action, defenders of the virtual porn ban would respond, but as the Supreme Court has repeatedly held, the possible or presumed effects of speech do not justify its suppression. Criminal law is supposed to address the action, not the word—the act of child abuse, not the idea of it. Civil libertarians have long accepted (and supported) bans on depicting actual children engaged in actual sex. Traditional child porn laws need not rely on speculation about the harm caused by the distribution of sexually explicit images involving minors; they can rely instead on the harm caused by the *production* of sexually explicit images involving minors.

But laws against depictions of imaginary children can only rely on imaginary evidence of harm. As the Ninth Circuit observed in *Free*

A version of this piece appeared in The American Prospect, *June 18, 2001*

Speech Coalition v. Reno, in 1999: "Factual studies that establish the link between computer-generated child pornography and the subsequent sexual abuse of children apparently do not yet exist." Indeed, in enacting the CPPA, Congress invoked the report of the pornography commission led by former attorney general Meese in the 1980s, which only addressed the suspected harms of pornography involving actual children. In other words, the Ninth Circuit stressed, the CPPA relied on findings that "predate" the technology it targeted.

Still, defenders of the CPPA equate actual and virtual porn, simply because they are difficult to distinguish visually. "Both actual and counterfeit child pornography will pass for the real thing and incite pedophiles to molest and children to be victims," according to the amicus brief filed by the National Law Center for Children and Families (and several other conservative advocacy groups). "If the pedophile and the child victim cannot tell the difference, there is no difference in the effect conveyed." What's wrong with this reasoning? (Put aside the callous disregard of the difference to real children who are forced to have sex in the production of real pornography.) It assumes its conclusion—that virtual child porn incites pedophilia and creates "child victims." It advocates criminalizing speech because of its presumed effect on a particular class of listeners—people inclined toward child abuse.

Courts have confronted this argument repeatedly in First Amendment cases, particularly in cases involving pornography. In 1985, in *American Booksellers Association v. Hudnut,* the Seventh Circuit Court of Appeals struck down a local antiporn ordinance based on the assumption that pornography leads to the objectification of women, contributing to sexual violence and discrimination. Accepting this assumption for the sake of argument, the court pointed out its inadequacies: "All of these unhappy effects depend on mental intermediation." In other words, the listener as well as the speaker determines the meaning and impact of any verbal or visual communication. That's why its consequences are unpredictable. The power of speech is collaborative.

A ban on virtual child porn relies heavily on the subjective reactions of viewers, which means that speakers are given little notice of precisely what speech is criminalized. When Congress bans sexually explicit material that "appears" to depict minors engaged in sex, you have to ask "appears to whom?" A lot of people over forty have trouble distinguishing nineteen-year-olds from precocious fifteen-year-olds. The CPPA could easily have been construed to prohibit nonobscene sexually explicit images of young adults. Congress did provide targets of the law with a defense: that the alleged child porn involved an actual person, who was an adult at the time the image was produced (so this defense would not apply in cases of virtual child porn) *and* that the image was not promoted in a way that "conveyed the impression" that it involved a minor. "Conveyed to whom?" you have to ask.

What are people talking about when they talk about child pornography? That depends. Some point to Calvin Klein ads or the movie version of *Lolita,* not to mention the book. Supreme Court Justice Scalia (who voted to uphold the CPPA) inadvertently confirmed the continuing vulnerability of *Lolita* during oral argument in *Ashcroft v. Free Speech Coalition.* When the attorney challenging the virtual porn ban offered "the movie *Lolita*" as an example of a work of art that the ban would imperil, Justice Scalia responded sarcastically, "A great work of art," adding "with all due respect" that *Lolita* "is not the *Mona Lisa* or the *Venus de Milo.*" He's right that *Lolita* does not enjoy the universal acclaim of established Renaissance masterpieces, but his observation was irrelevant: Books, films, paintings, and other forms of speech need not occupy places in the pantheon of great art (or popular culture) in order to enjoy First Amendment protection. The First Amendment is not designed to protect either the *Venus de Milo* or Mickey Mouse. It's designed for the protection of contested, controversial works, like *Lolita* or *Huckleberry Finn.* In Oklahoma City, *The Tin Drum,* the 1979 film based on the novel by Günter Grass, has been condemned as pornographic; in 1997, local officials confiscated copies of this allegedly dangerous film, which includes a scene suggestive of oral sex between a six-year-old boy and a teenage girl. A court in Oklahoma judged the film obscene.

People intent on restricting sexual imagery will dismiss cases like this as "horror stories," suggesting that they're rare or even apocryphal. In fact, they're fairly common, as anyone familiar with the recent history of censorship knows. In public schools and libraries across the country, censors intent on suppressing sexual explicitness or mere discussions of sexuality regularly target an odd assortment of books by such authors as Henry Miller, D. H. Lawrence, James Joyce, E. M. Forster, May Sarton, and Judy Blume.

These authors have impassioned defenders, of course, and they sometimes succeed in resisting censors who target works with acknowledged social or artistic value. (As a general rule, speech must be found to have no redeeming value to be considered obscene.) Defending material that allegedly violated a ban on virtual child porn would have been much more difficult, since evidence of social, scientific, or artistic value is irrelevant to a charge of child pornography.

The CPPA's bans on virtual child porn and suggestive advertising were doomed partly because they could easily have been applied to respected works of art (like *Romeo and Juliet*, the Supreme Court observed). But the broad reach of the law was not accidental. Retiring North Carolina senator Jesse Helms included some sex education materials in his definition of child porn. Not that attacks on sexually explicit or suggestive speech emanate only from the right. The CPPA was enacted with the support of centrist democrats, including Bill Clinton, who signed it into law. Sex does have inevitable perils (as the former president found out), but, thanks to the Supreme Court, fantasizing about sexual activity is, once again, not as risky as engaging in it.

VIRTUAL OFFENSIVENESS

Over fifteen years have passed since anti-libertarian feminists declared "pornography" a violation of women's civil rights, alleging that it demeaned and objectified women. In the 1980s, the antiporn movement enjoyed a lot of publicity and a little local legislative success. But federal courts quickly struck down antiporn ordinances that classified some sexually explicit speech as discriminatory and offered women private rights of action against its producers or distributors. In *American Booksellers Association v. Hudnut,* the court of appeals stressed that government officials cannot prohibit speech because they disapprove of its perspective: In America, people have a right to suggest that the sexual subordination of women is preferable to sexual equality.

This was an important but limited victory for civil liberty. The model antiporn law once promoted by feminists did not survive legal challenges, but its underlying view of pornography as a civil rights violation has reframed debates about free speech: During the 1990s, the equation of offensive or hateful speech with actual discrimination successfully infiltrated both the courts and the culture. Popular therapies confirmed that abuse could be verbal as well as physical, because people were fragile and apt to be deeply wounded by words—especially if they were members of historically oppressed groups, according to the politically correct left. Employment discrimination claims involving allegations of verbal harassment proliferated; in one notorious discrimination case, *Aguilar v. Avis,* the California Supreme Court upheld a prior restraint against the use of "derogatory racial or ethnic epithets" by an employee of Avis Rent-A-Car.

So it's not surprising that a former subscriber to America Online has filed a federal lawsuit complaining that AOL has violated his civil rights by not censoring hate speech in a chat room. Saad Noah, a Muslim, charges AOL with ignoring the harassment of Muslims in chat rooms devoted to discussions of Islam and the Koran. He has offered numerous examples of moronic epithets and obscenities directed against Muslims (occurring before September 11), all of which he claims to have reported to AOL. Noah has a contract claim, because in its terms of service contract, AOL imposes severe restrictions on "offensive" speech. He has also filed a complaint under the 1964 Civil Rights Act, claiming that AOL is a public accommodation, from

This piece appeared in The American Prospect, *November 19, 2001*

which Noah and other Muslims have been effectively excluded by AOL's failure to punish anti-Muslim speech.

Noah's civil rights complaint will resonate with liberals concerned about "inclusiveness," and with many people particularly wary of increased discrimination against Muslims, but it is likely to be greeted skeptically in federal court. Under the Civil Rights Act, the term "public accommodation" has generally been construed to apply to physical facilities or structures. In a 1993 case, a federal appeals court declined to classify the Boy Scouts as a public accommodation (although the BSA may qualify as one under state and local antidiscrimination laws), and in 1995, the Supreme Court ruled that Boston's St. Patrick's Day Parade was not a public accommodation (and could not be prohibited from excluding gays.)

Of course, the 1964 Civil Rights Act was written before anyone in Congress could even imagine cyberspace. Today many people probably can't imagine life without it. Distinctions between actual and real worlds are diminishing, and it's easy to understand how an AOL chat room might be deemed the equivalent of an actual place. Indeed, this is not the first lawsuit that has tried to hold AOL accountable as a public accommodation under federal law. In 1999, the National Federation for the Blind sued AOL under the Americans with Disabilities Act for failing to provide adequate access to blind people, through special software. (The suit was settled.) But if the concept of a virtual public accommodation makes sense to denizens of cyberspace, or enterprising lawyers, courts may decline to expand federal laws quite so drastically, leaving the task of creating new civil rights in cyberspace to Congress.

In any case, advocates of Noah's civil rights claim should note that the view of AOL as the proprietor of a public space could be used to expand, not restrict, the speech rights of its inhabitants. From the perspective of many AOL users, a chat room may seem more like a public forum than a place of accommodation, although current legal definitions of public forums are no more likely to include AOL than current definitions of public accommodations. AOL is a private entity, and the application of public forum law to private spaces is complicated and controversial. The Supreme Court has declined to classify privately owned, publicly used spaces (like shopping malls) as public forums under the federal Constitution, although a privately owned mall may be deemed a public forum under state law because of its public functions.

I know of no cases that have tried to extend public forum rules to privately operated sites in cyberspace, but I anticipate them. From the perspective of an individual speaker, media giants like AOL function like bureaucracies, controlling what feels like public space. And, the more public the space maintained by AOL, the sharper the conflict between the alleged civil rights of people offended by hate speech and the civil liberties of people speaking. Everyone has a right to walk down a public street, but no one has a right not to be insulted there.

I imagine that AOL regards this debate about speech as irrelevant. It considers itself neither a public accommodation nor a public forum, and it would have relatively little to fear from a civil rights suit based solely on AOL's current status under federal law. But if Saad Noah is likely to lose on his civil rights claim, he may prevail on his contract claim. AOL's service contract with its users includes a speech code that would please the most politically correct of college administrators: Users' accounts are subject to termination if they "harass, threaten, embarrass, or do anything else to another member that is unwanted" or if they "transmit or facilitate distribution" of "racially or ethnically offensive" speech. It would be hard to devise a vaguer, more subjective rule than a prohibition on "unwanted" speech, and I can't imagine why AOL thinks it can or should save people from ever being embarrassed. But having stupidly imposed extreme restrictions on speech, AOL may be liable for failing to try to enforce them.

So, under AOL's contract, Noah could succeed in establishing his right not to be offended in a chat room—at the cost of his own right not to offend or merely embarrass anyone else, even unintentionally. It's hard to see this as a victory for civil rights. It's hard to imagine how the Civil Rights movement might have prospered with equivalent restrictions on speech. Attacks on Jim Crow laws deeply offended a lot of segregationists. Social change can be achieved without violence, but it is rarely polite.

GRAND OLD RAG

In 1989, the Supreme Court rightly held that the First Amendment protected peaceful political protests involving flag burnings. In an opinion joined by conservative justices Scalia and Kennedy, the Court stressed that by punishing flag desecration, we "dilute the freedom that this cherished emblem represents."

That simple and obvious principle, however, is too subtle for some members of Congress to grasp, while others who understand the importance of preserving the freedom for which the flag stands often lack the political courage or desire to do so. In the late 1990s, a constitutional amendment providing for the prohibition of flag burning was passed by the House on several occasions and only narrowly defeated in the Senate. After September 11, there's a strong likelihood that both houses of Congress will eventually approve the flag desecration amendment, which the states will quickly ratify.

Supporters of the amendment naturally present themselves as patriots, in the belief that preserving every single flag made in America (or Hong Kong) displays greater love of country than protecting every instance of political dissent. They extol the flag as a primary unifying symbol of American community and invoke the ethos of political correctness: The communal right not to be offended, they argue, prevails over the individual right to offend. Opponents of the flag amendment extol the willingness to tolerate flag desecration as a measure of our commitment to political freedom. And they question the wisdom of amending the Constitution to address a symbolic problem that barely exists: Between 1990 and 1995 there were about eight reported flag burnings a year. The Republic withstood them.

No one, however, defends public shows of disrespect for the flag. For the most ardent defenders of free speech, flag desecration is like Nazi porn—"bad" speech that must be defended for the sake of protecting "good" speech. On both sides of the debate, people declare their love for the flag and their contempt for people who burn it. Everyone laments flag desecration, even if they uphold the right to engage in it; no one dares question the value of flag worship.

Yet, considering its history, sanctification of the flag reflects some of the more shameful characteristics of American culture: nativism, jingoism, and faith-based nationalism that portrays God as a virtual American. In *The American Flag*—my source for the history that

This piece appeared in The Nation, *April 28, 1997*

follows—Scot Guenter deftly chronicles the evolution of flag worship. Ever since Francis Scott Key wrote his ode to the star-spangled banner during the battle for Fort McHenry in 1814, campaigns to sanctify the flag have been fueled by war, fear of immigration, and an association of the flag and the cross, exemplified by the Ku Klux Klan. The crassest uses of the flag—in advertisements and political campaigns—have probably been the most harmless.

Politicians quickly recognized the advantages of identifying with the national banner. By the mid-1800s, candidates were placing their portraits in the upper corner of the flag, where the stars were supposed to be. Decorative and commercial uses of the flag were also coming into vogue; the stars and stripes appeared on wallpaper, hatboxes, and even a Parcheesi board. Eventually it would be widely used in advertisements for the most mundane products—shaving cream or sarsaparilla.

Commercial exploitation of Old Glory prompted efforts to pass flag desecration laws in the late 1800s. The first such statute, introduced in Congress in 1880, would have criminalized advertisements using the flag. (The bill passed the House but not the Senate.) A similar proposal was introduced and defeated ten years later, largely because of economic and political interests in exploiting the flag; but bills prohibiting commercial use of it were eventually passed in several states (and upheld by a 1907 Supreme Court decision). Concerns about free speech played no part in early debates over flag desecration. The notion that government suppression of unpopular speech was unconstitutional did not take hold until after World War I.

The first campaigns for flag-desecration legislation reflected a cult of the flag inspired by the Civil War. When the Confederate army fired on the flag at Fort Sumter in 1861, it gave the Union a powerful rallying symbol and ushered in a new period of flag idolatry. Volunteers pledged their lives to the stars and stripes, in the belief that it symbolized not just the nation, but also the kingdom of God. Magazines glorified loyalty to our "sacred flag," which was said to remind us that we are born "not of the flesh but of God." Churches mounted flags on their spires or attached the flag and cross. Some thirty years later, Scot Guenter notes, an advocate for flag desecration laws declared, "Three sacred jewels—the Bible, the Cross, and the Flag—command the national reverence."

Of course, sanctification of the flag is always apt to flourish during wartime, along with the notion that God chooses sides. Flag worship might have declined after the Civil War, but it was taken up to defend American values in the face of increasing immigration. The nativist, anti-Catholic know-nothing movement of the 1840s initiated use of the flag as a symbol of white Protestant Americanism. By the 1870s and '80s, nativists were promoting the notion that flag rituals would Americanize the children of immigrants. An early crusader for flag worship in the public schools, George T. Balch, regarded immigrants as "human scum," Scot Guenter writes. Balch believed that public schools, replete with flag rituals, would facilitate "elevation of the masses."

The "Pledge of Allegiance," introduced by a popular magazine, *The Youth's Companion*, in 1892, has its origins in an "American Patriotic Salute," championed by Balch. It required students to pledge their hearts and heads to God and country, with right arms outstretched, in a gesture prefiguring Nazi salutes. During World War II, students were taught to place their hands over their hearts instead, which didn't make the collective ritual of pledging allegiance any less sheeplike. The tradition of reciting the pledge in conjunction with a school prayer, which continued throughout the 1950s, maintained the linkage between love of Christ and love of country.

Balch did not live to see his vision realized, but around the turn of the century, states began mandating flag worship in the public schools. Nativism and jingoism continued to drive this movement. The first statute requiring daily flag salutes in the schools was passed by New York state the day after the Spanish American War was declared. Less than twenty years later, World War I inspired yet another outburst of flag waving, accompanied by paranoid fantasies about subversion that would result in the imprisonment of political dissidents under the Espionage Act. During this period, the state of Kansas criminalized mere expressions of disrespect for the flag.

Meanwhile, flag fetishists developed complicated rules about how to handle and display flags, carry them in processions, display them with other flags or in church, drape them over caskets, and, in the end, how to dispose of them. You do not simply throw out a tattered flag or use it as a bandanna. You're supposed to cremate it, with all due reverence. According to the Flag Code adopted by the National Flag Conference in 1923, "The flag represents the living country and is itself considered as a living thing."

Graduates of scouting, summer camps, and public schools generally take flag fetishism for granted, but mulling it over, you might wonder about the mental stability of people who regard the flag as sentient and obsess about folding it properly, taking it down at sunset, or never letting it touch the ground. You might ask how many times a day they wash their hands.

Repetitive, ritualistic behavior does seem a lot less peculiar when it is an expression of religious devotion. We expect people to kiss the Torah or the cross. In fact, we may hope that devotion to the higher authority represented by religion will inspire people to question the authority of government, which is why religion serves us best when it keeps its distance from the state. We should shudder when people kiss the flag, transforming a national emblem into a vessel of the divine.

We should, perhaps, appreciate the most irreverent commercial exploitation of our flag. It's a defense against religious nationalism. If politically inspired flag burnings fuel the passions of flag fetishists, flag boxer shorts debunk them. Flag neckties, toothpicks, T-shirts, and dog sweaters demonstrate that, as George M. Cohan originally wrote, it's only a grand old rag.

FREEDOM'S EDGE

In November 2001, two militant advocates for AIDS patients in San Francisco were charged with stalking and threatening public-health officials, researchers, and reporters who had made or disseminated statements about AIDS prevention and the behavior of infected gay men—statements with which the advocates disagreed. Naturally, with no apparent sense of irony, they asserted a First Amendment defense.

The suspects, David Pasquarelli and Michael Petrelis, were treated quite harshly—held for seventy-three days in pretrial detention, each on $500,000 bail. They admitted having made or encouraged "foul" late-night phone calls to the homes of officials who work at the federal Centers for Disease Control in Atlanta and others they consider the "enemies of gay people." (The phone calls began in November 2001, after San Francisco initiated a syphilis-awareness campaign inspired by an increase in the disease among gay and bisexual men.) But Pasquarelli and Petrelis denied making the threats of violence that their targets reported receiving: "They told me they were going to hunt me down, that I was in their sights," Carl T. Hall, a science writer for the *San Francisco Chronicle,* alleges. Dr. Jeffrey Klausner, otherwise known on the Net as Dr. KKK Klausner because of his references to quarantining sexually active infected gay men, claimed that he and his family received threatening, obscene calls at home. Petrelis and Pasquarelli are expected to stand trial in the late spring or early summer of 2002.

Of course, they have an obvious right to offend, unsettle, or denounce their ideological opponents—and a concomitant obligation to tolerate being offended, unsettled, or denounced. But they have no right to target people intentionally with plausible threats of violence, which hardly advance or encourage public debate. The prosecution of Petrelis and Pasquarelli did not present a difficult legal issue so much as a controlling question of fact: Did they or did they not intentionally issue the alleged threats?

The Ninth Circuit Court of Appeals, which could eventually hear this case if it winds up in federal court, grappled with a very similar question raised by a civil lawsuit. In March 2001, in *Planned Parenthood v. American Coalition of Life Activists,* a three-judge panel of the Ninth Circuit overturned a verdict by a federal jury that hit the ACLA, a group of antiabortion extremists, with a more than $100 million damage

A version of this piece appeared in The American Prospect, *February 11, 2002*

award for threatening abortion providers. In addition to circulating wanted posters that featured doctors who performed abortions, the appellants had contributed information about doctors and clinic workers to the notorious Nuremberg Files site on the Internet. That site maintained a hit list of over two hundred providers, including personal information about them, like names, addresses, license plate numbers, and children's names. After three doctors on the list were slain, lines were put through their names; the names of the wounded were listed in gray.

In overturning this verdict, Judge Alex Kozinski likened the alleged threats against abortion providers to the protected rhetoric of civil rights activists involved in a landmark 1982 Supreme Court case, *NAACP v. Claiborne Hardware*. It involved a boycott against white-owned businesses in Mississippi; one boycott organizer, Charles Evers, was said to have threatened retaliation against people who broke the boycott: "If we catch any of you going in any of them racist stores, we're gonna break your damn neck," Evers exclaimed. But the Court held that these remarks were protected speech—because Evers had not "directly threatened acts of violence." (Evers was making a speech to a crowd, not stalking or otherwise targeting particular individuals.) He was guilty of rhetorical excesses, not the issuance of intentional, plausible threats. The Court also stressed that Evers could not be held to have intentionally incited violence.

Claiborne Hardware was rightly decided, but it is the wrong precedent for the Nuremberg Files case. Abortion activists were not sued for inciting violence but for threatening it—against targeted individuals. And context is essential in determining whether or not a rhetorical flourish is an actual threat. Antiabortion activists issued wanted posters and hit lists during a wave of homicidal violence against clinics and clinic workers. The threats were quite plausible (people had been killed), the FBI was offering protection to targeted doctors, and one defendant, Andrew Burnett, even admitted that the threats were real: "If I was an abortionist, I would be afraid," he testified.

The Ninth Circuit's reversal of this verdict inspired a predictable outburst of protests among pro-choicers (and debates among free-speech advocates), and the full court reheard the case in December 2001. The timing was not propitious for antiabortion extremists. Fear of terrorism is much stronger these days than respect for speech. And in May 2002, in a 6 to 5 decision, the full court reversed itself and upheld the verdict against the ACLA, although it ordered a reduction in the damage award. This verdict was rightly restored—not in reaction to September 11, and not to stop violence against abortion providers, but to punish and perhaps deter intentional efforts to terrorize people.

Holding the ACLA liable for issuing intentional threats is not likely to begin a descent down the slippery slope of censorship, chilling offensive or unpopular political speech, or depictions and expressions of violence in popular entertainment. The usual debates about the causal connection between disputed speech and harmful behavior are irrelevant here. Neither the Nuremberg Files case nor the prosecution of AIDS activists in San Francisco were based on claims that speech causes violence: The defendants in both cases were charged not with causing physical harm to people but with intentionally instilling fear in them. For freedom's sake, we all have to tolerate being vilified, embarrassed, or harassed, but freedom will survive if we acknowledge a right not to be terrorized.

THE ROOT OF ALL SPEECH

Despite the materialism that defines American culture and our reverence for financial success, a suspicion that money really is the root of all evil retains its appeal, especially among progressives. The association of wealth with corruption is particularly clear in debates about campaign finance reform. Reformers are self-proclaimed proponents of "clean elections"; their opponents are presumed to favor dirty politics. Even centrist politicians eager to occupy the moral high ground (along with the occasional conservative like John McCain) fulminate against "big money" and "special interests."

Of course, the view that political contributions exert undue influence on policy is not exactly unfounded. Bribery, or what one Tammany Hall figure called "illegal graft," (as opposed to "honest graft") is an especially sturdy political tradition. Voters as well as politicians are subject to being bought (however unwittingly) by the political ads and image-making machines that contributions finance. But fear and loathing of concentrated wealth does sometimes blind "clean election" advocates to the complexities of campaign regulations and the role of money in politics.

Nothing seems to irritate reformers more than the assertion that limits on money—campaign contributions or expenditures—are the equivalent of limits on speech. Money isn't speech; it's property, Supreme Court Justice Stevens declared in a 2000 case upholding a Missouri law limiting campaign contributions. His insistence that money isn't speech has visceral appeal; it seems so egalitarian, so democratic. But it's wishful thinking, a rhetorical fantasy.

Money makes speech possible. *The American Prospect* publishes biweekly thanks to the generous support of wealthy benefactors. Money isn't speech? Try telling that to the folks at National Public Radio the next time they beg you for money to keep their programming on the air. If Congress passed a law limiting the amount of money we could spend annually on books or newspapers, we would probably not say, "Never mind. Money isn't speech."

In our society, money facilitates the exercise of rights. Children who attend schools in poor districts don't receive equal educations unless schools throughout the state are equitably funded. Poor women don't enjoy abortion rights if they can't afford abortions, unless we provide for Medicaid funding. Often, people need public

A version of this piece appeared in The American Prospect, *July 30, 2000*

subsidies that enable them to exercise rights and achieve some measure of equality, which is why progressives advocate expanding our notions of individual rights so that they protect basic economic needs, like housing or health care.

Like it or not, this relationship between money and the enjoyment of rights is an American fact of life, and as a practical matter (absent a revolution), it is essentially immutable. It is an argument for public financing of campaigns designed to subsidize candidates who do not have personal fortunes or major party support, and an argument against limits on contributions and expenditures. Public financing systems can expand access to little-known candidates by establishing a financial floor for candidates, without imposing a ceiling on them. Opponents of public financing argue that when the government compels contributions to a "clean money" fund, it essentially compels political speech. They have a point, but it seems mainly theoretical, given the small scale of individual contributions and the wide range of political views a public fund could support.

Ceilings on spending and contributions impose greater practical restrictions on political expression. They directly limit your right to support particular candidates who share your interests and ideals. When the government restricts our ability to spend money, it directly restricts our ability to speak. That fact doesn't end debates about campaign finance reform, but it does complicate them. They become debates about balancing individual rights (free speech) with other social goods that some presume will follow from reform—curbs on the political power of wealth and increased public faith in the electoral process.

On balance, the damage done to First Amendment rights seems much greater than the presumed benefits of reforms banning soft money donations to national parties or restricting hard money contributions to individual candidates. The promise that reforms will greatly limit the influence of wealthy "special interests" on elections is either naive or disingenuous. As numerous critics have pointed out, virtually all reforms include numerous funding loopholes, and "special interests" can exert influence on politicians without directly funding them anyway. (Big businesses provide big jobs for retiring officials and their aides.) The promise that reforms will increase faith in the system is quite speculative. Advocates of reform claim that campaign finance abuses cause voter apathy; the claim is plausible, but I've never seen much evidence to support it. The counterclaim that these abuses have little effect on voter participation seems equally plausible. Politics has long been regarded as a scoundrel's game. Regardless of campaign finance laws, people seem to expect a certain amount of thievery from elected officials. At the same time, they manage to put their faith in quite a few.

The harms of reform to free speech (and political discourse), however, are clear. Existing restrictions on campaign contributions have already created more problems than they solved. As almost everyone knows, federal reforms passed in 1974 limited both campaign contributions and expenditures. The Supreme Court struck down the limits on expenditures but upheld limits on contributions to candidates. This ruling greatly advantaged incumbents, who don't need to buy as much speech as insurgents. In the 1996 congressional election, for example, all incumbents who spent less than half a million dollars were re-elected, while only 3 percent of all challengers who spent less than half a million dollars succeeded in knocking off incumbents.

Still, the Supreme Court has so far remained somewhat blindly sympathetic to reform efforts. It recently upheld limits on contributions, in a case that clearly demonstrated their dangers. *Nixon v. Shrink Missouri Government PAC,* decided in January 2000, involved a challenge to Missouri's campaign limits by an outsider candidate who was substantially disadvantaged by the cap on individual contributions. Major party candidates had much greater visibility and access to soft money—unregulated dollars contributed in unlimited amounts to the parties, not to particular candidates. The law provided that soft money could be used for issue advocacy, not in support of particular candidates, but in this respect, the law was often unenforceable. In political campaigns, it's not always possible to distinguish between advocating for issues and advocating for candidates.

The 2002 campaign finance reform law is supposed to lessen access problems for insurgents (and bribery of incumbents) by banning soft-money contributions to the national parties (the market for which was created by the 1974 reforms). But it's likely that this reform will lessen the power of the national parties more than the influence of soft money on politics. State parties can still receive soft money (at a rate of $10,000 per donor) and so, of course, can private groups. Before the 2002 law was passed, private interest groups had already started to emerge as alternative receptacles for "big money." Dissatisfied with the disclosure requirements that accompany contributions to political parties, wealthy contributors had begun forming their own not-for-profit issue advocacy groups, which were not required to disclose their donors. These were stealth groups that operated under names like Americans United for Good Things—groups whose political interests or agendas aren't at all clear, groups like Republicans for Clean Air: Organized by a wealthy Bush ally, it ran anti-McCain ads in New York prior to the Republican primary in the 2000 presidential election. As Supreme Court Justice Kennedy observed in his dissent in *Nixon v. Shrink*, limits on campaign contributions have greatly increased incentives for a new kind of "covert" political speech. Campaign finance reform "forced a substantial amount of speech underground."

Covert speech can be made overt, however, and Congress has limited the anonymity of major donors. Prohibiting large, anonymous contributions to political parties or stealthy surrogate groups does raise substantial First Amendment concerns: Anonymity is an important element of free speech. If you're a closeted homosexual or Second Amendment advocate, you may not want your contribution to a gay rights group or to the NRA made public. On balance, however, the danger of a secret campaign finance system may outweigh the danger of restricting the right to speak anonymously, through large political contributions.

But reformers are not content with disclosure requirements. The 2002 reform law greatly limits the right of advocacy groups to engage in actual political advocacy. It prohibits nonprofit, public-policy advocacy groups from even mentioning a candidate's name in broadcast issue ads that run within thirty days of a primary or sixty days of a general election, when voters are paying attention. The law requires advocacy groups to establish separate, partisan political action committees to fund ads within a month or two of elections, which many nonpartisan groups will be unable to do. And rules limiting PAC contributions to five thousand dollars per donor would make it difficult if not impossible for advocacy groups to raise the funds they'd need for broadcast issue ads. Pursuant to this provision, wealthy individuals, from Barbra Streisand to Richard Scaife, retain the right to buy their own TV or radio ads, so long as they act individually. But the less wealthy are prohibited from pooling their resources to broadcast political speech.

Supporters of the law pretend that this restriction only affects sleazy stealth-attack ads, but in fact it will curb civil, issue advocacy by established citizens' groups. In March 2002, for example, the American Civil Liberties Union ran a newspaper and radio ad in House Speaker Denny Hastert's congressional district urging Hastert to allow a floor vote on a bill prohibiting workplace discrimination against homosexuals, without speaking for or against his re-election. As the ACLU observed in opposing the 2002 campaign finance reform law, this ad would have been prohibited under the new law, because it ran within thirty days of a primary in which Hastert was running, unopposed.

It's clear that effectively prohibiting political ads by private groups during election season constitutes a substantial, indeed unprecedented limitation on core political speech. [As this book goes to press, a politically diverse coalition is mounting a legal challenge to the new law.] Ordinary people exercise political power by acting collectively: A restriction on speech by citizens' groups is a restriction on speech by individual citizens. Under the pretense of cleansing the electoral system Congress is crippling our right to participate in it.

This is the dilemma for reformers: If they limit independent expenditures and private-issue advocacy, they deprive private citizens of First Amendment rights during political campaigns; if they don't limit these expenditures, they have no hope of limiting the influence of money on elections.

Now imagine that the Supreme Court accepts restrictions on organized issue advocacy as necessary evils of campaign reform. Who will be left to speak in the crucial weeks before an election? Cable bloviators and other electronic and print pundits, including all those liberal columnists who support campaign finance reform, will continue engaging in issue advocacy or offering criticism and praise of particular candidates. Rupert Murdoch and other moguls will still be free to slant news coverage in favor of their guys. But advocacy groups representing ordinary citizens will be restricted by law from buying ads on a Murdoch station criticizing or even naming his favored candidates. It's not surprising that major media outlets, like the *New York Times* and the *Washington Post,* have relentlessly supported campaign finance reform. It promises to give established media, pundits, and elected officials exclusive rights to effective political speech in the crucial month or two before an election. I doubt that will open up our democracy in ways that reformers have in mind.

THE WAR ON HIGH SCHOOLS

High school gave me my first lessons in bureaucracy: Rules were meant to be rigidly applied, not questioned; power was meant to be abused by petty functionaries. I don't mean to malign the entire faculty of my school. It included some very good teachers who encouraged curiosity and provocation and never lost their sense of humor. Because of them, high school also offered opportunities for self-expression and contained rebellion.

I regularly got into trouble for insubordination, but I was never suspended, much less expelled. It was the mid-1960s, a time of protest, not zero tolerance, and there was no clear rule prohibiting challenging or even insulting teachers and administrators. So the authorities simply reported me to my parents. My beleaguered mother came to expect their phone calls and made frequent visits to school, trying to placate whoever I'd offended. "You have such a nice mother," one of my teachers once said to me with wonder.

I doubt that my mother or any of my teachers could protect me from the wrath of school bureaucrats today. Fearful of violence and drugs, intolerant of dissent or simple nonconformity, public school officials are on the rampage. They're suspending and expelling even grade school students for making what might be considered, at worst, inappropriate remarks, dressing oddly, or simply expressing political opinions. Efforts to strip students of rights are hardly new, but they intensified after the 1999 shootings at Columbine High in Littleton, Colorado, amidst hysteria about school violence and "terroristic threats."

By the end of the 1990s, the American Civil Liberties Union was receiving hundreds of complaints about cases like this: In Ohio, a third grader was suspended after writing a fortune cookie message, "You will die an honorable death," which he submitted as a school project. (A terroristic threat? Or an innocent remark by a child who watches martial arts videos?) Eleven high school students in Ohio were suspended for contributing to a gothic-themed web site. In Virginia, a tenth grader was suspended for dying his hair blue. In Missouri, a high school junior was suspended and required to perform forty-two days of community service with the local police department for offering an opinion on school violence on an Internet chat room: When asked if a tragedy like the Littleton shootings could happen in

A version of this piece appeared in The American Prospect, *December 20, 1999*

his school, he responded "yes." In Louisiana, a twelve-year-old boy was suspended and held in juvenile detention for over two weeks after uttering a "threat" on a lunch line: "If you take all the potatoes, I'm gonna get you," the accused terrorist said.

Those students who dare to use their speech rights to protest such draconian restrictions on speech are liable to be punished severely. In Texas, a seventeen-year-old high school student, Jennifer Boccia, was suspended for wearing a black armband to school to protest restraints on free speech that followed the shootings in Littleton. Boccia was also reprimanded by her school principal, Ira Sparks, for daring to tell her story to the media; she was told that if she wanted to clear her record, she should refrain from speaking to the media before discussing her remarks with school officials.

Boccia made a federal case of it and won a settlement from her school, vindicating her First Amendment rights. Sometimes, schools back down when threatened with lawsuits, and many students willing to challenge their suspensions should ultimately prevail in court, so long as judges recognize the Bill of Rights. But repression is becoming respectable, and some federal judges are as wary of free speech as school administrators. Student speech rights have, after all, been steadily eroding for the past two decades. The landmark 1969 Supreme Court decision upholding the right to wear a black armband to school to protest the Vietnam War has not been overruled, but its assertion that students do not leave their First Amendment rights at the schoolhouse door has not been honored either.

Student press rights have been severely restricted as well as students' rights to express themselves sartorially. Unhampered by logic, judges have ruled that clothing choices are not expressive (and not protected by the First Amendment); but they've given schools the power to prohibit clothing when it conveys what administrators consider inappropriate messages. In a 1999 Utah case, a federal district court judge upheld the suspension of a high school student who wore a pro-vegan T-shirt to school and started a petition protesting a ban on vegan symbols. School officials associated veganism with the militant branch of the animal rights movement and labeled the T-shirt a gang symbol. (In Alabama and Mississippi, the Star of David has been banned as a gang symbol.) "Schools need to run and administrators need to make rules," the judge in the vegan T-shirt case explained, idiotically. "That's the only reason they exist."

Apparently. Education is becoming militarized: Teachers and

administrators give orders, and students are expected to follow them. The Louisiana legislature recently passed a law treating elementary school children like little army recruits. They can no longer simply say "yes" or "no" in answer to a question in school. Under law, they are now required to address all school employees as "sir" or "ma'am," as in "yes, sir" or "yes, ma'am."

The desire to regiment students is sometimes quite overt. Character First, an Oklahoma-based character education program for elementary school students, requires children to memorize this poem about attentiveness: "I will look at someone speaking/And I'll listen all I can/I will sit or stand up straight/like a soldier on command."

Soldiers don't generally enjoy much autonomy, even off duty, and neither do students these days. School administrators take an expansive, totalitarian view of their own jurisdiction: They're punishing students for after-school and out-of-school activities or remarks. Numerous suspensions of students for their exchanges in chat rooms and other instances of cyber-speech exemplify this disturbing trend. But administrators have also targeted more traditional forms of childhood play: In a 1999 Massachusetts case, two twelve-year-old boys were suspended for playing war with toy guns in the woods adjacent to their school after school hours. (At the time, the U.S. military was bombing Yugoslavia.)

While students are being suspended for playing with toy guns, police officers armed with real guns are being deployed in some schools in order to provide security—or the appearance of it. In Houston, officers wearing bullet-proof vests trained in assault tactics, and equipped with dogs as well as guns, patrol middle schools, high schools, and school neighborhoods. They plan to subject students to random, bimonthly searches for drugs and weapons. In Georgia, an entire class of fifth graders was strip searched by school officials and police officers, looking for a missing twenty-six dollars.

Why do we treat students like criminal suspects? We can't simply blame recent incidents of gun violence; minors were the victims of repressive laws and policies long before the Littleton shootings. Adults fear the sexuality of teens, or envy their youth, or worry about their judgment, or, like Dr. Frankenstein, they want to mold their little monsters, instead of allowing them their freedom to develop. In any case, obsessive concern about unruly children and especially adolescents is a long-standing American tradition.

In the late nineteenth century, moral-reform movements, fueled by urbanization and increasing immigration, focused on protecting minors from sin and rehabilitating or punishing those who had fallen. Juvenile courts established around the turn of the century policed the behavior of minors and the sexual attitudes of females without affording them the rights extended to adult defendants. (Juvenile justice was highly discretionary and only quasi-judicial, and children were hauled before courts for such crimes as "willful disobedience.") The first federal obscenity law, passed in 1873, was justified in large part by professed concern about minors, who were considered easily corrupted by "bad" literature. In *The Rise and Fall of the American Teenager,* Thomas Hine reports that in the early 1900s, an official at the New York Public Library removed a copy of George Bernard Shaw's play *Man and Superman* from circulation, to make sure it would remain unavailable to "the little East Sider." His presumed criminal tendencies would have been encouraged by Shaw's irreverence, the library bureaucrat feared.

Fifty years later, the U.S. Senate convened hearings on the effects of TV on "the shocking rise in our national delinquency rate." Television was labeled "mental poisoning," like the Internet, I guess. Experts warned about a supposed rise in serious crime being committed by young children. A cultural preoccupation with delinquency and fear of rebellious youth was reflected in films like *The Blackboard Jungle.* In fact, youth crime was low in the 1950s, but the self-appointed policers of children and teens are not always deterred by facts.

Juvenile crime is relatively low today. According to the Justice Department, violent juvenile crime began declining in the early 1990s and by the end of the decade was at its lowest point since 1986. Violence in high schools has also declined substantially; the chances of a child being shot in school are "literally one in a million," criminologist James Alan Fox remarked in 1999. Some may find a one in a million chance of being murdered unacceptable, and random shootings naturally arouse nearly everyone's anxiety. Still, according to a *New York Times* survey of teenagers conducted a few months after the Columbine attack, both violence and fear of violence appear to have declined among America's teens.

Fear of illicit drugs, however, remains high among adults, especially those who rule the schools. The war on drugs has greatly diminished students' rights (along with the rights of adults). Schools treat students like criminal suspects partly because they view nearly every student as a suspected or potential drug user. Urine testing is becoming common in schools, and courts have been struggling with it. In 1995, a federal district court in Texas struck down the mandatory drug testing of all seventh to twelfth graders, and in 2001, a federal appeals court in Denver invalidated mandatory testing of all students participating in nonathletic extracurricular activities. This decision, *Board of Education v. Earls,* was, however, reviewed by the Supreme Court and during oral arguments in March 2002, the Court seemed poised to reverse the appeals court and approve drug testing as a condition of participating in any extracurricular program—like choir or Future Farmers of America.

A majority of the justices showed little sympathy for students who object to being suspected of illegal drug use, absent any evidence, and forced to submit to urine tests. Indeed, Justice Kennedy practically accused the family challenging the drug-testing policy of being attracted to "druggies." Lindsay Earls, a student at Dartmouth College who challenged the policy when she was in high school, would rather attend a school filled with "druggies" than subject herself to a urine test, Kennedy suggested. Her parents would "send their child to a druggie school." The Court seemed to regard the constitutionality of drug testing as self-evident, partly because, in its view, students have few, if any rights. As Justice Scalia stressed, "We're talking about minors. You can keep them imprisoned if they don't do their homework. We're trying to train and mold them." Mold them into what, you might ask—adults with no vision of privacy, no understanding of repression, and no sense of entitlement to challenge the state. What's the harm of mandatory drug testing for all high school students? "This policy gives all kinds of people access to my private information when there isn't even any reason to think I'm doing drugs," one student challenging his school's drug-testing policy stated. "It's like something out of *1984.*"

It's heartening to find brave students willing to challenge their schools' repressive policies. Some teenagers instinctively understand speech and privacy rights or the right to be free of unreasonable searches, despite the efforts of administrators. Others are instinctively drawn to authoritarianism. How will most students learn about freedom when schools treat censorship, surveillance, and conformity as social goods? How will they learn about democracy and the exercise of individual conscience when schools equate virtue with obedience? How did following orders become the American way?

DON'T SPEAK ITS NAME

In 1997, in Cambridge, Massachusetts, ten-year-old Jeffrey Curley was abducted, sexually assaulted, and murdered by two men, one of whom was allegedly a member of the North American Man Boy Love Association (NAMBLA), founded in 1978. Both of his assailants, Charles Jaynes and Salvatore Sicari, are now serving life sentences for murder. They have also been found liable for Jeffrey's wrongful death in a civil suit that ended in a symbolic $328 million damage award to the Curley family. But according to Bob and Barbara Curley (Jeffrey's parents), Jaynes and Sicari were not solely responsible for their son's murder. They blame it on NAMBLA and filed a $2 million wrongful-death suit in federal court against NAMBLA and its alleged members.

This case has been compared to Planned Parenthood's 1999 lawsuit against antiabortion activists who maintained an alleged "hit list" of abortion providers or to recent lawsuits against white supremacist groups, like the suits filed by the Southern Poverty Law Center against the Klan. These cases, however, involved much more than claims about offensive or allegedly inflammatory rhetoric. The case against antiabortion activists was essentially about stalking: The defendants were found liable for intentionally threatening and terrorizing abortion providers. The Klan cases involved claims that Klan members were involved in violence. Even so, these lawsuits troubled many free speech advocates.

The case against NAMBLA is much more tenuous and mostly reflects abhorrence of its ideology. Unpopular speech, especially unpopular speech about sex, is regularly blamed for sexual violence and "deviance." Pornography causes rape, according to antiporn feminists. Sex education causes teen pregnancy, according to their counterparts on the right. NAMBLA's celebration of "man/boy love" causes homosexuality and violent predatory behavior, according to the Curleys' lawsuit.

"Prior to joining NAMBLA, Charles Jaynes was heterosexual," their complaint alleges implausibly. (I doubt heterosexual men are attracted to NAMBLA.) Because he was exposed to NAMBLA's propaganda, Jaynes "became obsessed with having sex with and raping young male children." The apparent theory of the lawsuit is that Jeffrey Curley would be alive today if only NAMBLA did not exist:

A version of this piece appeared in The American Prospect, *October 20, 2000*

The complaint claims that "immediately prior" to the murder "Charles Jaynes accessed NAMBLA's web site at the Boston Public Library."

The absurdity of these claims would raise questions about their sincerity, if the circumstances weren't so tragic. Maybe grief makes the Curleys really believe that Jaynes was converted to homosexuality and pedophilia simply by reading NAMBLA literature. You might expect that reason, not fear or grief, would prevail in court, but their lawsuit survived an initial motion to dismiss on First Amendment grounds. (Subsequently the court dismissed the Curleys' federal civil rights claim and refused to allow the addition of a federal racketeering charge, leaving intact the wrongful-death claim under state law. The Curleys filed a second lawsuit, naming additional defendants.) But if the course of this lawsuit has been convoluted, its immediate chilling effect on speech was simple: NAMBLA's web site was shut down after the first suit was filed, although, as far as I can tell, it comprised clearly protected speech. I can't swear that I've seen the complete web site, but viewing copies of what purportedly appeared on the Internet at the time of the Curley murder, I found no incitement to violence, no evidence of a conspiracy to rape and murder young boys, and not even any erotica. Mostly the site consisted of traditional political advocacy.

NAMBLA strongly opposed age-of-consent laws in the belief that they are arbitrary, simplistic, and a violation of the rights of minors as well as adults. It expressly condemned "sexual abuse and all forms of coercion," endorsed only "mutually consensual relationships," between men and boys, and stressed that it "does not provide encouragement, referrals, or assistance for people seeking sexual contact." The web site included the sayings of respectable writers and academics (Oscar Wilde, Allen Ginsberg, Dudley Clendinen, and John Money), a rather dry discussion of "positive and beneficial experiences" between adults and minors, and a list of journal articles on sexuality, as well as some sophomoric poetry. Maybe some people found this titillating, but all in all, the NAMBLA web site seemed a lot less incendiary than the Bible. NAMBLA's bulletin is more likely to offend. The issue I've seen includes a story about man/boy sex that could qualify as soft-core porn—but nothing sanctioning, much less encouraging, violence and abuse.

NAMBLA was clearly engaged in protected speech, and the Curleys practically conceded as much in their court papers. They could point to no specific NAMBLA publication or statement that caused

Jeffrey's death and constituted incitements to violence that the First Amendment would not protect. They based their claim merely on "the totality of the child sex environment" allegedly created by NAMBLA. You might as well sue an antiabortion group for stating that abortion is murder, calling for its criminalization, and creating an "environment" that causes the killing of abortion providers. Or, perhaps, you could sue the Catholic Church for routinely sheltering pedophilic priests: Consider the "totality of the child sex environment" created by Boston's Cardinal Bernard Law's history of protecting admitted pedophiles and concealing their crimes. Then imagine how quickly a judge would dismiss the claims made by the Curleys against NAMBLA if they were made against the Catholic Church.

But if the church hierarchy collaborates in child abuse, it doesn't publish even soft-core pornography; and some believe that any erotica involving minors is an invitation to abuse, or statutory rape, at least (just as some believe that denunciations of abortion are invitations to murder doctors who perform them). But if stories involving sexually active minors were not protected by the First Amendment, *Lolita* would be illegal (along with numerous TV shows and movies). In fact, Nabokov had predictable trouble finding a publisher for his controversial book; but even if *Lolita* were construed as an endorsement of statutory rape, it would remain protected speech. For speech to be prohibited it must have a clear, direct, immediate, causal relationship to violence or other unlawful activities. Mere advocacy of violence is constitutionally protected; only incitement to violence—intentionally provocative speech that is likely to result in imminent unlawful action—can be prohibited.

Still, the Curley lawsuit is hard for civil libertarians to ignore. Jeffrey Curley's murder was horrible and readily exploited by advocates of repressive legislation. (It nearly brought the death penalty back to Massachusetts.) The civil suit against NAMBLA, aimed at censoring unpopular speech about sexuality, reflects widespread biases about a supposed link between homosexuality and pedophilia—a link denied by such mainstream organizations as the American Medical Association and the American Psychological Association. Children have much more to fear from heterosexual predators within their extended families.

But for many people facts about child abuse are less compelling than their visceral reaction to NAMBLA's support for adult-child sexual relationships. NAMBLA is highly vulnerable (and Curley's lawyer threatened to demand its membership list during pretrial discovery). Virtually no group of people is more unpopular. Private attorneys generally sympathetic to First Amendment claims shied away from any association with NAMBLA, which could have been very bad for business. It has been represented by the American Civil Liberties Union of Massachusetts.

For representing NAMBLA, the ACLU has been excoriated by many and lost considerable support, but it does have one unlikely defender—Jeffrey Curley's father, a primary plaintiff in the case. (Robert Curley was previously represented by a Massachusetts ACLU board member in a dispute with the city of Cambridge over mandatory diversity training). Curley is surprisingly sympathetic to the ACLU's opposition to his lawsuit: "I really do have a lot of respect for them," he told the *Boston Globe*. "They are very consistent in who they defend. It takes a lot of nerve to defend the groups they have over the years. They have a lot of courage."

It's too bad that courage is required to defend this case, when a simple appreciation of freedom of thought and expression should do. You don't have to share NAMBLA's ideas about the possibility of consensual relationships between adolescents and adults to refrain from censoring them. Unfortunately, the fundamental principle underlying the First Amendment—the protection of "offensive," unpopular speech—is not widely embraced. Speech with more artistic value than anything found on the NAMBLA web site is regularly banned in our nation's schools: Recently, a high school teacher in Jacksonville, Florida, was prohibited from introducing his students to Allen Ginsberg's groundbreaking poem *Howl.* Considering perennial demands for censorship—of video games, rap music, and other material that supposedly corrupts America's youth—it wouldn't be hard to garner support for banning the mere advocacy of man-boy sexual relationships.

The notion that pubescent or prepubescent children may enter into consensual, mutually beneficial sexual relationships with adults seems deeply flawed to me, but so do a lot of ideas I don't share—like a belief in spirit channeling, reincarnation, creationism, or the spiritual wisdom of Oprah. If the First Amendment only protected sensible speech, we'd inhabit a very quiet nation indeed.

VIRTUAL RAPE

Like many criminal offenders, James Maxwell is not a particularly appealing character. At worst he's a dangerous sexual predator; at best, he's a sexual deviant. Maxwell, a fifty-one-year-old New Jersey resident, likes talking dirty to children. In April 2001, he acknowledged making obscene phone calls to eleven girls, ranging from eight to fourteen years old, pleading guilty to multiple counts of child endangerment. This would have been an unsavory but unremarkable case, except that Maxwell was also charged with aggravated sexual assault of a ten-year-old girl, known as SM, because during one phone call, posing as her mother's gynecologist, he persuaded SM to insert her finger into her vagina.

The application of a sexual assault statute to a phone call appears to be unprecedented. But it's not entirely surprising, considering pervasive concern about electronic, or virtual sex involving unsuspecting children. This case is a testament to the presumed power of the Internet and law enforcement's efforts to tame it. The application of sexual assault laws to cases involving children who are duped over the phone into fondling or penetrating themselves would greatly facilitate the prosecutions of people who engage in sexually explicit conversations in chat rooms, especially with minors. It hardly matters that Maxwell used a telephone instead of a computer. He might once have been dismissed as a dirty old man; now he's more likely to remind people of a dangerous pedophile prowling the Net.

Still, New Jersey's sexual offense statute was enacted in 1979, long before most legislators even imagined the Internet. Can a phone conversation qualify legally as an aggravated assault? New Jersey law defines sexual assault as "sexual penetration, either by the actor or upon the actor's instructions." Penetration involving a child is an aggravated sexual assault, with a maximum sentence of twenty years. Maxwell's victim acted on his instructions, under coercion (at ten years old, she was incapable of consenting to phone sex), and assistant district attorney Joseph Del Russo, who prosecuted the case, considers the absence of physical or even visual contact between the offender and his victim irrelevant: Maxwell is "equally culpable as the guy who gives a girl five dollars to lure her into his car and gets her to penetrate herself digitally."

Superior Court Judge Marilyn Clarke, a former sex crimes pros-

A version of this piece appeared in the New York Times, *November 25, 2001*

ecutor, apparently agreed and declined to dismiss the aggravated assault charge against Maxwell. He pled guilty to aggravated sexual assault and child endangerment, with leave to appeal, and received a twelve-year sentence, part of which will be served at the state sex offender treatment center in Avenal, New Jersey. Maxwell's attorney, Edward Jerejian, has promised to take this case to the highest court that will hear it: "The fight is just beginning." Essentially his client was guilty of making "phony phone calls," Jerejian says, and "they're treating him like a serial murderer." Jerejian argued unsuccessfully that the definition of sexual assault as penetration "upon the actor's instructions" was intended to cover cases involving multiple defendants, in which the offender instructs an accomplice to commit an assault. (Or, it could be applied to a multiple-victims case in which victims are forced to assault each other.)

As Jerejian suggests, New Jersey's legislators were probably not intent on punishing sexually explicit phone calls when they enacted the state's sexual offense statute, and neither the judge nor prosecutor in the Maxwell case could point to any other case quite like it. Creative prosecutions are staples in fictional courtrooms (it's easy to imagine James Maxwell turning up on *Law & Order*), but in real life, they arguably violate a basic principle of due process: that laws provide clear, reasonably specific notice of prohibited behavior. Jerejian claimed that the New Jersey law was impermissibly vague as applied to James Maxwell: "Violent crimes like sexual assault require physical presence," he instructed the court, in what he probably considered an appeal to common sense. But in a computer age and a therapeutic culture, Jerejian's notion of assault may be a bit anachronistic.

It's been over ten years since the recovery movement declared that verbal haranguing was apt to be as traumatic as physical battering, defining child abuse broadly to include any form of "inadequate nurturance": If you were ignored or belittled by your parents, you were a victim of abuse, just like a child who had been beaten or sexually molested by them. Once on a talk show, I observed that being yelled at by your father was not the equivalent of being raped by him, naively expecting that virtually everyone would concur. Instead, members of the studio audience hissed at me. "How dare I judge someone else's pain," people said. In this culture, there were no degrees or hierarchies of suffering and abuse, just as there were no hierarchies of addictions. People who shopped too much or drank too much, people who were verbally excoriated or beaten, were all equals in their pain.

Popular therapies that emphasized the ubiquity of abuse, our psychic fragility, and the inevitability of post-traumatic stress disorders, helped rationalize the political correctness that swept college campuses in the late 1980s and '90s and focused on protecting people from verbal assaults. The rise of the recovery movement naturally coincided with campaigns to prohibit "hateful" or "offensive" speech, like pornography or racial slurs. "Words wound," denizens of high and low culture—from pop therapists to progressive law professors—agreed. Feminist antiporn activists who emerged in the 1980s did not differentiate between virtual and actual assaults. In their view, pornography did not merely cause sexual discrimination and violence: Pornography *was* sexual discrimination and violence. People intent on outlawing racist speech made similar presumptions about the actual harm of name-calling and other expressions of insensitivity toward members of groups historically victimized by race discrimination.

The twelve-step movement is rather passé and has long been the subject of satire; the antiporn movement failed to achieve one of its primary objectives—passage of laws prohibiting speech that allegedly subordinated women—and speech codes on campus have been successfully challenged and ridiculed. But disregard for free speech persists on many college campuses (it was demonstrated by efforts to discipline students and faculty for expressing unpopular views after September 11) and even as the antiporn movement and crusades against hate speech were falling out of fashion they were successfully imprinting popular culture and the courts with their ideals. The concept of employment discrimination was expanded to include instances of purely verbal harassment or the use of words and images to create a "hostile environment"; efforts to curb hateful thoughts have shaped proposals to enhance penalties for crimes allegedly motivated by hate or prejudice, instead of, say, greed.

So, distinctions between words and deeds, verbal and physical abuse, or actual and metaphoric assaults were already blurred when the cyber-culture emerged, offering a virtual life that rivaled the real. For some residents of cyberspace, real life now requires its own logo—"RL"—to distinguish it from life on-line. Social psychologist Sherry Turkle has observed that some netizens "experience their lives as a 'cycling through' between the real world (RL) and a series of virtual worlds."

It's no surprise that virtual worlds harbor virtual criminals; you might even expect to find that virtual crimes greatly outnumber actual crimes. People tempted to behave badly in real life are apt to give in to their temptations on-line, where they are relatively harmless and generally legal. You can rape and pillage your way through a computer game and only risk virtual execution by other users; you are not likely to be prosecuted in an RL court, at least not yet.

Of course, virtual freedoms are hardly absolute, as high school students discovered a few years ago when school administrators began policing on-line speech. After the 1999 shootings at Columbine High, some school administrators went on their own rampage against students who made "offensive" remarks in chat rooms or maintained web sites that didn't enjoy official approval. The post-Columbine cases reflected an extreme, unreasoned fear of Internet speech. (In one, not atypical case in Missouri, a student was suspended for expressing his belief that an attack could occur in his school.) But not all prosecutions of speech on the Net can be dismissed as mere hysteria.

When does speech on the Internet (or over the phone) invite criminal prosecution? You may be liable for threatening or stalking people on-line, as in real life. The First Amendment does not protect intentional threats. In 1995, University of Michigan student Jake Baker was prosecuted for threatening a female classmate by posting a horrific fantasy about torturing and killing a character who shared her name. This case was loosely characterized in the press as a virtual rape case, but in fact it was based on allegations of an actual threat. The young woman named in Baker's murder story was reportedly quite frightened by it (who wouldn't be?), but a federal appeals court held that the story was not posted in order to intimidate her and did not qualify as a "true threat"; the charges against Baker were dismissed.

Baker's fantasy would have been just as chilling, and just as legal, had it been published in a pamphlet and distributed on street corners or delivered in a monologue at a comedy club. But it probably would not have garnered as much attention. As Internet use has soared over the past decade, so have efforts to prosecute Internet offenses and apply actual punishments to virtual crimes, especially those involving children. In this context, the prosecution of James Maxwell isn't novel; it's part of a worrisome trend.

Harvey Silverglate, who has been practicing criminal defense and civil liberties law for thirty-five years, sees the prosecution of virtual crimes as a step toward the thought-control that has gained cultural legitimacy on college campuses. During the sixties and seventies, students were disciplined for what they did, Silverglate recalls; then in the eighties they began to be disciplined for what they said; by the nineties, they were liable to be disciplined for their attitudes. In one popular view, he adds, computers are considered "weapons that magnify the dangerousness of bad thoughts," so it's not surprising that thoughts in cyberspace are in danger of being treated like actions in the real world.

The FBI began aggressively policing the Internet nearly ten years ago, through its Innocent Images initiative, established in 1993, with a $10 million annual budget. Seeking out pedophiles and child pornographers, FBI agents have been on-line, posing as teenagers and arranging trysts with suspected child molesters, who are promptly arrested if they travel out of state to meet their "prey." These methods are controversial, because of their potential for entrapment, but federal prosecutions of "travelers," and people accused of disseminating child porn, increased over 1000 percent in the latter half of the 1990s. Less work by the FBI would produce even more convictions if mere conversations constituted sexual assaults.

Dispensing with the notion that physical assaults involve physical proximity is no great leap for law enforcement today. The FBI apparently wants to go even further than the prosecutor in the Maxwell case, who can at least point to an actual, not a virtual instance of sexual penetration. Maxwell was not prosecuted simply for talking to his victim; he was prosecuted for the actions he persuaded her to take. The FBI has suggested that people should be prosecuted for thoughts as well as actions. As deputy assistant FBI director Thomas T. Kubic testified before Congress in June 2001, "The FBI fully supports (the) view that any legislation affecting the Internet should . . . treat physical activity and 'cyber' activity in the same way."

If there is any irony in the FBI's apparent adoption of the radical feminist view that pornographic images are the equivalent of pornographic acts, it generally goes unnoticed. Fear of pornography and sexual predators on-line has spawned a new generation of child protectors, right and left, intent on policing conversation and publication on the Net. In recent years, Congress has repeatedly tried to impose special restrictions on Internet speech in order to protect kids, beginning with the 1996 Communications Decency Act, which was struck down by the Supreme Court.

Concern about the corrupting effect of sexually explicit speech on children is familiar (it tends to be intensified by social change and new technologies, from television to computers). What's new is the notion that imagination—or "cyber-activity"—should be treated like "physical activity" by the criminal law. With few exceptions, like short-lived antiporn ordinances that equated pornography with discrimination, law has generally recognized a boundary between the virtual and real. Then, in 1996, Congress passed the Child Pornography Prevention Act, which criminalized virtual child pornography—sexually explicit images that only appear to involve children. (See "Courting Unsafe Speech.")

When the Supreme Court struck down the virtual porn provisions of the CPPA in April 2002, Congress and the Justice Department quickly promised to pass another version of it. It is no exaggeration to characterize a ban on virtual porn as a thought crime: pursuant to laws like the CPPA, on-line fantasies can land you in real-life prisons.

The post–September 11 notion that Americans should "watch what they say," is intended to discourage political dissent, but it applies with particular force to sexual deviants. They may even have to watch what they imagine. Consider the case of Brian Dalton. Dalton, a twenty-two-year old Ohio man, was on sex-offender probation for possessing child pornography when his parents discovered his handwritten personal journal, containing fantasies about abusing children. They turned him in to his probation officer, in the apparent hope that he'd receive treatment. Instead, his probation was revoked, and he was indicted on two obscenity charges. On July 3, 2001, Dalton pled guilty to one count of obscenity and received a sentence of seven years, to be served consecutively with a three-year sentence for his probation violation.

Dalton's case received considerable publicity; like the assault charge based on James Maxwell's obscene phone call, his prosecution for obscenity was apparently unprecedented. Dalton did not show his journal to anyone and there was no evidence that he intended to show or distribute it; he was convicted simply for entertaining bad thoughts. Dalton pled guilty on the advice of his lawyer, who, he claimed, did not tell him that he had a First Amendment defense to the obscenity charge. Instead, he claims, his lawyer advised against raising a constitutional defense, partly in deference to the judge's reported desire not to hear one.

Dalton also said that he was anxious to avoid a "futile" public trial and public exposure of his journal. Prosecutors intent on curtailing the dissemination of child porn might have shared an aversion for publicizing Dalton's fantasies, but instead, they made his journal public, filing it in Ohio's Franklin County Court, in an effort to prevent the revocation of his plea. If someone were to read the journal and act on it, fulfilling popular fears about pornography's effects on behavior, would the Franklin County prosecutor be morally, if not legally, responsible for facilitating a sexual assault?

It's easy to imagine a creative prosecutor charging Brian Dalton with assault if someone acted on fantasies that he published. (Consider the NAMBLA case, described previously in "Don't Speak Its Name.") James Maxwell's lawyer, Ed Jerejian, sees the assault charge against his client as the first step down a path that will lead to prosecutions of people "who create books or films or television with some sort of questionable content that a child views." That frightening scenario is possible, of course, but not inevitable. Maxwell is not being prosecuted for the attenuated, unforeseen, and unintended consequences of his phone call. There's no question that he intended to exploit his victim sexually, even if the exploitation was long distance. Indeed, he called her back some two months later, told her he had taped the first phone call and threatened to play it for her friends if she did not perform for him again. And he had not called SM at random. He selected his victims, culling feature articles about young girls from local papers.

It's fair to call Maxwell a predator, although his degree of dangerousness—the likelihood of his committing an in-person assault—is unknown (he has no record of violence). Prosecutor Joseph Del Russo says he was initially surprised by the controversy the Maxwell case engendered. "This girl was essentially coerced into touching herself," he stresses. Del Russo does not claim that this case is the equivalent of an assault as it is traditionally understood: He "appreciates" the "qualitative difference" between being tricked into touching yourself and being forcibly touched by another. "But just because this case is not as bad as the worst case scenario contemplated by the statute doesn't mean it can't be captured by the statute."

Del Russo has a point: As he observes, defense attorneys make similar arguments during sentence pleas: "I hear defense attorneys say this all the time: 'There are robberies and there are robberies.' A pickpocket who knocks someone down in the course of stealing his wallet and a guy with a gun who breaks into a convenience store are both guilty of robbery. But 'there are robberies and there are robberies.'"

"The term 'sexual assault' is like 'brain surgery,' we use it to describe a broad range of behaviors," Ben Saunders, a clinical social worker, observes. "The term 'sexual offender' can cover everyone from a father who fondles his daughter, feels terrible about it, and turns himself in for treatment, to Ted Bundy." Saunders, director of the Family and Child Program at the Medical University of South Carolina, considers the assault charge against Maxwell justified. "From a psychological standpoint," he sees "no difference at all" between the Maxwell case and a case where the offender is physically present. "We're talking about someone exploiting a child against her will for his own sexual gratification . . . She would feel violated and abused . . . If that's not an assault, what is? It's not the same as being raped by a motorcycle gang in front of St. Patrick's, but it's still an assault."

Other victim advocates demur. Linda Williams, codirector of the National Violence Against Women Prevention Research Center at Wellesley College, finds the Maxwell case "very confusing." It involves an abuse of power and authority (he was posing as a doctor), but "without a physical presence, it's hard to see how you can have an assault." Like defense attorney Ed Jerejian, she worries about where a prosecution like this will lead. Will we criminalize "CDs with lyrics that tell a child to do something?"

Civil libertarians instinctively raise these familiar questions about the consequences of the Maxwell case, and other prosecutions involving speech. You may consider the criminalization of popular entertainments unlikely (although Congress periodically threatens the entertainment industry with sanctions for its "toxic" products), and you can easily distinguish Maxwell, who lacked even creative pretensions, from, say, Eminem. But concern about the precedent that may be set by the Maxwell case points to the limits of a therapeutic approach to justice: An accurate psychological perspective on assault is not necessarily an appropriate legal one.

Ted Bundy and a man who fondles his twelve-year-old daughter and repents are both sex offenders, but they're hardly guilty of the same crimes and don't deserve even similar punishments—no matter how much the twelve-year-old is traumatized. The assertion that "there are robberies and there are robberies" is an argument for the defense, not the prosecution. The pickpocket who knocks his victim down should not be prosecuted and sentenced as aggressively as a thug with a gun. Someone who makes an obscene phone call and tricks a child into having phone sex should not—and need not—be treated like the participant in a gang rape in front of St. Patrick's. It was simply not necessary to stretch the law and convict James Maxwell of aggravated sexual assault in order to imprison him. He could have been convicted of child endangerment with relative ease and sentenced consecutively on several counts.

Del Russo acknowledges that he didn't charge Maxwell with assault in order to ensure his imprisonment. He invoked the assault statute, he says, in the belief that it described Maxwell's behavior most accurately, though he now understands that people believe he was "overreaching, going after a rabbit with a howitzer." Defense attorney Ed Jerejian suggests that the prosecutor intended to overreach, recognizing that this case presented an opportunity to expand the definition of sexual assault and facilitate prosecutions of suspected pedophiles on the Internet.

It's difficult to predict James Maxwell's fate, even if he prevails on appeal in the New Jersey state courts. If his assault conviction is overturned, the state could conceivably proceed against him again on the endangerment charges, which are likely to survive an appeal, or he could negotiate a plea to time served. At the time of his sentencing, he had already spent two years in prison and was likely to serve at least another year before his appeal was decided in state court. So even if he were to win his appeal in an early round, Maxwell would not have gone unpunished: He would have been imprisoned for at least three years and classified as a sexual offender for making a series of obscene phone calls. That would probably disappoint his prosecutor, but the intricacies of Maxwell's appeal and its eventual effect on his sentence may not matter much to his primary victim. "Children in general don't care about what happens in the criminal justice system as long as something happens," Lucy Berliner, director of the Harborview Sexual Assault Program in Seattle, observes. "It probably doesn't matter to the child how the guy is prosecuted. She just wants him to get into trouble and be held to account."

The case against James Maxwell is a lawyer's case, and the prosecutor and defense attorney seemed to be enjoying it, as any lawyer would. But if the question posed by this appeal—Can a phone call constitute a sexual assault?—seems like a legal technicality, so are many questions involving fundamental rights. Technicalities, like the rules that govern the right to appeal a murder conviction, the scope of a police officer's authority to stop and search people, or the legality of government involvement with a religious group, determine the parameters of freedom.

Viewed in isolation, the sordid case of *State v. Maxwell* may seem to implicate nothing so noble as freedom. (Maxwell was never legally free to target young girls with obscene calls.) But this case does not exist in isolation. It owes its existence to the Internet and the dissolution of boundaries between the virtual and real. People who feel active and alive in cyberspace may find this dissolution alluring, but they have the most to lose in it. The intrusion of police and prosecutors into diaries, chat rooms, and E-mails, the equation of bad thoughts with bad deeds, will leave us no refuge. As surveillance becomes nearly ubiquitous, as action is dramatically curtailed, as fear imprisons us, we need more than ever to be virtually free.

4

WHOSE GOD IS IT, ANYWAY?

THE JOY OF SECTS

When the 2000 election finally ended, politicians became less preoccupied with declaring their allegiance to God, but efforts to involve Him in public policy showed no sign of abating. Most Republicans and many Democrats enthusiastically advocated federally funded, sectarian social service programs, promoted initially by the religious right. George Bush quickly established a new federal Office of Faith-Based Action (in other words, an Office of Sectarian Initiatives). Exploiting the widespread belief that godliness is essential to virtue and the assumption that religious faith helps cure chronic welfare dependency, drug abuse, and other social ills, "charitable choice" programs have managed to make direct government aid to religious sects seem as American as football prayer. (What politician wants to oppose either charity or choice, much less a "faith-based" program?)

Charitable choice was introduced in 1995 by John Ashcroft, when he was a Republican senator from Missouri. Ashcroft's proposal, providing federal support for sectarian social service programs, was included in the 1996 welfare reform law and spawned a legislative movement channeling tax dollars directly to religious institutions. A charitable choice provision was included in the 1998 Community Services Block Grant Program and the 2000 Youth, Drug and Mental Health Services Act, and in the past few years, charitable choice provisions have been routinely added to numerous House and Senate bills, such as the Even Start Family Literacy Programs and the Community Renewal and New Markets Act. For several years, advocates of federally funded sectarianism hoped to pass legislation that would simply include charitable choice automatically in all current and future public health and social service programs receiving federal funds.

Ashcroft's remarkably successful initiative created unprecedented financial partnerships between church and state. Before becoming enamored of charitable choice, the federal government more or less respected First Amendment prohibitions on direct public funding of "pervasively sectarian" organizations. Religious service providers have been eligible for government support, but they've generally been required to establish independently incorporated secular affiliates to receive and administer public funds; they have been barred from using service programs for proselytizing and from delivering services in sectarian settings.

This piece appeared in The American Prospect, February 12, 2001

Charitable choice bills challenged this principle, expressly providing for federal support of pervasively sectarian organizations; they allowed services to be offered in sectarian environments, and even allowed government funds to be used for "sectarian worship, instruction, or proselytization," if the funds were provided in the form of vouchers to individual recipients. Or, under most proposals, religious groups receiving direct federal aid would be permitted to use private dollars for "worship, instruction, or proselytization," in the context of federally supported programs. Since money is fungible, these provisions would effectively allow all government funds (direct and indirect) to be used evangelically. That, of course, is the purpose of charitable choice bills, which reflect the presumption that sectarian social service programs are innately superior to secular ones.

It is politically futile to oppose charitable choice by questioning this presumption or pointing out the dangers in government-sponsored sectarianism. But they should surface soon enough, when unpopular or outré sects begin demanding their share of the federal pie [and they did indeed surface, soon after this column was published]. People who favor government funding of mainstream churches may be less inclined to support grants to the Nation of Islam or the Reverend Moon, much less the Church of Scientology. The government should be constitutionally (and morally) restrained from discriminating against maligned religious minorities, but people convinced that their faith alone can lead to salvation will not let the Constitution deter them from pressuring bureaucrats to distinguish between false religions and true. Their demands should clarify the relationship between religious freedom, religious harmony, and separation of church and state and dispel cheerful assumptions of ecumenicism, on which charitable choice proposals have relied. Listening to politicians prate euphemistically about "faith-based" services, you'd think that religion in America was somehow nonsectarian.

Many religious people surely know better. Some recognize the coercive potential of sectarian social service programs, and a surprising number of religious groups spurned charitable choice for fear of becoming dependent on government funds and entangled with government regulators (funding is usually accompanied by regulation). Indeed, it's hard to see how some of the safeguards of charitable choice bills—provisions barring proselytizing with direct government funds or conditioning the delivery of services on professions of faith by recipients—can be enforced without substantial federal oversight.

But other religious institutions, hungry for tax dollars and convinced of their own righteousness, expect funding without regulation, and have had some hope of getting it. One charitable choice proposal actually deleted a provision requiring religious-service providers to serve individuals who refuse "to actively participate in a religious practice." Initially, all charitable choice bills exempted religious groups receiving public funds from federal civil rights law prohibiting religious discrimination in employment: In other words, pursuant to these bills, religious organizations running federal programs could decline to hire outside the faith and could, in effect, fire people for heresy.

Privately funded religious organizations have long enjoyed similar exemptions; and they have practiced religious discrimination in employment, because, as private groups, they enjoy associational and religious freedom rights under the First Amendment. But private associations must, of course, give up private associational rights when they accept government support and become, in part, de facto public entities, as the Boy Scouts of America is learning. (Relying on its status as a private group, the Scouts recently won a Supreme Court case affirming their First Amendment right to discriminate against gay people, but they are losing some public support, because they openly violate various antidiscrimination laws. See "Guilt of Association.") Advocates of charitable choice want sectarian organizations to have what the Boy Scouts are losing: the benefits of public funds without the responsibility of obeying public laws. They want only to obey God's law, which is fair enough, so long as they don't depend on Caesar's money.

This is not only a matter of principle. Considering the explosion of charitable choice proposals, the drive to exempt federally funded religious groups from federal antidiscrimination laws has threatened to wrest equal employment rights from a significant number of workers. Some civil rights advocates view charitable choice bills as backdoor attacks on the civil rights gains of the past thirty years. (Congressional opposition to the civil rights exemption eventually foiled the Bush Administration's initial plans for charitable choice.)

Religious discrimination is bad enough, but legalizing its exercise can lead to discrimination based on sex, sexual orientation, and perhaps race as well. Courts have broadly interpreted the rights of private sectarian employers to hire and fire on the basis of religion, upholding, for example, the firing of pregnant women deemed guilty of engaging in illicit affairs. In July 2001, in *Pedeira v. Kentucky*, a federal district court upheld the firing of a lesbian youth counselor from a publicly funded Baptist organization that objected to her "homosexual lifestyle." Sometimes, people are fired for adhering to their own religious traditions: A federal court has upheld a Christian retirement home's dismissal of a Muslim receptionist who insisted on wearing a head covering. Courts may be less likely to excuse faith-based claims of race discrimination: Consider the Supreme Court ruling that denied Bob Jones University its tax exemption because it prohibited interracial dating, in the name of religion. But if Bob Jones University were a service provider under some charitable choice proposals, it would have legislative permission to prohibit interracial dating among employees. Religious groups that preach racial or ethnic hatred (white supremacist sects or groups like the Nation of Islam) should be eligible for charitable choice funding; as long as the law expressly permitted them to hire and fire on the basis of religion, the law would effectively authorize race discrimination, financed with public funds.

It's hard to know whether state and federal courts and ultimately the Supreme Court will uphold charitable choice laws. The Court seems to be fashioning a more permissive approach to government funding of sectarian activities (and one or two key Supreme Court appointments may end separation of church and state as we've known it). Still, charitable choice is vulnerable to attacks under First Amendment prohibitions on state-established religion and Fourteenth Amendment guarantees of equality, which don't generally apply to privately funded organizations.

Legal challenges have only just begun. The first case was brought in July 2000 by the American Jewish Congress against a state charitable choice program in Texas that funded a Protestant evangelical job-training program. Imagine the welcome that a Jewish organization, headquartered in New York, receives in Texas when it challenges government-funded proselytizing by a local group of evangelical Christians. We hear a lot of talk about the virtues of religion; charitable choice is more likely to release religion's fury.

FAITH-BASED FAVORITISM

I'm not gracious enough to resist saying "I told you so," when I see rival religious groups fighting over federal funds. Only a few weeks after President Bush announced his "faith-based" initiative in January 2001, the Anti-Defamation League was reportedly pressuring the new administration not to underwrite the Nation of Islam, with some success. According to the *New York Times*, ADL representatives left a meeting with John DiIullio, then head of the Office of Faith Based and Community Services, "reassured that the president would not allow financing for the Nation of Islam's programs."

The ADL, an organization devoted to opposing discrimination against Jews, might have spared itself the embarrassment of lobbying in favor of discrimination against Muslims. Bush made clear his aversion to the Nation of Islam during the 2000 campaign: "I don't see how we can allow public dollars to fund programs where spite and hate is the core of the message. Louis Farrakhan preaches hate," he declared. DiIullio would have been hard-pressed to reconcile the blacklisting of a national religious organization with his promise that the allocation of federal funds would have been based on "facts, not faith; performance, not politics; results, not religion." But public opinion probably opposes the funding of unpopular religions more than it supports religious equality.

Not that many people openly support discrimination or even tell themselves that they believe in it. But many will eagerly distinguish between true and false religions; and denying equal treatment to the latter seems no more discriminatory than refusing to hire someone with fake credentials. Religions apt to be labeled false are considered con games; by funding them, government officials look like easy marks. In 2001, Boston mayor Tom Menino came under fire for endorsing a literacy program affiliated with the Church of Scientology, which many consider a cult. (The mayor defended himself by claiming ignorance of the Scientology connection.)

Unease about unpopular religions benefiting from government largess grew quickly, as the administration pushed its "faith-based" initiative. Bush's faithful ally Pat Robertson voiced concern about nondiscriminatory faith-based programs. Robertson didn't exactly raise his voice in opposition to the charitable choice provision of the 1996 welfare reform law; perhaps he thought the Moonies wouldn't

This piece appeared in The American Prospect, *April 9, 2001*

learn about it. A few years later, however, he realized that "such groups as the Unification Church, the Hare Krishnas, and the Church of Scientology could all become financial beneficiaries of the proposal to extend eligibility for government grants to religious charities." This was apparently a painful epiphany: "I hate to find myself on the side of the Anti-Defamation League, and others," Robertson observed. But if there's one thing that worried him more than no government support for religion, it was government support for religions he doesn't like.

This impulse to pass judgment on minority religions is ubiquitous. In Massachusetts, several colleges have banned the Boston Church of Christ from their campuses, labeling it a cult. "They are destructive to freedom of thought, freedom of movement, and freedom of activity," the Reverend Robert W. Thornburg of Boston University asserted. Maybe so, but some overwrought atheists would offer a similar description of mainstream religions, and even established minority faiths are apt to be labeled cults by the majority. In France, a law passed in 2001 criminalizes aggressive evangelical activities by religious groups labeled cults—groups that the government reserves the power to ban if they or their de facto leaders are found guilty merely of minor offenses, like "misleading publicity." (The Chinese government has pointed to the French law in justifying its repressive treatment of the Falun Gong movement.) The French list of dangerous religions includes the Mormon Church and Jehovah's Witnesses, as well as the Church of Scientology. Former secretary of state Madeleine Albright condemned the French anticult law for stigmatizing "legitimate expressions of religious faith," which only begs the question: Which religions would Albright classify as illegitimate?

To some extent, official judgments about true and false faiths are unavoidable when the government offers a benefit to religious groups—another reason to prohibit state support of churches. The IRS, for example, has to decide what organizations qualify as religions for purposes of the tax code. (Under pressure of a lawsuit, it recognized the Church of Scientology.) But the appropriately broad definition of religion offered by the Supreme Court (essentially "a sincere and meaningful" belief in some transcendent power) will not please many people who are offended by the mere suggestion that Wiccans or Moonies, much less Satanists, should enjoy the same legal status as Pentecostalists or Presbyterians.

Given prevailing concerns that federal funds might be allocated evenhandedly to religious groups, there's no small irony in the fact that Bush's "faith-based" initiative (and charitable choice bills in Congress) were initially marketed as efforts to end religious discrimination. Advocates of state-sponsored religious activities, from official school prayers to sectarian drug counseling, have been quite successful in equating the separation of church and state with discrimination against particular churches seeking state support. John DiIullio cited "end(ing) discrimination against religious providers of social services" as a primary mission of his office.

"What discrimination?" you might ask, first of all. Federal funding has long been available to religious providers who establish secular affiliates to administer it. But this debate is not really about the government's obligation to accommodate religious belief and treat all sects equally. It's about the entitlement of particular religious groups to government support. Borrowing the rhetoric of stigmatized or subordinate groups that have had to fight for civil rights, believers who seek state sponsorship cast themselves as oppressed minorities seeking not privileges but rights. As Ralph Reed, former executive director of the Christian Coalition, and others have asserted, when a school system declines to sponsor an official prayer, it violates the rights of students who wish to pray.

It's always amusing to see right-wingers who have loudly derided the "victimism" of the left, play the victim when their own sense of entitlement is threatened. (Remember how the Reagan Administration cloaked its attack on affirmative action as a defense of white male victims of reverse discrimination.) Religious groups, even those that are part of a Christian majority, have become particularly adept at this game. During his confirmation hearing, Attorney General John Ashcroft was characterized by his defenders as a victim of anti-Christian bigotry. In his attacks on "offensive" exhibits at the Brooklyn Museum of Art, New York's former mayor Rudy Giuliani whined about religious discrimination, claiming that avant-garde artists singled out Catholics for abuse.

You don't have to examine these claims deeply to recognize their flaws. Take the argument that abolition of school prayer is discriminatory. It ignores the fact that students have an undisputed right to organize their own prayer groups in school, say grace in the cafeteria, or call on God's help in a football game; they can use school facilities for extracurricular religious activities. A great deal of religious expression is permitted in school (and protected by the First Amendment). What is prohibited is officially organized religious prayer or proselytizing that infringes upon the religious freedom of others.

People who want school-sanctioned prayers that all students are formally required or informally coerced to recite seek religious power over others, not religious rights.

There are hard cases involving the complex interplay of constitutional prohibitions on establishing religion with guarantees of its free exercise. (If churches get special treatment from zoning boards, is that establishment or accommodation of religion?) But efforts to require school prayer or publically fund sectarian social service programs don't cure religious discrimination; they create it, as the controversy over federal funding of church groups makes clear. Why didn't it occur to charitable choice proponents that unpopular religions and even "cults" would qualify for federal funds? They put their own sense of entitlement above other people's rights.

GOOD NEWS?

Should we protect young children from efforts by private groups to evangelize them in public schools? Civil libertarians and secularists who are tempted to answer "yes" should remember how much censorship has been justified by concern about protecting minors. When people talk about the dangers of sex and violence in the media or free speech on the Internet, they invariably imagine the dangers to children. It's not surprising that one of the latest congressional efforts to prohibit indecency in cyberspace was dubbed the Child Online Protection Act. If you're wary of restricting pornography in the name of child safety (as I am), you need to think twice about restricting evangelicalism.

Sectarian religious groups that seek access to public schools are unlikely to compare themselves to pornographers, but they do rely on their First Amendment rights, as a 2001 Supreme Court case made clear. *Good News Club v. Milford Central School* was a challenge by an evangelical group to a decision barring it from conducting classes on the premises of a public elementary school immediately after the school day ended.

At first glance, the Good News Club appeared to have the First Amendment on its side: In a 1993 case, *Lambs Chapel v. Center Moriches,* the Supreme Court properly ruled that a Christian group could not be prohibited from using public school premises in the evening to show a film series offering a sectarian point of view about family life. In *Lambs Chapel,* the court relied on the fact that public schools were made available to a broad range of community groups for social, civic, and recreational purposes (when school was not in session). Secular groups enjoyed the right to use school facilities to show films about subjects like family and child rearing; a religious group could not be denied the same right simply because it presented films with a religious perspective.

But if *Lambs Chapel* was a relatively easy case, *Good News Club v. Milford Central School* was a hard one. There were important factual differences between them. The film series at issue in *Lambs Chapel* was shown in the evening and open to the entire community. The Good News Clubs are not aimed at the general public; instead they target young children and, by meeting immediately after school, on school premises, they make their meetings seem like extensions of the school day. Fi-

This piece appeared in Free Inquiry, *summer 2001*

nally, the Good News Club is devoted to religious worship and indoc-
trination, not the discussion of social issues (like child rearing) from
a religious perspective. The clubs were created by the Child Evangelism Fellowship, which, as you may have guessed, is devoted to con-
verting children between the ages of five and twelve.

The stated purpose of the Child Evangelism Fellowship is "to
evangelize boys and girls with the gospel of the Lord Jesus Christ and
to establish (disciple) them in the local church for Christian living."
What exactly happens at a meeting of a Good News Club? According
to Rob Boston of Americans United for Church and State, children
are divided into two groups—the saved and the unsaved; then, they
read Bible stories, sing Christian songs, and play "Bible-themed
games"; finally, they are encouraged to make "faith professions."

"It sounds like Sunday School," Justice Souter remarked during
oral arguments in *Good News Club*. Justice Ginsberg also expressed
doubts about the rights of religious groups to use public schools in
efforts to convert young children. But most of the justices seemed
sympathetic to the claim of the Good News Club, especially Justice
Scalia, who professed surprise that opening the public schools to
the Child Evangelism Fellowship might divide the local community.
"This is divisive in a community," he exclaimed. "I don't understand. What would the community get upset about?"

Scalia's obliviousness to the divisive power of religion suggests
lack of imagination and his own complacency as a member of a religious majority. He would probably understand why a community
might object if the Hare Krishna, the Unification Church, or a local
Wiccan group engaged in religious proselytizing in an elementary
school, once a week, at 3 P.M. Some Christian evangelicals might be
first on line to protest the use of school facilities by "cults" or "false"
religions. But they'd be guilty of religious bigotry.

The specter of bigotry and discrimination against unpopular faiths
shadows demands by religious groups for state support. The campaign by
Congress and the Bush Administration to provide sectarian social service providers with public funds has been plagued by fear that controversial religions, like the Nation of Islam, might qualify for federal aid.
When Pat Robertson expressed concern that new church/state partnerships might benefit the churches he doesn't like, he demonstrated, inadvertently, the virtue of our constitutional prohibition on establishing
religion. It protects minority faiths and keeps sectarian rivalries in
check.

Would the opening of elementary schools to the Child Evangelical

Fellowship violate the Establishment clause? The schools wouldn't exactly be sponsoring the Good News Club, but they would be providing the club with access to young children whom it might not reach by holding weekly meetings off school grounds. Schools might offer similar services to the Boy Scouts, but state sponsorship of scouting is not unconstitutional.

Still, as the Milford Central School conceded, it had created a limited public forum on school grounds, and once public schools make their facilities available to community groups, it's hard for them to exclude religious groups, whether they offer religious worship or religious perspectives, which may not readily be distinguished. The Good News Club had a substantial discrimination claim, and it gained the support of some groups that are committed to separation of church and state. (The National Council of Churches and the Baptist Joint Committee on Public Affairs signed a friend-of-the-court brief in support of the club.)

By a 6 to 3 vote, the Supreme Court decided in favor of the Good News Club, although the Court's reasoning may give religious groups pause. To prevail on its discrimination claim, the club had to persuade the court that its evangelical activities did not differ significantly from the motivational efforts of secular groups. The privileges that religious groups enjoy—like tax exemptions—are justified by differences between religions and secular movements. But when religions seek equality—not privilege—from the state, they're apt to emphasize what they share with secularists. Writing for the majority in *Good News Club,* Justice Thomas suggested that, under the First Amendment, Christianity is just another cause or ideology: "What matters for purposes of the Free Speech Clause is that we can see no logical difference in kind between the invocation of Christianity by the club and the invocation of teamwork, loyalty, or patriotism by other associations to provide a foundation for their lessons."

This suggests that in extracurricular activities in public schools, a belief in the divinity of Jesus is no different than, say, a belief in the importance of self-esteem. So long as the Court doesn't extend this equation of religious and secular ideologies to curriculum planning or official school functions, students should be free to exercise, or not exercise, whatever religions they choose. Meanwhile, people who worry about exposing children to evangelicalism after school might consider that it's the job of parents, not the state, to protect kids from speech considered harmful, whether it promotes religion or group sex. First Amendment advocates often say that the answer to bad speech is good speech. Atheists enjoy equal rights to meet in and after school; maybe it's time to use them.

AMERICAN GOTHIC

Feminists have long asserted that crusades against witchcraft reflect a primal fear of feminine power and aim to punish women, most brutally, for transgressing gender roles. But if accusations of witchcraft are useful, as instruments of social control, they're not necessarily cynical; often, they're entirely sincere. As a casual perusal of the Christian Broadcasting Network web site and other right-wing Christian literature shows, some people believe in Satan, witches, and various evil spirits as fervently as they believe in God. (Why shouldn't they, after all; one belief in the supernatural is no stranger than another.) "The Bible makes it clear that there are demons, or evil spirits in the world that interfere in people's lives," a CBN posting on "Freedom from Demon Bondage" asserts. The symptoms of "demon oppression" or "possession" include "involvement in occult practices (fortune-telling, Satanism, etc.)," and "seeking spiritual knowledge through Eastern religions and other counterfeit religious groups."

"Demon possession" must be quite common: One of its symptoms is "mental distress." It is also reflected, apparently, in the growing popularity of witchcraft. To the dismay of some conservative Christians, "white witchcraft," in the form of the Wiccan religion, has become rather fashionable, especially among the young. How-to books for teenage witches are "flying off the shelves," a reporter for CBN.com warns. By the dreaded year 2000, television was offering several attractive, good-hearted young witches—the three sisters of *Charmed*, the character of Willow on *Buffy the Vampire Slayer*, and Sabrina (*the Teenage Witch*). Paganism has been growing in popularity on college campuses, according to an October 2000 report in the *Boston Globe*. Even the U.S. Army has fallen under the spell and allowed Wiccan rituals on its bases, "inviting Satan into our military," according to one Christian critic.

Given this concern about devilry, the Christian right's crusade against popular fascination with New Age and the occult is no more surprising than its support for federally funded Christian schools, and no less intense or pervasive. It underlies the campaign to censor Harry Potter books, those benign stories about a teenage wizard that lead the American Library Association's list of most frequently challenged titles nationwide. According to its critics, the Harry Potter se-

This piece appeared in The American Prospect, *December 18, 2000*

ries wrongly teaches children that magic can be a force for good; it encourages them to regard witchcraft (the devil's work) as a "normal, non-evil religion."

This preoccupation with the occult also emerges in far-right condemnations of feminism, which Pat Robertson famously described as a "socialist, antifamily political movement that encourages women to leave their husbands, kill their children, practice witchcraft, destroy capitalism, and become lesbians." The loony Pat Robertson can't claim to speak *for* conservative Christians, but he does speak *to* many of them, exacerbating the fear of witchcraft. Once, he claims, witches cast a spell on his daughter, inflicting bad headaches upon her, which he cured with a successful exorcism: "I ran into my daughter and said, 'Come here. In the name of Jesus,' I said, 'You foul spirit of witchcraft, I command you, loose this child and go back where you came from.' Just like that, she was free."

It's tempting to laugh off this fear of witchery. How seriously can you take people who take *Buffy the Vampire Slayer* (or *Touched by an Angel*) literally? The trouble is that only the witches are imagined; the witch-hunts are frighteningly real. In Oklahoma, in December 1999, a fifteen-year-old girl was suspended from school for allegedly casting spells and making one of her teachers ill. She and her family, represented by the ACLU, filed a federal lawsuit against the school, to the amazement of her father: "It's hard for me to believe that in the year 2000 I am walking into court to defend my daughter against charges of witchcraft brought by her own school. But if that's what it takes to clear her record and get her life back to normal, that's what we'll do."

The persecution of Brandi Blackbear began in the aftermath of the Columbine shootings. According to her complaint, she was targeted by school administrators in the spring of 1999 because of rumors that she had written a story "about an incident at school." (Blackbear is an aspiring fiction writer, with an interest in horror stories.) Her locker was searched and her private notebooks confiscated. School officials found a story involving a shooting on a school bus and promptly suspended her.

Ostracized and harassed by fellow students, Blackbear returned to school in the fall of 1999 and began a private study of Wicca. Within a few months, a teacher was hospitalized for a still-unknown ailment. Blackbear was blamed. An aptly named assistant principal, Charles Bushyhead, accused her of practicing Wicca, casting spells, and causing the hospitalization of the mysteriously ill teacher. Calling her an immediate threat to the school, Bushyhead suspended her for fifteen days.

If only the charge of witchcraft were true, Blackbear wouldn't need the ACLU to vindicate her rights. Indeed, if Assistant Principal Bushyhead actually believes in her magical power, you have to wonder why he doesn't fear them. Maybe he feels protected by Jesus.

Oklahoma officials may need God's help in opposing Blackbear's lawsuit; only a miracle, or a very bad judge, can save them. [They are scheduled for trial in the summer of 2002.] Putting aside the cruelty of the school's behavior toward Blackbear, which has been rather un-Christian, there's little question that her First Amendment rights were violated. In addition to being suspended from school, after having her writings impounded, Blackbear was prohibited from wearing any emblems associated with the Wicca religion (students are free to wear crosses).

This is what religious freedom means to some devout Americans: the freedom to practice "respectable" or "true" religions, not "counterfeit" religions, like Wicca. If the accusations of witchcraft in Blackbear's case are outré, the majoritarian religious fervor that punishes adherence to alternative faiths is common. It shapes disputes about official school prayers, which are usually challenged by people of minority faiths whose children are scorned and taunted by the majority. It surfaced recently in the response of the right-wing Family Research Council to an invocation by a Hindu priest offered in the U.S. Congress: "Our founders expected that Christianity—and no other religion—would receive support from the government, as long as that support did not violate people's consciences and their right to worship. They would have found utterly incredible the idea that all religions, including paganism, be treated with equal deference."

This is what religious tolerance represents to some religious zealots: the growing acceptability of paganism and other "evil" or "false" beliefs, the domestication of evil. They're probably not amused when Martha Stewart claims credit for the resurgence of Halloween, now a $6.8-billion retail holiday, second only to Christmas. To Christian critics of the occult, Halloween is a dangerous time, "when Satanists and witches' covens meet to cast their spells and perform grotesque rituals . . ." To Martha Stewart, "Halloween is a traditional and lovely thing for children and adults to enjoy." She effuses over her "sandwitches." It seems that Satan's influence is subliminable.

SECTUAL DISCRIMINATION

Rebecca and David Corneau of Attleboro, Massachusetts, are Christian fundamentalists who belong to a small sect called The Body. Like Christian Scientists, they reject modern medical care in accordance with their religious beliefs. Unlike Christian Scientists, they are being deprived of all rights to raise a family.

In the fall of 1999—after their infant son allegedly died shortly after birth because he was denied medical care—the Corneaus' three daughters were taken from their home and placed in the custody of relatives. The following fall, the then-pregnant Rebecca was incarcerated and forced to give birth in custody; her baby girl was also taken by the state. The Corneaus, who claim that their infant son was stillborn, are currently engaged in a legal battle to regain custody of their children.

That battle escalated recently when Massachusetts officials "accused" Rebecca of giving birth to a sixth child. The Corneaus initially refused to confirm or deny this charge, which seemed to have been based on changes in Rebecca's appearance and statements from neighbors who claim to have seen her leaving her home in labor. No one testified to the child's existence, and police did not find a baby during a search of the Corneaus' home. Still, in January 2002 a juvenile court judge awarded the Department of Social Services temporary custody of the alleged newborn and ordered Rebecca Corneau jailed for contempt if she refused to bring the child to court. On February 5, the Corneaus told the court that Rebecca had miscarried. Judge Kenneth P. Nasif imprisoned them both for contempt, observing that he could not confirm their claim without evidence of a dead fetus.

The prosecution of the Corneaus is zealous, but not entirely arbitrary. State officials have reason to fear for the welfare of children whose parents belong to The Body: Sect leader Jacques Robidoux has been convicted of murder in the starvation death of his ten-month-old son Samuel in 1999. (He was fed only breast milk, in response to a vision from God.) The Corneaus' infant son was buried in secret with Samuel Robidoux, his cousin. The Department of Social Services gained custody of the Corneaus' three daughters after civil proceedings under a child-abuse-and-neglect statute.

Still, this case would generate outrage or, at least, considerably

This piece appeared in The American Prospect, *March 11, 2002*

more controversy if the Corneaus were not identified as "cultists." No one has a religious right to harm a child. (Abraham would not have had a First Amendment defense for terrorizing Isaac.) But no one loses the right to raise children because of an association with a suspect religious group. The Commonwealth of Massachusetts has proceeded as if membership in The Body strips people of the right to parenthood. It stopped just short of requiring the Corneaus to be sterilized.

Compare the Corneau case to the 1990 prosecution of another Massachusetts couple, Christian Scientists David and Ginger Twitchell. They were convicted of involuntary manslaughter for failing to provide their two-year-old son Robyn with medical treatment that could have saved his life. Robyn suffered from peritonitis, but instead of calling a doctor, the Twitchells retained a Christian Science healer and prayed over their son until he died. They were apparently acting in good faith.

The prosecution of the Twitchells for homicide was quite controversial because the fatal neglect of their child was mandated by their religious beliefs. The Commonwealth's Supreme Judicial Court reversed the Twitchells' conviction in 1993 (ruling that their right to present a defense had been unduly restricted), but the SJC made clear that parents do not have a religious right to deny their children essential medical care. Still, state officials do not seek to prohibit Christian Scientists from bearing children or retaining custody of them, although a belief that illness should be treated with prayer, not medical intervention, is central to their faith.

Indeed, the Twitchells—who were proved to have caused the death of their son, however inadvertently—were treated with much greater leniency than the Corneaus. After being convicted of manslaughter, they were not incarcerated; they did not lose custody of their surviving children and were not enjoined from having any more children. Instead, the Twitchells were placed on probation for ten years and required to submit their other three children to periodic medical checkups and to seek medical care for any of them showing signs of serious illness. As far as I know, police have never searched the Twitchells' house (nor the houses of other Christian Science couples) to determine whether or not they are harboring infants who may or may not exist and may or may not require medical care.

Americans who pride themselves on the religiosity of our country and its pluralistic tradition should consider the disparate treatment of the Corneaus and the Twitchells. If our respect for religious pluralism were genuine, members of established churches, like Christian Science, would not enjoy greater protection than do members of small sects, which are denigrated as "cults." All parents, of any or no religion, would be prohibited from denying their children medical care and could be prosecuted for homicide if any of their children died because of intentional medical neglect. But no parents would be presumed to be abusive, neglectful, or otherwise unfit and denied the right to raise their children because of their religious beliefs. Rebecca Corneau has been treated like a criminal because she is suspected of having given birth. What can millions of women say but mea culpa?

THE AG IS THEIR SHEPHERD

When Attorney General John Ashcroft began conducting daily prayer sessions with Justice Department employees, he confirmed the hopes of religious conservatives and fears of secularists: The new Republican regime would make government more godly. As a senator, Ashcroft loudly lamented the separation of church and state and advocated government funding for religious groups, as well as the reintroduction of official prayer in public schools. As attorney general, he organized prayer in the public workplace. According to a May 14, 2001, report in the *Washington Post,* Ashcroft and a group of employees have regularly met at 8 A.M. in his personal office or a conference room to pray and study scripture. The meetings were conceived formulaically, in the self-help tradition: They are RAMP meetings, at which people read, argue, memorize, and pray.

Ashcroft's daily devotionals were said to be ecumenical, despite periodic references to Jesus, and they were open to all employees (his supporters have boasted that one regular attendee is an Orthodox Jew). No one was required to attend, but according to the *Post* some Justice Department employees were uneasy about the prayer meetings and concerned that participation or nonparticipation in them could affect their career prospects. Some were offended by the use of a government workplace for sectarian religious activities.

Reactions to these daily rituals were predictable. Civil libertarians argued that it is inappropriate, although not illegal, for the nation's chief law enforcement officer, and putative protector of liberty, to lead a sectarian prayer group at the nation's chief law enforcement agency. Conservatives stressed correctly that Ashcroft has his own First Amendment right to pray at work and denied that anyone at the Justice Department had reason to feel pressured to join in their boss's prayers. One right-wing polemicist dismissed Ashcroft's critics as "prayer police," and suggested rather stupidly that the wall between church and state is not constitutionally mandated, since the phrase "separation of church and state" does not appear in the Constitution; never mind that the concept helped shape it. The phrase "sex discrimination" is not in the Constitution either, but even conservatives generally concede by now that it is prohibited by the Fourteenth Amendment; indeed, they claim the Fourteenth Amendment obviates the need for the ERA.

This piece appeared in The American Prospect, *July 30, 2001*

But Ashcroft's fundamental right to pray at work was not in dispute, and it demanded respect. Religious beliefs are not neatly compartmentalized; people naturally take their religions with them into the workplace (or voting booth). Federal law rightly requires employers to make "reasonable accommodations" for religious expression by employees. But "reasonableness" is a rather elastic concept that generates a lot of litigation.

Questions about religion in the workplace are not new to employment lawyers, regulatory agencies, or courts. The religious revivalism of the 1990s gave public expressions of religious belief renewed respectability; it's not surprising that the last decade saw an increase in discrimination claims involving employers' alleged failures to accommodate their employees' religious practices. Religious discrimination claims before the federal Equal Opportunity Commission increased 43 percent between 1991 and 1997.

It is no small irony that these cases sometimes reflected efforts by employers to regulate the religious expressions of some employees in deference to the beliefs of others. Increased sensitivity to harassment was both a blessing and a curse to employees anxious to practice their religions at work. In 2000, Lule Said, a Muslim man in Massachusetts who was targeted by fellow employees for praying at work, won a harassment claim against his employer (he was awarded $300,000 by the Massachusetts Commission Against Discrimination). But in a 1995 Nebraska case, *Wilson v. U.S. West,* a federal appeals court ruled against an employee, Christine Wilson, who claimed a religious right to wear an antiabortion button featuring a color photo of a fetus that upset her coworkers, including some who shared her opposition to abortion rights. Offended coworkers complained that the button constituted harassment, and Wilson conceded that it caused serious disruption at work. The federal court upheld U.S. West's efforts to accommodate Wilson's religious beliefs by giving her the option of wearing an antiabortion button that contained no pictures, or allowing her to wear the pictorial button in her own little cubicle and covering it at other times. (Rulings like this can give credence to complaints about closeting religion.) In another 1995 case, *Brown v. Polk County,* however, the same court upheld the right of a devout Christian employee, Isaiah Brown, to conduct prayer sessions in a government workplace. His employer, Polk County, Iowa, claimed that the prayers could cause resentment and religious divisiveness in the workplace, but presented no evidence that they had actually done so.

As these cases make clear, the line between the right to express religious beliefs at work and the power to impose those beliefs on others is often in dispute, especially in a culture suspicious of First Amendment rights—a culture that sometimes values inoffensiveness as much as self-expression. The rights of employees to wear or display religious paraphernalia or pray at work should generally prevail over the sensibilities of colleagues. Employer's concerns about the divisiveness of sectarian rituals are not unfounded, but people ought to tolerate the religious practices of their coworkers.

They should, however, be spared the religious enthusiasms of their supervisors, which are apt to be inherently coercive. Indeed, federal guidelines on religion in the federal workplace stress that supervisors need to express their own religious beliefs with great care, to avoid even misperceptions of coercion. The attorney general is violating the spirit if not the letter of these guidelines, his critics claim. He may have a legal right to conduct morning prayer sessions, but it should be exercised with regard for his authority over some 135,000 Justice Department employees, not to mention his power to set policy for the nation. As conservatives often point out, you lose your moral claim to exercise a right when you exercise it irresponsibly.

In any case, John Ashcroft has limited credibility as a champion of religious freedom. He aggressively supports the right of publicly funded religious groups to limit the religious practices of their employees and even to hire and fire on the basis of belief. Under the 1996 charitable choice bill introduced by then senator Ashcroft (and incorporated in the welfare reform law), religious groups receiving federal funds to deliver social services were exempt from federal law prohibiting religious discrimination in employment. (See the "Joy of Sects") In other words, the attorney general supports the right of Christian employers receiving public funds to hire only Christians or to prohibit any Muslim employees from praying at work or merely wearing headscarves. Ashcroft may read scripture every morning, but he doesn't seem to know the Golden Rule.

5

CRIMINALLY UNJUST

ORDINARY ABUSES

It's no coincidence that, in the days before September 11, declining support for capital punishment was accompanied by increased mistrust of law enforcement and discomfort with the war on drugs. A relative lull in violent crimes during the 1990s contributed to a reconsideration of harsh police and prosecutorial practices. But many people are willing to tolerate bad policing so long as it's directed at bad guys—few complain when guilty suspects are deprived of their rights and coerced confessions prove true. It was the abuse of innocent people or ordinary people guilty only of minor, nonviolent offenses that prompted some tentative public review of the current regime.

It's not just the regularity with which DNA evidence was exonerating people wrongly imprisoned that aroused concern about criminal justice. By 2000, the bias and bloodthirstiness of law enforcement simply became unseemly—because the public became aware that it was sometimes directed at innocent people, like Abner Louima, who was tortured by a New York City police officer in a Brooklyn station house. Racial profiling became impossible to ignore: The police killing of the innocent African immigrant Amadou Diallo in New York dramatized its brutality and its cost to civil order. In the 2000 presidential campaign, even conservatives like Dick Cheney and Joe Lieberman belatedly condemned racial profiling. The awful misdeeds and mistakes of FBI agents—from the attacks at Ruby Ridge and Waco to the framing of Bostonian Joseph Salvati, wrongly imprisoned for thirty years in order to protect a murderous FBI informant—made the nation's premier law enforcement agency look like public enemy number one. The continued imprisonment of nonviolent drug offenders, the federal government's gratuitously cruel campaign against medical marijuana, and the expansion of the drug war to public schools, where students are treated like suspects and randomly tested for drugs brought the police state home to the white middle class. Confronted with the sheer meanness of their government, people began to rediscover traditional American values, like fairness and respect for individuals.

On occasion, the press collaborated with law enforcement in trampling people's rights: Irresponsible reporting by the *New York Times* was partly to blame for the federal government's wrongful

This piece appeared in The American Prospect, *August 27, 2001*

prosecution of Los Alamos scientist Wen Ho Lee; right-wing media partnered with Ken Starr in his fanatical pursuit of Bill Clinton. But the press has also helped expose the crimes of law enforcement, which politicians of both parties have supported or ignored. Stories about thuggish cops and prosecutors, and ordinary citizens spending years in prison for minor drug offenses are hard to resist. In the months before September 11, the press was paying particular attention to the trampling of rights by officials who are paid to protect them.

"Suspects' False Confessions Ignite Interrogation Debate," a June 14, 2001, headline in the *Miami Herald* proclaimed, in a story about a mentally retarded man wrongfully imprisoned for twenty-two years, thanks to a false, coerced confession. In Prince George's County, Maryland, according to a June 2001 series in the *Washington Post,* police routinely coerced confessions from unsophisticated people, interrogating them for days at a time in isolation, terrorizing them, and illegally depriving them of counsel, not to mention sleep. Honest, skeptical prosecutors or DNA evidence can free some people who are wrongly imprisoned by cops who don't distinguish between innocence and guilt in their zeal to clear cases. (The *Post* examined four cases in which people forced to confess were exonerated.) But prosecutors are not always honest, or alert; DNA evidence is not always available; and it's not always possible to prove the innocence of criminal defendants (it's also not required and shouldn't be expected). People are sometimes convicted on the sole basis of highly questionable confessions; and, often, in the absence of videotaping, challenges to the legality of an interrogation and truth of a confession involve the conflicting testimony of defendants and police. Guess whom judges generally believe.

Die-hard defenders of the system dismiss the kinds of cases chronicled by the *Post* as "horror stories"—the usual description of injustices people would rather not acknowledge. Or they assert that one bad department or a few bad cops don't indict an entire system. But as defense attorneys will attest, the abusive tactics used in Prince George's County, the targeting of apparently innocent people (or people whose guilt is not supported by evidence) are not anomalous. Of course, many law enforcement officials are competent, energetic, and honorable; but some are not. After all, virtually no one in the system is surprised when police officers perjure themselves on the witness stand (it's called "testilying").

The legal representation of poor people prosecuted for serious crimes is often inadequate to the challenge of righting these wrongs. In April 2001, a *New York Times* series chronicled the failings of indigent defense in New York. The Legal Aid Society (my former employer) has been crippled by former mayor Giuliani's budget cuts. According to the *Times*, Legal Aid's caseloads and resources were drastically reduced: Its lawyers now handle only 50 percent of all felony and misdemeanor cases annually. A few small defense organizations handle an additional 18 percent of cases, and the rest are turned over to private attorneys, who are often inexperienced, underpaid, and unsupervised. (When I worked for Legal Aid, the court-appointed lawyers tended to be guys in shiny suits.) According to the *Times*, many court-appointed attorneys don't investigate the crimes with which their clients are charged, don't visit the scenes, and don't hire expert witnesses, psychiatrists, or pathologists. Many don't visit their clients in prison or interview them in private. Some don't exactly know the rules of evidence.

The *Times* interviewed several important players in the New York justice system, including its chief judge and the state's director of criminal justice, who confirmed the awful failings of indigent defense. Readers were regaled with stories about people wrongfully imprisoned, thanks partly to bad lawyering. Still, some observers were unimpressed: In *Slate*, Mickey Kaus derided the *Times* series as boring, uncontroversial, and unsubstantiated by sufficient "horror stories." He didn't exactly question the system's failings (in fact, he dismissed the *Times* exposé as old news), but he was skeptical of the harms caused by bad lawyers—as if he'd ever agree to be represented by one of them. I doubt any pundit would question the dangers posed by untrained physicians who treated gravely ill patients without actually examining them, but the average pundit is more likely to identify with a sick person than a suspect in a homicide.

When people start identifying with the victims of law enforcement, they stop accepting its systematic abuses: Laws against medical marijuana are vulnerable because their targets include respectable, disease-stricken citizens. So, if we want to rein in bad cops and bad laws, we might first unleash them on the white middle class. Imagine the political consequences of subjecting affluent whites to the same degree of police surveillance and abuse that poor blacks and Latinos endure. The war on drugs is a war on minorities partly because police pay relatively little attention to drug-law violations by whites. That's why nearly 70 percent of people in prison are blacks and Latinos—who constitute about 25 percent of the nation's population. Prison conditions would improve dramatically if statistics like these were reversed.

We would also witness dramatic improvements in crime control if police and prosecutors were held accountable for misconduct. Criminal justice abuses are threats to the public safety as well as individual rights. When the innocent are persecuted, the guilty roam free.

VICTIMS VS. SUSPECTS

In the 1960s, the Supreme Court recognized that people accused of crimes were imbued with constitutional rights, which the states were obliged to respect. In the course of a few years, the Warren Court applied the exclusionary rule to the states, prohibiting the introduction of evidence seized in violation of the Fourth Amendment; it fashioned the Miranda warnings, to protect the Fifth Amendment right to remain silent and prevent coerced confessions; it required prosecutors to disclose exculpatory evidence; and it held that states must provide indigent defendants with lawyers at both the trial and appellate levels.

These rulings are commonly and stupidly derided for elevating legal technicalities over questions of guilt: With the exception of the exclusionary rule (which is quite flexible and all too easily avoided), these "technicalities" focus precisely on the question of guilt. Coerced confessions are inherently unreliable; prosecutorial misconduct, like failure to disclose evidence exonerating the defendant, leads to wrongful convictions, as does the denial of competent counsel to poor defendants.

But ensuring the integrity of the trial process has never been a high political priority. Legislators and judges intent on being perceived as "tough on crime" pass laws or issue rulings that increase the likelihood of conviction but not the reliability. Indeed, some rules, like those limiting federal appeals of state court convictions, facilitate unreliable convictions—convictions of innocent people, or people whose guilt was never proven. Few voters seem to care. The reforms demanded by the Warren Court were undermined by Richard Nixon's law and order campaign of the late sixties, the ongoing war on drugs, and a widespread tendency to presume the guilt of people prosecuted for crimes. In a different world, the Warren Court decisions could have inspired increased respect for the rights of criminal suspects; instead they helped spark a movement to create countervailing rights for crime victims.

In the past thirty years, the victims' rights movement has generated some welcome reforms, notably the extension of services to crime victims in localities across the country and the renewed attention that prosecutors pay to victims' concerns. In addition, all the states have adopted legislation or constitutional amendments recog-

This piece appeared in The American Prospect, *March 13, 2000*

nizing the interests of victims in criminal proceedings. Still, Congress is anxious to declare its allegiance to crime victims, partly to affirm its abhorrence of criminal suspects. So, for several years, in the late 1990s, the Senate threatened to pass the Crime Victims' Rights Amendment to the Constitution. It would give victims of violent crimes a right to be present at all public proceedings, a right to be heard regarding negotiated pleas and release from custody, a right to restitution from the convicted offender, and a right to consideration of their interests in a trial "free from unreasonable delay."

What's wrong with these rights? Putting principle aside for the moment, consider the practicalities: Offering federal constitutional rights to crime victims will greatly complicate and impair prosecutions, which is why the Victims' Rights Amendment encountered opposition from some prosecutors, (including a federal prosecutor in the Oklahoma City bombing case). Granting crime victims vaguely defined rights to speedy trials may pressure prosecutors into trying cases before they are ready; requiring victims to be present during all trial proceedings will often conflict with the need to sequester witnesses, since the victims of crime often testify against their alleged attackers; requiring victims to be heard on plea negotiations may lead to delays, and possibly more trials (and perhaps fewer convictions, since delay often benefits the defendant). Problems like these will be exacerbated in cases involving multiple victims, with multiple prosecutorial agendas of their own. What's a prosecutor to do if one victim urges him to negotiate a plea and another demands a trial?

The practical problems posed by the Victims' Rights Amendment are, however, less daunting than its repressive ideology. It attacks the presumption of innocence. When we identify and legally empower a victim before conviction, we assume that a crime has been committed, although that is sometimes disputed at trial (think of an acquaintance rape case); we also assume the veracity and reliability of the self-proclaimed victim. It's worth noting that the Victims' Rights Amendment was opposed by many feminist advocates for battered women (including the NOW Legal Defense and Education Fund), because in cases involving domestic violence, the identity of the victim is not always clear. Women who strike back against their abusers are sometimes prosecuted and offer claims of self-defense: These women should not "lose their 'victim' status once they have defended their lives and become defendants," the National Clearinghouse for the Defense of Battered Women has asserted. It has argued that additional time, money, and energy devoted to helping crime victims should be used to increase support and services for victims outside the court-room, not to invent questionable constitutional rights within it. But many victims' rights advocates perceive the rights of defendants and the interests of victims as elements in a zero-sum game: many don't simply want to increase victim services; they want to decrease defen-dants' rights and reorient criminal trials so that the victim, not the defendant, occupies center stage. "How might the most serious crimes . . . be resolved differently if the victims, rather than the offenders, were the center of attention?" Judith Herman wondered in *The American Prospect,* in January 2000. "What if the courtroom drama were a dialogue between the victim and the community about restitution rather than a duel between the prosecution and the de-fense about punishment?" she asked rhetorically.

Questions like these presume the defendant's guilt. The prose-cutor and defense are not engaged in a "duel about punishment"; they're engaged in a duel about guilt. Should we determine the resti-tution owed by the defendant to the victim before we have determined her guilt? What if the victim is lying, or mistaken about the identity of the defendant? (Eyewitness identifications, for example, are noto-riously unreliable.) What if police falsify evidence against the defen-dant? What if the prosecutor has concealed evidence of her inno-cence?

Defendants occupy the center of attention in criminal trials be-cause they're the ones being prosecuted. The rights conferred upon criminal suspects are limitations on the power of the state to kill or imprison its citizens. The Bill of Rights reflects the Founders' belief that government could not be trusted to exercise its police powers fairly. It reflects the understanding that power is easily abused, and that individuals cannot protect themselves against the state without rights that prosecutors are required to respect.

Crime victims have a strong moral claim to be treated with respect and compassion, of course; but they should not be imbued with con-stitutional rights equivalent to the rights of defendants (their liberty and their lives are not at stake), and they should not expect their need to be "healed" or "made whole" by the trial to take precedence over the defendant's right to dispute allegations of guilt. Once guilt has been adjudicated, victims have an appropriate role in sentencing, but even then, courts concerned with equal justice have to guard against letting bias for or against the victim determine punishment. We should, for example, be wary of victim-impact statements, which de-scribe the effects of a crime on the victim, or the victim's family.

These statements can easily favor defendants whose victims lack family or friends to speak for them. The bias they introduce into the sentencing process is especially troubling in capital cases. Should killing a homeless, friendless person be less of a crime than killing someone well loved by his family and community?

Victims' rights advocates generally view therapy for the victim as a primary form of justice, but in the criminal courts, the demands of therapy and justice conflict. Some crime victims, for example, may find cross-examination traumatic, but it is essential to the defense—and to the search for truth. The victim's credibility must be tested, inaccuracies or inconsistencies in her story must be revealed. Taking a cue from the therapeutic culture, victims' rights advocates tend to impute virtue to victimhood, but of course it is sometimes misplaced. Taking the presumption of innocence seriously means that we can never take an accusation at face value.

It's hard to argue with the desire to reform trials in order to help victims heal—unless you consider the consequences. Because the Victims' Rights Amendment decreases the rights of defendants, it's not simply a grant of rights to crime victims: It's a grant of power to the state. Victims need and deserve services, but with nearly two million people already behind bars, the state needs no more power to imprison us.

PICTURES AT AN EXECUTION

Timothy McVeigh was killed on June 11, 2001, on closed-circuit TV (for the benefit of his victims) and with luminaries like Bryant Gumbel presiding over what networks presumed would be a national death watch. We didn't actually see McVeigh being poisoned. But we were regaled with numbing reports about his last moments and discussions of execution protocols. We heard from some who witnessed his death, as well as numerous commentators for and against capital punishment. Downtime was filled with stories about the victims of the Oklahoma City bombing, discussions of domestic terrorism, and arguments about televising executions. When they got desperate, they told us about Terre Haute, home of the federal death chamber, where hotels and motels for the execution week sold out early.

McVeigh's death reinvigorated debates about public executions (they were phased out in nineteenth-century America, partly because people enjoyed them too much). But public viewing of executions is less important than public scrutiny of capital cases. It's too bad we can't televise the closed-door discussions of federal as well as state prosecutors who target people for death row. According to a 2000 Department of Justice Study, racial minorities constitute about 80 percent of federal death row inmates, because prosecutors (not judges or juries) have singled out minorities for death: About 80 percent of the cases in which federal prosecutors sought the death penalty in the past five years involved minority defendants. The DOJ study also found geographical disparities in the application of the death penalty: Five jurisdictions were responsible for 40 percent of capital cases, with Texas leading the way. (Almost 90 percent of all state-administered executions in 2000 occurred in the South.)

Former attorney general Janet Reno was "troubled" by these figures, acknowledging that "minorities are overrepresented in the federal death penalty system," and in one of his last gestures as president, Bill Clinton stayed by six months the execution of convicted drug dealer Juan Garza (a Hispanic from Texas). But Reno's successor, John Ashcroft, a strong supporter of the death penalty, was not troubled by the DOJ study. He ordered a controversial follow-up study shortly after taking office, which, not surprisingly, found no evidence of racial bias in the federal death system. Ashcroft had the satisfaction of authorizing the executions of both McVeigh and

This piece appeared in The American Prospect, May 21, 2001

Garza. The stay issued by Clinton did not save Garza, but it did save Clinton the trouble of killing him, and it ensured that white man Timothy McVeigh was the first person executed by the federal government in thirty-eight years.

McVeigh, the Charles Manson of his day, did not evoke much sympathy, yet June 2001 was an odd time for the federal bureaucracy to reinstate the death penalty. Mounting evidence indicated that people are wrongly convicted of capital crimes almost routinely. The facts are familiar but still bear repeating:

Since the mid-1970s, ninety-six people sentenced to death have been exonerated and freed—about 13 percent of all people executed in the same period. A 2000 study by James Leibman of Columbia University found a devastatingly high reversible error rate of 68 percent in trials that ended in death penalties. Diehard supporters of capital punishment perversely insist that evidence of a high error rate is proof that the system works, because it shows that errors are uncovered. Put aside questions about errors that remain concealed, partly because appeals have been drastically curtailed. Imagine, instead, if hospitals made potentially fatal errors in treating 68 percent of their patients. Would anyone sensible or humane remain content with our system of health care? Would any death penalty advocate who lost years of his own life in prison for a murder he did not commit, point to his tenure on death row as proof that the system worked?

Not everyone is so crazy or cruel. The late Supreme Court justice Thurgood Marshall once optimistically opined that Americans would cease to support the death penalty if they were informed of its gross inequities, and recent exposés of wrongful convictions proved him partly right. In the late 1990s, support for capital punishment declined dramatically, from about 75 percent in 1997 to 66 percent in the early months of 2001, the lowest level of support in nineteen years.

Given this trend, abolishing the death penalty was, at least, conceivable before September 11. Even a few conservative commentators had begun belatedly to realize that if you don't trust the government to deliver the mail, perhaps you shouldn't trust it to select people for death. (The conservative Rutherford Institute called for a federal moratorium on the death penalty.) George Bush, who enthusiastically presided over 834 executions during his five years as governor of Texas, was always unlikely to discover flaws in the death-selection system, although he was better positioned for a conversion experience leading him to oppose capital punishment than most Democrats. But

Congress had the power to halt federal executions. (In the midst of a war on terrorism, that power seems merely theoretical.) The proposed National Death Penalty Moratorium Act of 2001 would have suspended federal executions and established a commission to review the administration of the death penalty at the state and federal level.

Introduced by four liberal Democratic senators (Feingold, Levin, Wellstone, and Corzine), this bill probably enjoyed about as much chance of success as a condemned man seeking clemency from the Texas Board of Pardons and Paroles. Still, if it's always hard to rally support for restricting executions, it's virtually impossible to fashion an intellectually honest argument justifying capital punishment in the face of overwhelming evidence that it is applied unfairly, and in bad faith.

Twenty years ago, the late Yale Law professor Charles Black wrote an eloquent book describing the inevitable capriciousness of the system for trying death penalty cases. He noted that people often asked him if he'd support the death penalty if the system were fair. The question, he suggested, rested on an impossible hypothetical: "Sometimes I think the question, 'What would you do if the death-choice system were perfected?' is like the question 'What would you do if 40 percent of the people in New York learned to speak pretty good Japanese by next New Year's Day?' . . . But sometimes I think the question is more like, 'What would you do if an amoeba were taught to play the piano?' "

"Why shouldn't we kill people who deserve to die?" proponents of the death penalty continue to ask. The question is dramatic but irrelevant, and in more peaceful times, people may eventually realize why we shouldn't kill people whom the death penalty bureaucracy has selected to die.

SECRETS AND LIES

Assuming that the late former Enron vice chairman Cliff Baxter died by his own hand and not the hands of others who feared he might testify against them, you might blame Baxter's suicide on guilt, shame, or fear of financial ruin. Linda Lay, wife of former Enron CEO Kenneth Lay, has blamed the media. "Cliff was a wonderful man," Mrs. Lay lamented in her January 28, 2002, interview with NBC's Lisa Myers: His apparent suicide was "a perfect example of how the media can play such havoc and destruction in people's lives."

There's nothing new about efforts to scapegoat the media, and they sometimes seem justified by the sins of tabloid journalism. But for every victim of the press there are many legitimate targets, from Richard Nixon and O. J. Simpson to Gary Condit and Cardinal Bernard Law. Often, media scapegoating simply reflects an effort to evade individual accountability. People who resent being caught sometimes blame the press for their downfall—as if reporting crime is worse than committing it.

Linda Lay's clumsy attack on the press did not distract many people from the sins of Enron executives or the consequent sufferings of employees and shareholders. But people with power often succeed in suppressing vital public information that would incriminate or embarrass them. President Bush has an infamous affinity for secrecy: He issued an executive order delaying the legally mandated release of papers from previous presidential administrations and sequestered his own gubernatorial records in his father's presidential library to evade the requirements of Texas's Public Information Act. His administration ordered federal agencies to resist Freedom of Information Act requests, refused to answer questions about Vice President Dick Cheney's energy-policy meetings, and initially resisted a congressional request for Justice Department memos concerning the FBI's murderous thirty-year collaboration with Boston-area gangsters.

But attempts by presidents to keep public information private are likely to attract press attention and lawsuits, as the Bush Administration learned. Lesser officials keep secrets with less public scrutiny. Consider efforts by prosecutors to hide evidence of wrongful convictions. Peter Neufeld, cofounder of Cardozo School of Law's Innocence Project, has estimated that during the past ten years prosecutors opposed post-conviction DNA typing in about half of the cases in

This piece appeared in The American Prospect, March 25, 2002

which it was requested. One defense attorney has observed that some-times prosecutors even oppose requests for new trials after testing has virtually exonerated a convicted defendant.

Take the case of Bruce Godschalk. He was wrongly imprisoned for fifteen years for two rapes committed in a Philadelphia suburb in 1986, when he was twenty-six. His conviction was based on a now dis-credited confession, which he long insisted was coerced and effec-tively written by the interrogating detective, who supplied him with unpublicized facts about the crime. In addition, one victim chose his photo from a group of mug shots; the other victim was unable to make an identification. Godschalk had no record of violence and two prior arrests—for possession of marijuana and driving while impaired.

While in prison, Godschalk spent seven years trying to arrange for DNA testing of the evidence in his case, at his own expense. Montgomery County prosecutor Bruce Castor refused to allow test-ing, relying on what he claimed was an irrefutable confession (al-though if the confession were true, he had no need to fear the test). Finally, in November 2001, Godschalk obtained a ruling from a fed-eral judge ordering DNA tests, which definitively exonerated him. The prosecutor's own laboratory and a lab hired by the defense con-cluded that both rapes were committed by the same person, who could not have been Bruce Godschalk.

At first, Castor persisted in opposing Godschalk's release, al-though he acknowledged having "no scientific basis" for doubting the test results. He simply assumed that "the tests must be flawed" be-cause they contradicted the claims of the interrogating detective in the case. Finally, On February 14, 2002, after additional testing and some bad publicity, Castor grudgingly gave in: "I'm not convinced that Bruce Godschalk is innocent . . . but a tie goes to the de-fendant."

Given the new DNA evidence, Godschalk seemed bound to be set free eventually, partly because as the criminal justice system begins to rely on DNA tests to convict people, it will have to accept DNA tests that exonerate people (one hopes). Opposition to testing is begin-ning to ease, and twenty-two states have passed laws providing con-victed inmates with access to DNA tests, in some cases. But inmates who may have been wrongly convicted still have no generally acknowl-edged right to obtain DNA testing, and the public has no acknowl-edged right to know when innocent people have been imprisoned or executed. In January 2002, the Fourth Circuit Court of Appeals held that convicts have no constitutional right to DNA testing; and in May 2001, a state court in Virginia denied a motion by a group of newspapers for DNA testing in the case of Roger Coleman, who was executed for murder in 1992, despite questions about his guilt.

This ruling in the Coleman case makes sense only if the goal of prosecutors and judges is to spare the state the embarrassment of exposing the execution of an innocent man and to spare the public knowledge of fatal flaws in the criminal justice system. Imagine if hospitals openly refused to uncover and divulge readily obtainable information about the number of people who died as a result of botched procedures, grossly negligent care, or doctors and nurses who purposefully maim or murder their patients—like prosecutors and police officers who knowingly convict the innocent. The truth may hurt, but it's lies that are liable to kill us.

6

WOMEN'S RIGHTS

EQUAL RIGHTS POSTPONEMENT

Ask state and federal legislators if they believe that legal rights should be extended or withheld on the basis of sex. Most would probably say no; many would be lying. Passage of an Equal Rights Amendment to the Constitution remains a feminist fantasy. Its simple declaration of rights—"Equality of rights under the law shall not be denied or abridged by the United States or by any state on account of sex"—cannot win congressional support. The ERA has been introduced in every session of Congress since 1985, only to be buried in committee. In 2001, it was introduced in the House by Democratic congresswoman Carolyn Maloney and in the Senate by Edward Kennedy, but don't expect passage of it anytime soon.

Sometimes it's hard to believe that in the early seventies the ERA was actually approved by Congress and sent to the states for ratification (constitutional amendments must be ratified by three-fourths of the states). Feminists famously failed to win ratification (they lost by three states) after a hysterical public debate that focused on legal absurdities, like mandatory coed bathrooms. At the time, a majority of Americans professed support for the amendment, but as political scientist Jane Mansbridge observed in her astute book *Why We Lost the ERA,* support for equality itself was rather shallow. Polls showed that a majority of Americans who endorsed the ERA also endorsed traditional gender roles: A 1977 survey showed that over half of ERA supporters agreed that advancing her husband's career was more important to a woman than advancing her own. Almost two-thirds believed that wives should not work outside the home if their husbands could support them and jobs were limited.

Equality has become much more respectable in the last two decades, even as feminism itself has fallen out of fashion. That's the message young women send when they decline to identify as feminists while endorsing feminism's goals. According to a 2001 survey commissioned by *American Demographics,* only 34 percent of adolescent girls call themselves feminists but 97 percent believe that men and women should be paid equally; 92 percent believe that a woman's "lifestyle choices" should not be limited by her sex; and 89 percent agree that a woman does not need a man or children to be successful.

But support for female independence doesn't necessarily translate into activism or demands for an ERA. A 2000 Gallup Poll asking

This piece appeared in The American Prospect, *September 10, 2001*

women about the "challenges (they) face in their daily lives" found that only 4 percent of women were "most concerned" about equality and discrimination. Money, family, and health were women's top concerns, which is hardly surprising. Some feminists will argue that women would have fewer money, family, and health problems if they enjoyed full equality; and, in theory, many women might agree. According to a 1999 Gallup Poll, only 26 percent of Americans believe that men and women are treated equally and 69 percent believe that society treats men better than women. But when people answer a pollster's questions about their daily struggles, they're not thinking theoretically. Equality is an abstract, long-term goal compared to a daily struggle to pay the bills.

Besides, the ERA suffers from the common belief that it is no longer necessary, given the growth of civil rights laws in the past thirty years. That's one irony of progress: as acceptance of sexual equality grows, active support for the ERA declines. Young women who believe they already enjoy equality are not inclined to fight for a constitutional guarantee of it. Meanwhile, conservatives who fought the extension of constitutional equality rights to women and passage of statutory prohibitions of sex discrimination rely on the past progress toward equality to prevent more progress in the future. Now that the Fourteenth Amendment has been applied to sex discrimination, they argue, we have no need for an ERA.

But in fact, the Supreme Court has not applied Fourteenth Amendment guarantees of equality with equal force in sex and race cases, because a majority of justices have always regarded some instances of sex discrimination as "only natural." The Court employs a "strict" standard of review in race discrimination cases: Essentially the state must show that any law discriminating on the basis of race is a *necessary* means of protecting a compelling state interest. Laws subjected to this standard are doomed. In sex-discrimination cases, the Court uses an "intermediate" standard of review: A law discriminating on the basis of sex is struck down only if it lacks a substantial relationship to an important government goal. Laws discriminating on the basis of sex sometimes survive this test: In June 2001, in *Nguyen v. Immigration and Naturalization Service*, the Supreme Court upheld a federal law that discriminates between men and women who desire to pass on American citizenship to foreign-born children. The offspring of American women who give birth abroad enjoy automatic citizenship. Men whose children are born abroad to foreign-born women must take legal steps to establish paternity before the children turn eighteen in order to confer citizenship on them.

In upholding these distinctions between the rights of fathers and mothers, the Court relied on gender stereotypes—notably the belief that men are less likely than women to form bonds with their children. A majority of the justices found the discrimination against men legal because they considered it natural—a product of biology, not prejudice. The dissent, by Justice O'Connor, forcefully disagreed, pointing out that paternity could be established by DNA testing, if it were in question, and that the sex of a parent cannot be relied upon to predict parental affection or responsibility.

Does a case like this demonstrate a need for the ERA? Not exactly. The ERA, like other constitutional protections, will mean what the Supreme Court says it means. There's no guarantee that judges who cling to gender stereotypes will apply the ERA more rigorously than they apply Fourteenth Amendment guarantees of sexual equality. In interpreting an ERA, they can always find that some discriminatory laws merely reflect the natural order, which law is presumably powerless to challenge. Once, the Supreme Court held that prohibitions on female lawyers were only natural. Culture had to change before courts could acknowledge that women had the right to practice "male" professions. But law changed too, notably with the passage of the 1964 Civil Rights Act that imposed a federal ban on sex discrimination in employment. Culture and law change in tandem to revise our visions of what's possible and fair. By itself, an ERA would not deliver full equality to women, but it would prompt courts and legislatures to reconsider it.

REPRODUCTIVE EMERGENCY

Life is one long emergency for most advocacy groups, whose members are apt to be united by the belief that they're besieged. To an outsider who lacks their political passions, however, they seem less besieged than overwrought. So casual supporters of abortion rights may be unimpressed when NOW declares an official state of emergency in the battle over reproductive choice. The "Emergency Action for Women's Lives," a four-year campaign targeting the U.S. Senate, was launched in 2001 with an April 22 rally in Washington. Even before September 11, this campaign didn't seem to generate much excitement, or publicity. But the more you know about threats to choice, the more you share NOW's sense of urgency.

A majority of Americans support abortion rights, but rather queasily, and the antiabortion and pro-choice movements have been stalemated for several years. Pro-choicers narrowly defeated efforts to criminalize particular abortion procedures (in the guise of bans on mythical "partial birth" abortions) and they recently won a Supreme Court decision striking down the nonconsensual drug testing of pregnant women. But over the years, restrictions on minor's rights have been upheld, along with restrictions on the use of public funds to finance abortions and the rights of publicly funded doctors even to talk about abortion with their patients.

Attacks on the basic constitutional right to obtain an abortion outlined by *Roe v. Wade* have failed, just barely, but access to abortion has declined: Violence against abortion providers is a strong disincentive to doctors and many are no longer being trained to perform abortions anyway. In Massachusetts, a major Boston hospital has shut down a late-term abortion program that served women who needed abortions after fourteen weeks of pregnancy because of serious health problems. "This is reminiscent of the problems of thirty years ago," the chief of obstetrics and gynecology at Beth Israel Deaconess Hospital told the *Boston Globe*. Antiabortion activists have managed to make the legality of abortion irrelevant for many women by making the availability of abortion scarce.

This bad situation is likely to get worse. Encouraged by the ascension of George Bush, antiabortion activists renewed their efforts to erode reproductive rights "incrementally." They've already tasted victory: The new president, grateful and obliged to opponents of

A version of this piece appeared in The American Prospect, *May 7, 2001*

abortion rights, moved swiftly to deny U.S. aid to international family planning agencies that merely provide abortion counseling. President Bush and his congressional allies also favor stringently limiting access to the FDA-approved abortifacient Mifepristone (RU-486.) Secretary of Health and Human Services Tommy Thompson has signaled his willingness to order a new review of the drug, although the FDA approval of it in 2000 followed an unusually lengthy review. RU-486 is approved in nineteen countries and has been used by half a million women in Europe since 1989. U.S. clinical trials found the drug effective in 92 percent of cases; women for whom the drug did not work were successfully treated with surgical abortions. No deaths were reported as a result of the drug's use—unless, of course, you count the deaths of embryos.

People opposed to abortion because of a sincere belief that a live human being inhabits a woman's body in the earliest stages of pregnancy naturally find RU-486 morally repugnant. But metaphysical questions about when life begins are not exactly within the purview of the FDA and are often absent from public debates about RU-486—partly because early, first-term abortions are considerably less controversial than abortions conducted after the fetus has begun to resemble a baby (that's why antiabortion activists carry around pictures of developed fetuses, not fertilized eggs). Opponents of RU-486 often disingenuously attack its safety for women instead of stressing the homicidal threat it poses to embryos.

Of course, antiabortion opponents are not above expressing concern for embryonic life, as debates about stem cell research illustrate. The premise that human beings exist, in microscopic form, immediately after conception often provides a benign pretext for curbing abortion rights. The antiabortion movement is, in part, a movement to enshrine embryonic and fetal rights.

Embryos would have a right to health care, under a Health and Human Services proposal announced in January 2002. HHS secretary Thompson wants to expand the definition of a child under a federal children's health insurance program to include everyone (or everything) from conception to age nineteen. This proposal has been offered in the spirit of compassionate conservatism; its purpose is to provide prenatal care for poor women, proponents claim. But as critics counter, prenatal care can be provided directly to the poor simply by extending federal health insurance to pregnant women, not their fetuses, which a Senate bill proposes to do. Of course, the purpose of

Secretary Thompson's proposal is not to extend prenatal care, but to incorporate the theoretical underpinning of the antiabortion movement—a belief in embryonic or fetal personhood—into federal law.

The proposed Unborn Victims of Violence Act exemplifies the strategy of destroying reproductive choice without ever attacking it directly. Introduced by Republicans in the House and Senate (and drafted by the National Right to Life Committee), this bill would make it a federal crime to injure or kill a fetus during an attack on a pregnant woman, at any stage of fetal development (even if the attacker was unaware of the pregnancy). It's not a novel concept. Fetal-protection laws are in place in a majority of states, although some consist of sentence-enhancement schemes in cases involving fetal injury or death—an approach that expresses the public's particular abhorrence for attacks on pregnant women without necessarily undermining their reproductive rights. But protecting pregnant women is not what antiabortion advocates in Congress have in mind. They're seeking to confer personhood upon the fetus.

The Teen Endangerment Act also favors the presumed interests of the fetus over the interests of pregnant women (or, in this case, pregnant girls). It would make felons out of family members, like grandmothers, aunts, or older sisters, who transport a minor across state lines in order to obtain an abortion, if the girl cannot obtain parental or judicial permission for an abortion in her home state.

Encouraging communication between parents and kids is a worthy goal, but laws like this do not further it. Rates of parental involvement in teen abortions are about the same in states with and without parental consent laws. (Pregnant teens usually do seek the help of at least one parent, and the rate of parental involvement in abortions is especially high, 90 percent, for girls fourteen and younger.) What will be the effect of a federal law that punishes family members other than parents for helping pregnant teenagers? This is one law that threatens to live up to its title: If it's enacted, the Teen Endangerment Act surely will endanger teens, encouraging them to obtain illegal abortions, continue high-risk pregnancies, or seek help from hostile, violence-prone parents. One-third of teenage girls who do not talk to their parents about abortions have already been the victims of family violence.

Battles over antiabortion measures like these are important, but they may be skirmishes compared to the upcoming fight over the next Supreme Court nominee. If a member of the slim moderate pro-choice majority on the court retires, Bush will, no doubt, nominate a judge opposed to abortion rights. If he or she is confirmed, *Roe v. Wade* will be overruled as soon as the next case challenging it wends its way to the Court.

The crusade to make abortions illegal and unsafe (they are unlikely ever to be rare) does pose political risks for Republicans. If outright abortion prohibitions and a reversal of *Roe v. Wade* were popular, Bush would not have cloaked his support for them during the 2000 campaign. Female voters deprived of all abortion rights promise to become a more potent political force than male voters who fear being deprived of their guns. If reproductive choice falls victim to the Bush Administration, it could fall victim to reproductive choice. But once revoked, rights are not quickly or easily restored, and the Supreme Court outlives the administrations that shape it. A Bush Court would survive, while women and girls would die from illegal abortions. There are surely better ways to win elections.

ABORTION AND AUTONOMY

Two important abortion cases were decided by the Supreme Court in June 2000. In *Hill v. Colorado*, the Court upheld statutory buffer or bubble zones—no speech zones around abortion clinics and individuals entering clinics, in which even peaceful antiabortion protests are prohibited. In *Carhart v. Stenberg*, it struck down a Nebraska bill prohibiting "partial birth" abortions. A great deal was at stake in these cases. They determined the availability of abortions and the legality of common abortion protests, at a time when public support for reproductive choice appeared relatively weak. (Support for obnoxious, controversial speech is never strong.)

The abortion rights movement would have withstood a loss in the buffer zone case, and probably deserved one. The Colorado law upheld by the Court establishes a one-hundred-foot buffer zone around the entrance to any health-care facility; within this zone, speakers are prohibited from coming within eight feet of any prospective listener, without the listener's consent, in order to hand out literature or engage in "oral protest, education, or counseling." Thus, the law establishes an eight-foot bubble zone around all individuals entering or simply passing by abortion clinics. Although it applies to all speakers within one hundred feet of all health-care facilities (and was deemed by the Court to be content-neutral), the law was admittedly motivated by a desire to restrain antiabortion protesters outside clinics.

In rejecting a constitutional challenge to these restraints, the Court deferred to the sensibilities of an "unwilling audience," rather than the First Amendment rights of speakers. Its reasoning reflected the political correctness of campus speech codes that value an imagined right not to be offended over a right to give offense. Writing for the majority in *Hill*, Justice Stevens upheld a law silencing political speech in order to avoid the speculative harm to listeners: Colorado's no speech zones outside abortion clinics were justified partly by the need to avoid "potential trauma to patients associated with confrontational protests."

In previous cases, the Supreme Court has rightly struck down a fifteen-foot bubble zone surrounding individuals entering and leaving clinics but upheld judicial injunctions establishing buffer zones around clinic entrances, when protesters have a history of harassing

A version of this piece appeared in The American Prospect, *June 5, 2000*

people and blocking their access. The Colorado case, however, involves a statute that restricts all abortion protests, regardless of any particular history of abuse. Effectively assuming that all protests within one hundred feet of any clinic and eight feet of any individual will constitute unlawful harassment, Colorado law imposes a clear prior restraint on protected political speech. How do you hand a pamphlet to someone if you're prohibited from coming within eight feet of her? Women and girls seeking abortions have a right not to be criminally harassed or blocked from entering clinics. But contrary to the Court's ruling, they should have no right not to be upset, offended, or even traumatized by abortion protests.

Anyway, the right not to be upset or "potentially traumatized" seems trivial when compared to the basic right to obtain an abortion, even in the early stages of pregnancy. That right was at risk in the Carhart case, which struck down Nebraska's "partial birth" abortion law. Thirty-one states had enacted similar laws that purported to ban late-term abortions. Congress sent two partial birth abortion bans to former president Clinton, who vetoed both. These laws had been challenged in twenty-one states: In nineteen states, courts had blocked their enforcement. Partial birth abortion statutes were marketed as narrow efforts to ban one particularly gruesome procedure used to abort viable fetuses late in the pregnancy. But in fact the laws were broadly and vaguely drafted so that they prohibited common procedures used in the first two trimesters of pregnancy, long before fetal viability. If the Court had upheld the Nebraska law, it would have effectively reversed *Roe v. Wade.*

Abortion rights were spared, at least temporarily, by the ruling in *Carhart,* but the proliferation of partial birth bans reflected the vulnerability of the reproductive choice movement. It's not just the threat of the Bush Administration appointing two or three antiabortion justices to the Supreme Court that should worry pro-choicers. Equally sobering is public resistance to recognizing women's moral agency, when abortion is at issue.

A 1998 survey by the *New York Times* found the public quite confused about abortion rights—hesitant to prohibit them outright yet eager to pass judgment on women's choices. Professed public support for abortion in the first trimester was 61 percent; but it dropped to 15 percent in the second trimester, and people seem inclined to prohibit abortions, whenever, if women seek them for the "wrong" reasons. (It's worth noting that these were not new findings: A 1989

Times poll showed slightly stronger support for abortion rights, but a similar pattern of discomfort with them.)

Putting aside concern about late-term abortions, people appear most disapproving of women who have abortions because they are ambitious—to finish school or pursue their careers. A strong majority, 70 percent of those surveyed by the *Times,* said they did not believe abortions should be available to women who want to terminate their pregnancies for the sake of their careers; less than half (42 percent) believed that teenage girls should be able to get abortions so that they might finish school. The majority did not consider poverty an excuse for terminating a pregnancy: Only 43 percent said abortion should be available to low-income women who cannot afford more children. (It's not clear how this can be reconciled with general public hostility to "welfare mothers.") There was strong majority support only for women who obtain abortions because their own health is endangered or because of a strong chance of birth defects.

What should we make of this? It suggests that the heart of opposition to abortion rights is not a deep-seated belief that a three- or four-month-old fetus is a person, just like a four-month-old baby. Although 50 percent of people responding to the *Times* poll agreed that abortion is "the same thing as murdering a child," this view of abortion as murder seems mostly hypothetical. When the great majority of people surveyed believe that abortion is an acceptable choice for women who carry impaired fetuses, then a great majority of people don't really consider the fetus a person. Most Americans, after all, would not suggest that parents have the right to kill their disabled children.

Of course, many people find abortions morally troublesome or abhorrent, but mainstream opposition to abortion seems to reflect something else as well: a refusal to acknowledge that women are autonomous individuals first, not mothers. The abortion debate is not simply about the nature of a human fetus; it is, in large part, a debate about the nature of a woman.

Is it natural for her to put motherhood second—or to choose not to become a mother at all? Is it natural for her to demand the same right to self-determination that fully democratic societies have always granted men? Some feminists have engaged in public breast beating over abortion, advertising their own moral qualms about it to avoid appearing selfish or morally shallow. But by declaring their doubts about the morality of abortion, in an effort to gain sympathy for women making hard choices, feminists have probably contributed to public discomfort with abortion rights.

The feminist movement today, although as fractured and confused as ever about femininity and sexuality, must still fight the battle commenced at Seneca Falls in 1848. There, in the Declaration of Sentiments, the first women's rights advocates called for equal economic rights, equal educational and employment opportunities, equal divorce and child custody laws, and a single standard of sexual behavior, in addition to suffrage. The basis for these demands was the belief that men and women were "invested by the Creator with the same capabilities, and the same consciousness of responsibility for their exercise."

We have, of course, made great progress toward equality since 1848. We've made a lot of progress since 1968. But feminists today face the same challenge—debunking the feminine ideal—that many have ducked for 150 years. Every female politician who runs for office stressing her talents for listening or building consensus is running on a platform of femininity. Every feminist who celebrates women's allegedly superior relational skills celebrates femininity and the maternal ideal and confirms doubts about the moral character of women who choose to terminate their pregnancies. And, every pro-choice activist who supports restrictions on abortion protests in order to protect women from the "trauma" of unwilling exposure to offensive speech reinforces traditional notions of feminine fragility. It's difficult to argue that women are strong enough to exercise autonomy—professionally, politically, and personally—but too weak to withstand all its consequences.

7

WOMEN'S WRONGS

FEMINISTS, PURITANS, AND STATISTS

Feminism's ideological diversity makes fools of those who generalize grandly about the movement, but many critics are undeterred. A facile view of feminists as a monolithic group of male bashers and prudes was eagerly adopted by impeachment pundits in the late 1990s. Confusing feminism with a sexual purity movement, they naturally pronounced all of us guilty of hypocrisy for not abandoning former president Clinton, embracing Paula Jones, and fretting about the victimization of Monica Lewinsky. It was as if women's rights advocates had no mission but the policing of male sexual behavior, as if securing reproductive choice, economic equity, and political power were afterthoughts to the elimination of harassment and adultery.

Where did they get this idea? In part, the pundits relied on tenacious, popular caricatures of combat-booted harridans or spinsters. Rejecting traditional feminine roles, feminists have always been dismissed by some as "antisex" or "unnatural." Still, like most caricatures, these were overwrought and oversimplified, but not entirely inaccurate. They did not describe all feminists, as they purported to do, but they did describe some, however hyperbolically. There have always been strains of Puritanism within the women's movement, and during the 1990s, they became quite pronounced. Clinton's impeachment dramatized their dangers.

The personalization of politics, the devaluation of privacy (long associated with family violence), and the prosecution of sexual sins have all been advocated by some feminists who locate female oppression in male freedom. In the 1990s, the media may have focused on sexuality debates because of their prurient appeal, but one popular school of feminist thought did identify the vigorous prosecution of sexual misconduct (and censorship of pornography) as essential to equality. The drive to lessen sexual violence and bring some solace to its victims also aligned many women's rights activists with right-wing advocates of law and order in their efforts to restrict the rights of men accused of rape. It's true that before the passage of rape shield laws some twenty-five years ago, complaining witnesses in rape cases were subject to brutal interrogations about their own irrelevant sexual histories (not entirely unlike the subsequent interrogations of defendants in harassment cases). But to suggest, as some activists do, that

This piece appeared in Dissent, *spring 1999*

we should reflexively "believe the women" in rape cases is to endorse conviction by accusation and imbue prosecutors with awesome, unconstitutional power.

The feminist movement has always included civil libertarians and even libertines, who are instinctively wary of authority, but it has never really been defined by them, partly because so much historic progress for women has been secured through the intervention of the state: The criminal law gradually began punishing rape and other forms of abuse (within or outside of marriage), and civil rights laws have provided women with unprecedented educational and professional opportunities. Neither colleges and universities nor the marketplace responded voluntarily to women's demands for equality. They responded under force of law. It's no wonder that many feminists have looked upon the state more as a partner than a potential oppressor.

Statism is a predictable temptation for civil rights activists, but among racial minorities it may be tempered by mistrust of prosecutors and police, grounded in hard experience and practices like racial profiling. In New York City, for example, during Mayor Giuliani's reign, a white woman probably felt protected by police much more than an African-American male, who had reason to feel threatened by them. As individuals, many white women may have been treated unjustly, even cruelly, by law enforcement officials when they reported sexual assaults or beatings by their husbands. But as a class they have virtually no history of being systematically brutalized by police or wrongfully prosecuted and convicted of crimes, on account of their sex. I suspect that middle-class white women, who populate the feminist movement, are more likely to see themselves as crime victims allied with the state, than as suspects wrongly accused.

The impeachment-related prosecutions of Susan McDougal and Julie Hiatt Steele and the coercion of Monica Lewinsky might have encouraged some to reconsider. Indeed, the spectacle of the Starr investigation should have awakened anti-libertarian feminists to the horrors of a prosecutorial state with no respect for sexual privacy; it should have injected the women's movement with renewed regard for liberty, even when it is utilized by men. The most predatory male in the impeachment saga was Ken Starr, not Bill Clinton.

Mistrusting the state and embracing, or at least appreciating, liberty does not require feminists to abandon their drive for civil rights. Civil liberties and civil rights do sometimes conflict (consider the debate to regulate verbal workplace harassment), but intelligent activists can entertain and balance conflicting ideals. They can recognize the difference between government regulation of corporate or institutional behavior in the public sphere and the regulation of individual sexual proclivities, or speech. They can demand restrictions on the power of the state when it is turned against individuals.

The feminist movement has always been torn between the desire for individual autonomy and demands for the collective advancement of women. By the end of the twentieth century, autonomy was in disrepute, associated with selfishness and anomie. Was it naive to hope that the impeachment debacle would revive respect for it? Clinton didn't betray feminists by fooling around with Lewinsky. He betrayed the principles of liberty for which feminism should stand when he advocated and signed legislation drastically limiting appeals of wrongful state court convictions, expediting the summary deportations of legal immigrants, and allowing for secret trials of suspected terrorists. Clinton championed restrictions on due process and expansions of unaccountable police power. He was the victim of the kind of prosecutorial excesses his administration encouraged. His politics, not his personal life, are what should have made feminists shudder.

FEMINISTS, RACKETEERS, AND THE FIRST AMENDMENT

First Amendment freedoms are inevitably invoked by provocateurs and dissenters seeking to change or complain about the status quo, so it's not surprising that antiabortion protesters have discovered free speech, to the dismay of abortion providers and advocates. After abortion was legalized and normalized in the early 1970s, pro-choicers suddenly had the law on their side, and pro-fetal life advocates began adopting the tactics of earlier protest movements. Picketing abortion clinics and conducting sit-ins, they likened themselves to civil rights activists of the 1950s and '60s.

The analogy broke down when radicals in the antiabortion movement turned from civil disobedience to violence, in addition to protests that bordered on criminal harassment of women seeking entry into abortion clinics. The enraged activists who organized clinic blockades resembled the segregationists who surrounded Central High in Little Rock in 1956 much more than the besieged African-American students trying to enter the school. Some antiabortion activists today are not only engaged in loud or angry speech. The arsenal of their movement includes clinic invasions, assaults on clinic workers, bombings, and the shootings of obstetricians. Shortly after the 1998 murder of Dr. Bernard Slepian (the seventh practitioner killed), the FBI warned dozens of other doctors that an antiabortion web site was distributing detailed information about them and their families. (See "Freedom's Edge.") Abortion providers have taken to wearing bulletproof vests; the Planned Parenthood clinic in Boston, site of a fatal shooting in 1995, operates behind bulletproof glass.

As protesters became aggressive and assaultive, crossing the line between protected speech and criminal conduct with increasing frequency, conflicts between speech and abortion rights became increasingly common. Not that distinctions between speech and conduct are always self-evident. People opposed to abortion have fundamental rights to rally or picket outside abortion clinics, accuse women of killing their babies, or exhort them to consider adoption instead. They don't have the right to block the path of women seeking to enter clinics, as many do. The Supreme Court has upheld injunctions prohibiting protests directly outside the entrances to two abortion clinics that had been targeted by highly intrusive protesters. In

This piece appeared in Dissent, *winter 1999*

one case, *Schenck v. Pro-Choice Network of Western New York,* the lower court found evidence of "physical obstruction, intimidation, harassment, crowding, grabbing, and screaming," which continued after issuance of a temporary restraining order and made it impossible for police to ensure clinic access. The Court has also upheld the establishment of statutory no protest zones outside health-care clinics. (See "Abortion and Autonomy.")

Feeling under the gun, quite literally, many pro-choice advocates cheered the 1998 verdict in *NOW v. Scheidler,* a landmark civil action for extortion brought by the National Organization of Women against several militant leaders of the radical antiabortion movement and their organizations. NOW successfully sued Joseph Scheidler, Andrew Scholberg, and the Pro-Life Action League and former Operation Rescue leader Randall Terry (who settled the case against him) under the federal Racketeer Influenced and Corrupt Organizations law (RICO). Enacted in 1970, RICO was aimed at organized crime. It allows individuals to be prosecuted for their involvement in a criminal "enterprise" and makes them liable for treble damages in civil actions brought by their victims. NOW obtained an $85,926 damage award (on behalf of two target clinics), which is tripled under RICO. It also obtained an order enjoining the defendants from engaging in future protests in violation of RICO.

The verdict in *Scheidler* survived an appeal to the federal circuit court and could greatly curtail protests by antiabortion radicals [The Supreme Court is scheduled to hear arguments on aspects of the Scheidler case in October 2002.] Few will lament a decline of clinic violence, but many if not most abortion protests involve pure speech, however obnoxious or belligerent. Some civil libertarians have rightly decried the use of RICO against political movements because it will inevitably chill political speech.

RICO doesn't target individual crimes, like clinic bombings; it targets and aims to destroy entire enterprises that often involve legal as well as illegal activities. (RICO was originally intended to combat organized crime's infiltration of legitimate businesses.) RICO focuses on "patterns of racketeering activity"; individual defendants may be held liable for all activities of the enterprise if they agree to the commission of two illegal (predicate) acts involved in it. Thus, numerous people who are essentially unknown to each other and involved in unrelated predicate acts can be tried together and held liable for each other's crimes, so long as they were committed under the auspices of the "enterprise." RICO differs from traditional conspiracy laws by allowing alleged members of an enterprise to be tried en masse for one another's offenses.

The particular acts at issue in the Scheidler case generally involved "extortion," allegedly aimed at driving clinics out of business. According to the complaint, the defendants "conspired to use threatened or actual force, violence, or fear to induce clinic employees, doctors, and patients to give up their jobs, give up their economic rights to practice medicine, and give up their right to obtain medical services at the clinics." Notice that the defendants were not charged with actually engaging in arsons or bombings; most of the acts of "extortion" for which they were held liable involved clinic blockades. (Federal law now prohibits clinic blockades, however; RICO prosecutions are not needed to police them.)

The Scheidler defendants' incentive was not economic but ideological: They were engaged in political protests, not a campaign to open a competing chain of reproductive health-care clinics. The Scheidler case poses a clear threat to other protest groups who boycott or picket businesses accused of engaging in objectionable practices, like discrimination, for example, or the use of child labor. Indeed, NOW itself has reason to fear expansive interpretations of federal laws intended to regulate economic activity. It was once the subject of an unsuccessful civil action occasioned by an ERA boycott that was brought by the state of Missouri under the Sherman Act. Ruling against the state, a federal appeals court held that NOW's right to boycott was "privileged" by the First Amendment, and that the Sherman Act was not intended to apply to NOW's pro-ERA activities, which were primarily political, not commercial.

Just as the Sherman Act was not intended to regulate political movements, RICO was not supposed to brand ideologically motivated activists as racketeers or extortionists. If a group of NOW members organizes pickets and blockades outside porn shops, with the intent of shutting them down or greatly discouraging their patronage, and if some shops are firebombed, should NOW leaders be held liable under RICO if they have indulged in inflammatory rhetoric about the dangers of pornography?

The question of RICO's applicability to politically motivated actions is not new to the Scheidler case. In fact, the Third Circuit Court of Appeals upheld the use of RICO against antiabortion protesters in a 1989 case, *Northeast Women's Center v. McMonagle*. A contrary reading of RICO was subsequently adopted by the Second Circuit in *U.S. v. Ivic*, a

1993 case involving an attempted assassination by a group of Croatian nationalists. In *Ivic,* the Second Circuit Court of Appeals considered the legislative history of RICO (and the common definition of racketeering) and held that RICO only applied to economically motivated crimes.

The Supreme Court disagreed and sided with the Third Circuit, in a pretrial ruling in *NOW v. Scheidler.* NOW's complaint had been dismissed by a lower federal court, but in 1994, the Supreme Court reversed the lower court and held that the use of RICO is not limited to acts "motivated by an economic purpose." (NOW's case against Scheidler then proceeded to trial.)

This holding was urged on the Court by strange bedfellows—the government and the American Civil Liberties Union (both filed amicus briefs). Government officials generally favor expansive interpretations of criminal statutes, and they have had a particular interest in using RICO against political terrorists. The ACLU is torn between its respective commitments to reproductive choice and free speech. In 1969, during congressional hearings on RICO, it advised limiting RICO to prosecutions of organized crime, cautioning against its application to political protests (which in the late 1960s were occasionally violent). In *NOW v. Scheidler,* however, the ACLU argued that the absence of an economic incentive was a "poor proxy" for First Amendment interests: Some money-making enterprises, like video stores that sell sexually explicit material, are engaged in protected activity. Some political organizations committed to illegal acts of violence are not.

Still, as the ACLU stressed, constitutional rights of speech and association impose strict limitations on RICO prosecutions of political groups. Extortion must be narrowly defined to exclude mere advocacy and angry rhetoric, and protest leaders should not be held vicariously liable for acts they did not authorize or approve. In *NOW v. Scheidler,* the Court did not decide whether or not RICO prosecutions of political groups were barred or severely restricted by the First Amendment, at least in some cases (the question was not formally before it); but in his concurrence, Justice Souter observed that "RICO actions could deter protected advocacy," adding that a First Amendment defense would be available to any protest groups sued under RICO.

The Supreme Court itself clarified the limits of civil actions against political groups in a 1982 case (noted briefly in "Freedom's Edge."). In *NAACP v. Claiborne Hardware,* the Court held that the

NAACP could not be held liable for a few acts and threats of violence that occurred during a prolonged boycott of white merchants in Claiborne County, Mississippi, in the late 1960s. The Court's holding in this case speaks to the essence of a RICO prosecution, which mingles lawful and unlawful activity (speech and violence) and makes speakers liable for the violent acts of their associates.

Protesters in Claiborne County were charged with coercing adherence to the boycott: Members of the black community who patronized target stores were publicly identified and vilified; four people who ignored the boycott were the victims of vandalism; in a couple of cases, shots were fired at the victims' homes. Boycott leader Charles Evers threatened to "break the damn neck" of any black who patronized a white-owned business.

But as the Supreme Court observed, the boycott primarily involved protected activity—pickets, marches, speeches, and "the practice of persons sharing common views banding together to achieve a common end." Even some of the activities that were the subject of the complaint—like the exposure and branding of blacks who violated the boycott—consisted of protected speech, however "offensive" or "coercive." The threatening rhetoric of Charles Evers was also protected advocacy: It did not immediately and directly incite violence, and neither Evers nor the NAACP authorized any of the violence that did occur.

RICO may permit criminal or civil actions against members of an "enterprise" that is engaged in some illegal activities, but as the Court stressed in *Claiborne Hardware,* "civil liability may not be imposed merely because an individual belonged to a group, some members of which committed acts of violence." Those acts are unprotected and may, of course, be punished, but when they occur "in the context of constitutionally protected activity . . . 'precision of regulation' is demanded." And, as the Supreme Court held in a landmark 1969 case (*Brandenburg v. Ohio*), protesters cannot be held liable for merely advocating the use of force or violence, unless their advocacy is "directed to inciting or producing imminent lawless action and is likely to incite or produce such action."

What does this mean for the Scheidler case? Remember that Scheidler and his codefendants were not accused of committing any violent acts. Instead, according to the *New York Times,* NOW attorney Fay Clayton charged that they created a climate conducive to violence. Creating or changing a climate of opinion or emotion, however, is precisely what political protesters aim to do; it is protected activity.

Did Scheidler do more? He allegedly told his followers, "You can try for fifty years to do it the nice way or you can do it next week the nasty way." Whether this was mere advocacy, like Charles Evers's threat to break the necks of people who did not observe the boycott, or direct incitement to imminent violence is a hard question of fact. Only if Scheidler's remarks constituted unprotected incitement to violence should he be held individually liable for their consequences. But "precision of regulation" is required: Neither he nor his organization nor any of its members should be punished for all the protected activities in which they engaged. RICO is a very blunt instrument; the First Amendment requires a scalpel.

SEXUAL CONGRESS

Feminists have long regarded rape as a hate crime, like lynching. The view of sexual violence as a particularly vicious form of bigotry and social control may oversimplify the dynamics of any given sex crime (and overlook the historic use of rape allegations to justify lynching), but it resonates with many women. Both self-identified and closeted feminists who differ wildly about the nature of equality and the means of achieving it often agree that rape is an act of misogyny.

So there was widespread feminist support for the Violence Against Women Act (VAWA), which essentially adopted this view of sexual violence as discriminatory. Enacted in 1994 as part of an omnibus federal crime bill (in the immediate aftermath of Nicole Simpson's murder), VAWA was a comprehensive law that included provisions expanding federal criminal jurisdiction over domestic violence involving interstate travel; amending federal rules of evidence in rape cases; and allocating federal funds for local efforts to combat domestic violence. It also established a federal civil right to be free of gender-based violence.

The Violence Against Women Act declared, "All persons within the United States shall have the right to be free from crimes of violence motivated by gender." The victim (male or female) of a "crime of violence motivated by gender" was entitled to bring a civil action against his or her attacker in federal court, seeking damages or injunctive relief. This "civil rights remedy" was available regardless of whether the alleged attack was prosecuted, much less proven, in criminal court.

When it was enacted, conservatives derided VAWA as feminist victimism, questioning the extent of domestic violence and the claim that women (not men) were the primary victims of it. These attacks were easily dismissed—asserting that men were equally targeted by domestic violence was a bit like claiming that the earth revolves around the moon. But by the late 1990s, VAWA encountered more serious opposition: The federal appeals court for the Fourth Circuit struck down VAWA's civil rights remedy, holding that Congress had no constitutional authority to enact it. The Supreme Court upheld this ruling (by a 5 to 4 vote) in *United States v. Morrison*, decided in May 2000.

The facts of this case were compelling: In 1994, Christy Brzonkala, a student at Virginia Polytechnic Institute (Virginia Tech) was

This piece appeared in The American Prospect, *February 14, 2000*

allegedly raped by two members of the university football team. The encounter she describes was not ambiguous: She was pinned down, forcibly undressed, and sexually assaulted. She did not report being raped for several months. Instead, she sank into a depression, cut her hair, stopped attending classes, and attempted suicide. Eventually, some five months after the incident, Brzonkala identified her alleged assailants as Antonio Morrison and James Crawford and subsequently filed a complaint under Virginia Tech's sexual assault policy. She did not pursue a criminal case, apparently because she had not preserved physical evidence, and the administration did not report the alleged attack. (All violent felonies except sexual assaults of females by males are automatically reported by Virginia Tech authorities to university or town police.)

At the university's administrative hearing, Antonio Morrison admitted to having intercourse with Brzonkala over her objections. There was also evidence that after assaulting her, Morrison declared publicly that he "liked to get girls drunk and fuck the shit out of them." Crawford testified that Morrison had engaged in "sexual contact" with Brzonkala, while denying his own participation in her alleged attack. No action was taken against Crawford. Morrison was found guilty of sexual assault and suspended for two semesters. But school authorities reconsidered (at the behest of the football coach, Brzonkala alleges); the finding was subsequently vacated, the suspension lifted, and Morrison returned to school on a full athletic scholarship. Brzonkala filed a civil action against Morrison and Crawford under the Violence Against Women Act.

Much was at stake in this case, not just for Christy Brzonkala, to whom the VAWA lawsuit must have seemed like a last chance for justice. *United States v. Morrison* tested the concept of sexual violence as a civil rights violation that Congress is empowered, if not obliged, to redress. Yet, this was not simply a case about civil rights. It was a case about federal power, which can be used to extend or restrict the rights of individual citizens. The power of Congress to create civil remedies for sexual violence is the same power that imprisons people for growing marijuana, the same power that some would use to criminalize late-term abortions. Brzonkala's lawsuit tested the limits of congressional police power, which has been steadily expanding and creating what the Founders never envisioned—a federal justice system that regulates local conduct, reaching local as well as national crimes and purported vices.

Which is more frightening—the persistence of sexual violence or the growing power of federal law enforcement? Before you answer this question, imagine yourself serving a long prison term for a minor drug offense; or imagine your family doctor in prison for performing an abortion. When VAWA was enacted, I welcomed its recognition that crimes "motivated by gender bias" were federal civil rights violations. But I didn't stop long to consider the jurisdictional basis for VAWA and the dangers of expanding federal power beyond its constitutional limits.

This case divides heart and mind. It's difficult to agree with ultra-conservative, often anti-libertarian justices on the Fourth Circuit Court of Appeals and the Supreme Court, especially when liberal feminist allies oppose them, especially when they deny vindication to the victim of an apparent, brutal rape. I'd have liked Christy Brzonkala to get her day in court. But putting sentiment aside, I could not have advocated for her. In *United States v. Morrison*, the Supreme Court was right to strike down VAWA's civil rights remedy.

Supporters of the civil rights remedy argued that it was a legitimate exercise of congressional authority under the Commerce Clause (which gives Congress regulatory power over interstate commerce) and the Fourteenth Amendment. The Fourteenth Amendment argument was easily dismissed: The constitutional guarantee of equality under law prohibits discriminatory actions by public entities—state and local governments, not private citizens—and does not give Congress the power to regulate the unauthorized conduct of individuals. (The disputed provision of the VAWA applied to private actions not condoned or supported by the state.) The Commerce Clause argument had more merit.

Congress has long invoked the Commerce Clause to regulate noncommercial or quasi-commercial activities that affect interstate commerce. The landmark 1964 Civil Rights Act prohibiting racial discrimination in places of public accommodation and employment was based on the Commerce Clause; so was a 1994 federal law prohibiting blockades of abortion clinics—the Freedom of Access to Clinic Entrances Act (FACE). But the constitutional limits of congressional power are decided by the Supreme Court, and in a 1995 case, *Lopez v. United States*, the Court showed a new willingness to examine congressional use of its power to regulate interstate commerce.

Lopez struck down a federal penal statute establishing "gun-free school zones," pursuant to the Commerce Clause. The Court held that a prohibition on handgun possession in a school zone had no substantial relationship to interstate commerce. Liberals who favor gun control are apt to regard this decision as an unwelcome example of right-wing judicial activism (Chief Justice Rehnquist wrote the majority opinion). Civil libertarians, however, may view *Lopez* as welcome restriction on congressional power in general and the harsh, unnecessarily expansive federal penal code, in particular. (It's not as if the states don't or can't criminalize possession of guns and other weapons in schools.)

You'd have to adopt an extremely broad notion of interstate commerce to uphold the gun-free school zone law at issue in *Lopez*. Consider the government's case. It argued that gun possession in schools causes violent crime, which carries economic costs, and also threatens the "learning environment," which makes students less likely to mature into productive citizens, which adversely affects the economy. As the Court noted in *Lopez* (and the government acknowledged), given this reasoning, Congress could regulate "all activities that might lead to violent crime, regardless of how tenuously they relate to interstate commerce." If Congress can regulate handgun possession under the Commerce Clause because of its potential, indirect impact on the economy, then what can't Congress regulate?

Does this seem like legalese? Try the commonsense test: When you think of a rape in a college dormitory, do you think about interstate commerce? As the Court noted in Brzonkala's case, the relationship between sexual violence and interstate commerce is rather attenuated. Sexual violence does have a general connection to the economy. It affects women's employment decisions, spending habits, and mobility, and the nation's health-care expenses, as supporters of VAWA assert. But virtually all crimes and most conduct, within and outside the home, can be said to have economic impacts. So what? Do you want Congress to enjoy unrestricted regulatory power over you? (Do you want Congress making local zoning decisions for your town? Do you want your divorce in federal court?) The Supreme Court in *Lopez* rightly held that the Commerce Clause is not a grant of general police power. It does not (and should not) bring "any activity by any individual" within reach of federal regulators, because of its eventual, indirect impact on the economy. Congress may regulate noncommercial activities under the commerce clause only when they "substantially affect interstate commerce."

This standard does not unduly limit congressional power, including the power to prohibit discrimination. It does not invalidate the 1964 Civil Rights Act: segregation in hotels, restaurants, on transportation systems, and in the workplace involved commercial activities with clear and substantial interstate effects. The FACE Act, prohibiting blockades of abortion clinics, has withstood challenges under *Lopez* (in fact, the Fourth Circuit recently upheld it). Reproductive health services are quasi-commercial activities; cutting off access to them would have substantial economic effects.

But the Supreme Court struck down the civil rights remedy in VAWA, with no noticeable impact on interstate commerce. I'm not belittling the importance of policing sexual violence. I am suggesting that it should, in general, remain the province of the states, which have been paying more attention to it recently. (Christy Brzonkala could have pursued a criminal prosecution under state law but chose not to do so.) Congress can provide funding for innovative state programs and improved law enforcement without using the problem of sexual violence to expand its own authority.

As the Fourth Circuit stressed in *Brzonkala*, the federal government is a government of enumerated powers. The price of upholding VAWA's civil rights remedy was an unconstitutional grant of unlimited power to Congress, power that would not always be used wisely or with regard to individual rights. We need to combat sexual violence without making a federal case of it.

SEX AND SENSIBILITY

Having attended a woman's college and having spent half of my professional life affiliated with a female institution, I know better than to believe that women are naturally more sharing, caring, and cooperative than men, although, in general, they may be more polite. I'm not denying the existence of distinct masculine and feminine cultural styles or different male and female perspectives, based largely on experience. I'm simply asserting what was once recognized as a basic tenet of liberal feminism: Sex is no predictor of character, or moral sensibility.

Sex is a poor predictor of ideology, despite the influence of traditional gender roles. The female solidarity sometimes forged by women's common experiences doesn't always overcome demographic differences among women, not to mention their differences in talent and temperament (that, too, is one familiar feminist truth). Considering the chasm between the women of NOW and the women of the Christian Coalition, I never trust popular pronouncements about a gender gap between women and men. Race trumps sex, Washington, D.C., congresswoman Eleanor Holmes Norton remarked in the aftermath of the Thomas/Hill hearings. Religion and wealth sometimes trump sex as well.

So while I look forward to the day when women have equal access to high elective and appointive office, when sex is not an obstacle to political achievement, I have never considered sex a fair or sensible political advantage, or a reliable signal of political preferences. It's true that studies of women in state legislatures have suggested that they are apt to pay more attention to issues such as child care and family leave and that they tend to be more responsive to demands for women's rights. But a profile of the average female legislator has little relevance in any particular election. We evaluate candidates as individuals, on the basis of their own political records and ideas, not on the basis of the voting records of their demographic group.

At least, in an ideal world, we'd evaluate candidates as individuals. In fact, voters have always been influenced by ethnic, racial, or sexual biases, which is why candidates are apt to treat African Americans, Asian Americans, Latinos, and even the most amorphous groups, like white men and white women, as separate voting blocs. Identity politics have made tribalism respectable. Still, politicians,

This piece appeared in The American Prospect, *December 6, 1999*

who are supposed to represent everyone, commonly disavow discriminatory voting. Even Elizabeth Dole, who sometimes seemed to be running for role model instead of president in 2000, periodically acknowledged that people shouldn't vote for her simply because of her sex.

But while advocates for female candidates routinely acknowledge that sex should not be a qualification for office, they expect and encourage female voters to put more trust in female candidates and feel better represented by them. (Minority candidates often make similar appeals to minority voters.) Women feel more "comfortable" with candidates, who "look like them," the advocates say approvingly. Female politicians can be relied upon to "get it."

This double-talk about whether sex matters is exasperating and does seem rather unprincipled: You can hardly object when female candidates are disadvantaged by negative gender stereotypes if you're in the business of exploiting the positive ones. Any woman running for office who suggests that by virtue of her sex she has an "open," nonhierarchical management style or that she's particularly adept at forging consensus has waived the right to complain when reporters focus on her fashion sense.

The inconsistent messages often generated by women's campaigns, however, are likely to reflect genuine confusion about sex and gender, rather than political hypocrisy or cynicism. Feminism has always been beset with cognitive dissonance: Nineteenth-century women's rights advocates fought to expand the rights due them regardless of sex, as citizens and human beings, while arguing that armed with feminine virtues, female voters and office holders would purify public life. Similar dissonance is evident among some professional feminists today. Consider the White House Project.

Launched in 1998, the White House Project is officially a public education project, with the vague but ambitious aim of "changing the climate of American politics . . . preparing a political and social climate to elect a woman president within the next decade." One of its primary initiatives so far was the conduct of a mock presidential election featuring only female candidates. Nearly one million ballots were reportedly distributed on the Internet, in magazines and shopping malls, and on college campuses; some 100,000 ballots were cast. The results were hardly surprising: Hillary Clinton and Elizabeth Dole were among the top five vote getters.

Why was the left-wing, feminist Ms. Foundation effectively aiding the candidacy of Elizabeth Dole? The White House Project is painstakingly nonpartisan. It is based both on a reasoned appeal for equal access and an emotional nineteenth-century assumption that women are endowed with virtues that will ennoble public life: "Women office holders are leading voices for more accountable and responsible government," the White House Project ballot asserts nonsensically.

Ms. Foundation president and White House Project cofounder Marie Wilson eschews gender stereotypes in conversation and is surely aware of the differences among women like, say, Gloria Steinem and Republican senator Kay Bailey Hutchison (who was on the mock ballot). But allusions to female solidarity and virtue underlie every fund-raising appeal for this project I've witnessed. A series of taped interviews with international female leaders shown to prospective donors concludes with the suggestion by the president of Iceland that women really are nicer than men (I imagine Margaret Thatcher gagging on this.)

Is the White House Project good for women? I suspect that like most campaigns, it is good for some women and not others. Maybe young girls, future women of America, feel inspired by it, as Marie Wilson hopes. Maybe some adult women feel "validated" by it. But actual as opposed to virtual female candidates who practice real partisan politics are apt to scoff at a $3 million campaign that merely talks about electing women—any women, of no particular party or ideology. "If they want more women in public office, why don't they contribute money to my campaign," one woman engaged in a tough statewide race remarked to me.

You can make a case for nonpartisan civic education organizations, like the League of Women Voters. But unlike the league, the White House Project has a particular political agenda—electing a female president by 2008. It's an agenda that makes little sense, precisely because it is nonpartisan and disregards ideology—or stupidly assumes that ideology is ultimately dictated by sex and that all women are liberal feminists at heart. The White House Project is either naive or dishonest. Either Marie Wilson and her colleagues actually believe that any female president will do; or their nonpartisanship is merely a pose, and they intend their $3 million project to facilitate the election of a feminist president.

Partisan politics are frustrating, I admit, with centrist Democratic and Republican candidates parroting each other's views. In other words, what partisan politics lacks today is genuine partisanship. Sexual politics cannot substitute for it, especially if you're concerned with issues other than day care, elder care, and reproductive choice. I pay particular attention to civil liberties and criminal justice, for example, and have never found males any less attentive to these concerns than females. In fact, there is a statist, anti-libertarian strain in popular feminism that encourages censorship and is generally hostile to the due-process rights of men accused of sexual misconduct.

Sexual politics will not advance many progressive causes, including feminism, especially when the Republican party is endeavoring to promote women. And sexual stereotypes are treacherous. One hundred years ago, they helped gain women the vote, as suffragists argued that politics would benefit from women's gentle, purifying influence. But they also limited women's political opportunities: Gentleness and purity were hardly qualifications for high executive office. Today, despite incremental gains by women at the state and national level, they're still hobbled by expectations of femininity, as Hillary Clinton may attest. It was discouraging but not surprising to see her popularity increase when she was cast as a long-suffering victimized wife, not an equal political partner.

It was appalling to see the attention that continued to be paid to her appearance throughout her husband's presidency and her own campaign for a U.S. Senate seat. During the campaign, an edition of *Larry King Live* focused on Clinton's New York Senate race included a critique of her by then CNN style editor Elsa Klensch. Klensch was generally supportive of Hillary Clinton's campaign, stressing that "every woman I know is for her. That smile is a great visual." She praised Clinton for "disguising" her "figure" flaws—but didn't hesitate to point them out: "She has a bad figure. That's one of her problems. She's bottom heavy and her legs are short." Klensch's co-panelist, celebrity divorce lawyer Raoul Felder (like Larry King, a homely, late-middle-aged male) added that Clinton was "fat," and wondered, "If your legs are too short, how do you evolve?"

Listening to this discussion was like time traveling back to the seventh grade; grown-ups are not supposed to engage in such petty cruelties. Female candidates, however, remain vulnerable to them. So while Hillary Clinton's physique was being scrutinized, it was, I confess, refreshing to see New Hampshire Republican senator Bob Smith's figure described in the *New York Times* as "the opposite of an hourglass, expanding rather than contracting in the middle." But such descriptions of male candidates are rare, and Smith's homeliness was treated as a virtue: It made him seem like a regular "small-

town American'' and helped him ''stand out as an unsmooth nonlaw-
yer in Congress.''

Should we publicly mock funny-looking male candidates? Maybe
criticizing George Bush's beady eyes or Dick Cheney's bald pate
would be unworthy of us, but treating men with the disrespect traditionally afforded women is an effective strategy against sexism—which
pieties about femininity perpetuate. Femininity is a package: The
view of women as more compassionate, cooperative, and better at relationships and family life than men follows inexorably from popular
notions of female sexuality, from which we draw our preoccupation
with female beauty.

''Hire him. He's got great legs,'' the NOW ad used to say. That's
not sexual politics. It's equal rights feminism—an appeal to the
golden rule.

REPRODUCTIVE ENTITLEMENT

Once women were considered disabled by pregnancy, or the mere possibility of it. Before the modern civil rights era, women could be fired because they were pregnant or not hired because they seemed likely to become pregnant. From the late-nineteenth through the mid-twentieth century, women were excluded, under law, from presumptively masculine occupations that were considered incompatible with their maternal functions; they were also subject to protective labor laws that limited their hours of work and their work assignments, in order to preserve their ability to bear and care for children.

The drive to define women as human beings first and mothers second has been central to demands for equal rights, and, in the 1970s, feminists succeeded in outlawing pregnancy discrimination in the workplace. Women are no longer considered disabled by fertility. Today, however, they might lay claim to being disabled by infertility.

It is not exactly a sign of progress that demands for expanded health-care coverage have helped inspire a drive to define infertility as a disability under federal law and make infertility coverage a federal mandate. Of course, infertility affects men and women, but it continues to be considered a woman's problem, often blamed on decisions by professional women to delay child bearing, and, as a medical matter, women are generally the subjects of expensive infertility treatments.

Federal courts have been divided on the question of extending the Americans with Disabilities Act to infertile people, but a 1998 Supreme Court decision strengthened the case for infertility rights advocates. In *Bragdon v. Abbot* (a lawsuit brought under the ADA for denial of dental treatment to an HIV positive patient), the Court held the patient, who was asymptotic, was covered by the act because she was effectively precluded by her disease from having children. The ADA defines a disability as an impairment that "substantially limits one or more of the major life activities," which in the majority's view, clearly included reproduction.

Should the ADA be construed to protect people who cannot bear children, along with people who can't walk, see, hear, or breathe without assistance? If the primary purpose of the law was to end discrimination against the disabled, expanding their employment opportunities and access to public accommodations, it is not served by extending its reach to people who can't reproduce without treatment.

This piece appeared in The American Prospect, *March 27, 2000*

Infertility may be a great personal trial, but it does not generally inspire economic discrimination or interfere with access to subways, sidewalks, elevators, or workplaces. Indeed, for women, childlessness is still a professional advantage, not a liability.

When the ADA was enacted, conservatives attacked it as liberal "victimism," offering a familiar and, in this case, rather perverse critique. The ADA is designed to help disabled people achieve self-sufficiency. Discrimination victimizes disabled people, consigning them to telethons: Civil rights enable them. But expanding the definition of disability to include disappointments, like the inability to bear children, does seem to reflect a self-centered attraction to victimhood.

"I can do mostly everything—run, jump, skip," one infertility patient interviewed on National Public Radio explained in 1998. "But physically, we are disabled; we're diseased in a way because we can't procreate naturally." The enthusiasm with which many people declare themselves diseased or otherwise dysfunctional is one of the more perverse legacies of popular therapies. If infertility is a disease, it is not a disease like, say, diabetes, cancer, or AIDS. It's not degenerative, and left untreated, it won't kill you or impair your physical health and independence, much less your capacity to perform in the workplace. It does not necessarily threaten your mental health either: Some people may be tormented by the inability to bear children; others successfully adapt.

Finally, unlike most serious physical diseases, infertility is defined by cultural norms, as well as science. There is no one, objective standard of infertility; it is defined differently in different epidemiological studies. In practice, in our culture, you may be declared infertile after one year of unfruitful, unprotected intercourse. Would we lower the incidence of this alleged disease, and the need for treatment, simply by increasing the definitional period? What if we declared people infertile only after two or three years of unprotected intercourse, instead of one?

Declaring infertility a disease could, however, have a practical benefit—mandatory insurance coverage. After the Supreme Court defined reproduction as a major life activity under the ADA, the Equal Employment Opportunity Commission ruled in favor of a woman who charged her employer with discrimination for not providing infertility coverage. A federal district court disagreed: In *Saks v. Franklin Covey Co.*, a U.S. District Court in New York ruled that employers need not cover infertility treatments. But advocates of cover-age have pleaded their case before Congress, where several bills man-dating infertility coverage have been proposed. Some thirteen states already require health plans to cover diagnosis and treatment of in-fertility. These laws do not involve the troublesome determination that infertility is a disability, but they do raise equally hard policy questions about our social and medical priorities.

In an ideal world of unlimited resources, only the mean-spirited would deny coverage to infertility treatments, but in our world, we're forced to rate competing claims of suffering and injustice when we al-locate funds: We prioritize. Infertility treatments are expensive and essentially elective and the occasional traumas of infertility seem less than compelling compared to the sufferings of 44 million Americans with no health insurance at all. "The real social justice question here is how do we provide decent health care to the 40 to 50 million com-pletely uninsured people in the United States and the other 50 mil-lion underinsured people," medical ethicist George Annas asserts. Annas, chair of the Health Law Department at the Boston University School of Public Health, adds, "This is a much higher-priority ethi-cal and social justice issue than how to increase the private health in-surance people already have to include infertility services."

It is also troubling to see legislators responding to the demands of the middle class for infertility treatments when they have disregarded the plight of poor women with children who have been forced off wel-fare and into the workforce and provided with little if any reliable day care. Indeed, recent welfare reforms have been aimed, in part, at de-terring poor women from bearing children: If infertility is a disease, it's one that many Americans would like to inflict upon the poor. State and federal legislators may require private insurers to cover in-fertility treatments, but they are unlikely to extend similar benefits to Medicaid recipients.

It's worth stressing that public antagonism toward the fertile poor is historic. Consider the early twentieth-century eugenics move-ment. By the 1930s, some twenty-seven states had passed eugenics laws, pursuant to which over 12,000 people were sterilized. Steriliza-tion movements tended to be overtly racist and discriminated against the poor. During the Depression, eugenicists proposed ameliorating poverty by sterilizing poor people. Some forty years later, in the early 1970s, a lawsuit involving the coerced sterilization of two African-American girls revealed abuses in the Medicaid program. A federal court found that "an indefinite number of poor people" were sterilized "under the threat that various federally supported welfare benefits would be withdrawn unless they submitted to irreversible sterilization."

The contemporary movement for infertility coverage ought to be considered in the context of abuses like these. I'm not suggesting that middle-class people don't suffer and aren't appropriate subjects of compassion. I'm not necessarily opposed to mandatory infertility coverage and don't mean to characterize it as completely unaffordable: In Massachusetts, the additional cost of coverage is estimated at $1.71 per month (that figure does not include the costs associated with multiple births resulting from treatment). Still, I'd be more sympathetic to the movement for infertility coverage if it weren't so difficult to reconcile with our rather punitive policies toward child bearing and child rearing by poor women, not to mention the neglect of children in foster care or the increasingly harsh treatment of children caught up in the criminal justice system. Compassion, like justice, ought to be meted out equally.

FATHERS IN COURT

It's often difficult for a feminist to garner much sympathy for the father's rights movement. At first glance it seems, at best, redundant. Fathers monopolized familial rights and power for much of our history. Nineteenth-century common law gave men the right to control and the duty to support children born in marriage, while women were left with the rights and responsibilities regarding children born out of wedlock. Women and children even derived their citizenship from male "heads" of families, pursuant to federal laws. (In the early 1900s, American women forfeited their citizenship when they married foreign men.) Marital rape was generally legal until the 1970s. It's not surprising that the domestic subordination of women, under law, helped fuel the nineteenth- and twentieth-century women's movement.

Fortunately, feminists have enjoyed considerable success in their efforts to reform discriminatory laws governing family life and divorce. Equitable distribution laws, for example, reflect a feminist view of women as equal partners in a marital enterprise, not subordinates in a familial hierarchy. But according to men's rights advocates, feminists have won more than equality for women; they've won unfair advantages, initiating an era of discrimination against fathers and husbands.

Feminists tend to dismiss this complaint as "backlash," often with good reason; still, it deserves to be considered. I haven't run across good, recent quantitative data on the comparative treatment of men and women embroiled in marital disputes or other familial battles, so I hesitate to take sides in this debate. But I have heard anecdotal evidence (partly from lawyers) about the abuse of restraining orders against men and the preferences enjoyed by women in custody and marital property disputes, especially when minor children are involved. It's not hard to imagine that judges who've had their collective consciousness raised might overcompensate for prior discrimination against women by discriminating against a few men. But I suspect that gender bias varies by judge and jurisdiction and that, nowadays, both sexes have legitimate complaints about it.

Traditional notions of gender differences still help determine claims of unequal treatment, sometimes to the detriment of women and sometimes to the detriment of men. The Supreme Court has

This piece appeared in The American Prospect, *September 24, 2000*

upheld federal law denying men equal rights to transmit citizenship to children born outside of marriage, partly because it assumed that mothers naturally develop closer relationships with their offspring than fathers. The assumption that men typically try to evade responsibility for out-of-wedlock children also strengthens efforts to hold some men—or any men—accountable for child support. Consider the current controversy over the use of DNA testing in paternity cases. In July 2000, in *Langston v. Riffe,* the Court of Appeals in Maryland ruled (4 to 3) that under Maryland law, men are entitled to use DNA tests to contest prior findings of paternity, at virtually any time. The court expressly declined to put a time limit on paternity challenges and rejected the notion that an application for a DNA test should be granted only if the test is deemed to be in the best interest of the child.

Why is this ruling controversial? Doesn't justice require finding out the truth about paternity whenever it becomes available? Not according to some advocates for children and women, who fear that men will abandon children whom they have been supporting for years, if they are able to disprove their paternity. In his dissenting opinion, Chief Judge Robert Bell argued that the court's decision would result in an increase in requests for blood and genetic testing by men seeking to avoid paying child support: "They have nothing to lose and everything to gain. The only losers under the majority opinion are the children." Joan Entmacher of the National Women's Law Center observed that successful but belated paternity challenges will cause considerable economic disruption and "children will also be hurt when genetic tests disprove something that is a cornerstone of their identity."

These statements are hard to dispute, but they're remarkably unpersuasive. If the cornerstone of your identity is a lie, it may be in your best long-term interest to uncover it, especially if you're concerned about your genetic inheritance. In any case, if a man is ordered to pay child support by mistake, on the basis of inaccurate information or a knowingly false charge of paternity, fairness demands that the mistake be acknowledged (and damn the consequences). Excessive deference to the finality of judicial rulings is quite dangerous. Concern about efficiency and "closure" is what keeps people in prison after evidence of their innocence has emerged, pursuant to Supreme Court decisions and federal legislation greatly limiting the right to appeal wrongful convictions. It is not occasion for celebration that we now have a judicial system in which an interest in finality is allowed to trump the truth.

This lamentable trend dramatizes the perils of a result-oriented approach to justice. If you're primarily concerned with clearing criminal cases, you may not mind occasionally convicting the wrong men, especially if you assume that a defendant who is not guilty of the crime for which he is punished is probably guilty of something. (I imagine that the assumption that everyone on death row is a bad guy, whether or not he was fairly convicted, explains some cavalier attitudes toward executions.) If your primary goal is to secure financial aid for children, you may not care if some men are ordered to provide it because of false findings of paternity. If you're focused exclusively on supporting women, you may be oblivious to gender bias directed against men; or you may welcome it.

Ideally, the judicial system should be driven by a vision of fairness and equal treatment, whomever it benefits. Ideally, due process should prevail over the desire for any particular result. Interest-group politics belongs in legislatures, not courts. In fact, courts are supposed to operate as checks on the political process and the power of some groups to deprive others of fundamental rights. So, you can't judge the progress of feminism by the number of disputes in which women prevail over men. If the complaints of father's rights advocates are well-founded, they're testaments to the failures of feminism, not its successes. Only chauvinists want sex to matter more. Feminists should strive to make it matter less.

8

ANTI-INDIVIDUALISM/LEFT

Self-invention has always been an American ideal. We're supposed to enjoy opportunities to make our own fortunes and control our own fates, in this world and the next. The Calvinism of seventeenth-century colonials proved less quintessentially American than the notion that you can choose to be born again in Christ. This is not a culture inclined to embrace notions of predestination, spiritual or financial. In the mythic, utterly egalitarian America—the democratic America de Tocqueville described—we create our own futures, unburdened by our familial pasts.

That is the American dream, and a primary ideological obstacle to winning reparations for slavery. Demands for reparations challenge the vision of an American meritocracy. African Americans have not enjoyed equal opportunities for self-invention, advocates of reparations insist: Tenacious economic discrimination, widespread denials of voting rights, and oppressive brutalities (like lynching) followed the abolition of slavery and made sure that the descendants of slaves would be burdened by their history, not freed from it.

I don't dispute the truth of this assertion; the persistence of discrimination throughout the twentieth century is a primary justification for affirmative action, which I have always supported, a little unhappily. Race-conscious hiring, promotion, or admissions policies are not entirely equitable, but they are necessary and, on balance, less inequitable than race-blind policies. Still I don't regard affirmative action as compensation for the past; I regard it as insurance for the future. I don't support affirmative action programs because I believe that white women and racial minorities have somehow earned the right to preferential treatment by inadvertently inheriting discrimination. I support affirmative action because I can't figure out a better way to achieve equality.

So I hesitate to endorse recent demands for slavery reparations, although they have been thoughtfully presented. Opening a new conversation about reparations, activists and intellectuals like Randall Robinson and Charles Ogletree have stressed that they are not asking for direct cash payments to African Americans; reparations may take the form of compensatory social and economic programs (Robinson has called for "public initiatives, not personal checks"). They have not accused those Americans whose ancestors were not enslaved of

This piece appeared in The American Prospect, *May 22, 2000*

collaborating in the perpetuation of racism. "No one holds any living person responsible for slavery" or its legacies, Robinson stressed. They have made an appeal to our collective conscience, not issued an indictment of collective guilt.

Still, it's hard to imagine how this appeal might be implemented over one hundred years after abolition, without encouraging a belief in inherited guilt. Reparation demands do rest on the conviction that the nation owes a debt to its black citizens. This view implicates all citizens who constitute the nation, except the victims of slavery. First-, second-, or third-generation Americans whose families were busy being persecuted in some other country when slavery was abolished here may be particularly resistant to the demand that they contribute to reparations; but if you don't believe in inherited guilt, it's even difficult to make a case against the descendants of slaveholders.

How will we identify the beneficiaries of reparations? Will they be limited to people of African ancestry? Will they include those Americans of African descent whose ancestors participated in the slave trade? Will they include all those Americans of mixed race descended from slaves and slaveholders? If reparations are intended to atone for racism, will they extend to all self-identified people of color, like Hispanics, Native Americans, or Pacific islanders? Will the drive for reparations provoke a close examination of our ancestry to determine racial purity and entitlement to compensation?

Irritating questions like these are sure to follow from demands for reparations. They illustrate the difficulties of atoning for sins committed over a century ago. The perpetrators and their victims have been dead for generations, and we can't identify their survivors, which makes the payment of slavery reparations much more complicated and controversial than the compensation of Jewish Holocaust victims, Japanese citizens interned during World War II, or blacks who were murdered in riots in Greenwood, Oklahoma, in the 1920s. (A commission in Oklahoma recently recommended that reparations be paid to the victims of the Greenwood massacre.) Reparations for slavery should have been paid in the late 1800s, when they were first demanded, or at least in the early 1900s. It's not fair but it may be inevitable that the failure to recognize claims for compensation within a generation or two makes them virtually impossible to recognize at all.

I'm not offering this as an excuse for amnesia about our history, but the difficulties of designing reparations do suggest that history is sometimes irremediable. I am always nonplussed and a little annoyed when some head of state offers an apology for the crimes of his predecessors. While I understand the symbolic value of Tony Blair's apology to the Irish or Clinton's apology for slavery, I still find their contrition rather cloying. It's easy to atone for someone else's sins. Vicarious apologies are cheap thrills for the sanctimonious.

This does not condemn us to inaction when confronted with racism and economic inequities in the present. I might support many of the public initiatives offered by advocates for reparations, but I'd justify them differently. Why must we suggest that, by accidents of birth, people have somehow earned the right to government assistance in achieving equality?

There's an ideological paradox at the heart of demands for reparations: They challenge the myth of an American meritocracy, as the civil rights movement once challenged the myth of legal equality. Reparations aim to make the meritocratic ideal a reality for African Americans, as the civil rights movement aimed to realize the constitutional ideal of equality under law. But the campaign for reparations also reflects some of the premises of the aristocracy it attacks: It allows the past to define our entitlements in the present; it relies on a belief in the justice of inheritance.

If equality is an American birthright, we shouldn't have to rationalize efforts to achieve it by labeling those efforts compensation for the past. Whether or not your great-great-grandparents were enslaved, you ought not to be consigned to substandard schools, excluded from home ownership by discriminatory lending or sales practices, or subject to arbitrary searches by police because of the color of your skin. If equality is a birthright, you don't have to purchase it with the sufferings of your ancestors anymore than you should be allowed to purchase privileges with your ancestors' achievements.

It's a coincidence worth noting that demands for reparations closely followed a drive to reduce or even eliminate estate taxes and allow for tax-free transfers of wealth between generations. George Bush, who essentially inherited his place at Yale and arguably inherited the presidency, opposes the "death tax." I suspect that like many aristocrats, Bush feels deserving of the privileges he's inherited. I suspect he is irrationally proud of what he considers the accomplishments of his father and grandfather (accomplishments for which he can claim no credit); maybe he's proud of his "bloodlines."

I have no quarrel with noblesse oblige (it helped shape Franklin Roosevelt). But noblesse oblige reflects a commitment to making yourself worthy of what you've inherited, a commitment to earning your privilege with your own labors—not justifying it with the labors of your forebears. Bush, for one, doesn't exhibit noblesse oblige; he exhibits a sense of inherited entitlement, which is echoed in demands for reparations.

Underlying the drive for reparations is one of the great taboos of American politics—the demand for redistribution of wealth. The compensatory programs envisioned by reparations advocates are essentially redistributive; they're intended to raise the economic status of blacks, as Randall Robinson suggests. They would acknowledge and undo the "mechanisms" that have pushed blacks to "the back of the line." But if the problem is a system of inherited poverty and inherited wealth, why not address it directly?

If I were queen, just before abolishing my office, I'd raise taxes on intergenerational transfers of great wealth and use the proceeds to help build a meritocracy. Maybe I'd devote the additional revenues to public education, health care, or transportation. Maybe I'd compensate people victimized today by racial profiling. Maybe I'd fund some of the public initiatives proposed by Randall Robinson, but I wouldn't call them reparations. We shouldn't have to justify equality.

POLITICS OF IDENTITY

George Bush opposes affirmative action, at least in theory; in practice he has an affirmative action record that might have made Bill Clinton proud. According to *Time,* during his first year in office Bush "appointed more women to positions of power and influence than any president in history." He even has a diversity policy requiring that 30 percent of administration jobs be filled by women. He seems to have sought racial diversity as well: According to his personnel director, Clay Johnson, minorities constitute 20 to 25 percent of people selected for top government jobs.

Conservative opponents of affirmative action who once derided President Clinton for bean counting have generally exercised their right to remain silent about Bush's efforts to diversify. Their reticence is not surprising. They also declined to criticize his dad's affirmative action appointment of Supreme Court Justice Clarence Thomas. (I imagine that even people who did not believe that Justice Thomas harassed Anita Hill *did* believe that he was selected by Bush at least partly because of his race.)

Liberals have been flummoxed by the demographic diversity of the younger Bush's appointments. They're loath to praise his concern for diversity, even though it reflects their own success in expanding opportunities for women and racial minorities. It's difficult to celebrate the political ascension of your opponents: "We knew if we kicked the doors open, conservative women would walk through," former NOW president Patricia Ireland ruefully remarked. But liberals could learn from Bush's affirmative action program: It illustrates the falsities of identity politics. Race, ethnicity, sex, and sexual orientation are not reliable, or appropriate, predictors of ideology.

That may sound obvious, but it challenges a fundamental premise of left-wing crusades for diversity: the belief that heterosexual women, lesbians and gays, and racial minorities are united, respectively, by common histories of subordination, resulting in reliably liberal group-think (so long as they are true to themselves). Diversity is not only valued as a demonstration of equal access and an essential element of economic equality. It's also considered a virtual guarantee that particular political perspectives will be voiced, and strengthened. The power of this belief—that all members of "victim groups" do or should think more or less alike politically—is reflected in the vituper-

This piece appeared in The American Prospect, *September 24, 2001*

ative denunciation of conservative African Americans as race traitors, the dismissal of conservative women as "male-identified," and the presumption that conservative homosexuals are "self-hating."

Unfortunately, as Bush's diverse judicial nominations are considered, we're bound to hear more epithets like these. Conservatives will pounce on them as evidence of liberal bias and intolerance of dissent. They'll have a point. The patronizing condemnation of conservative women, gays, and racial minorities is a triumph of circular reasoning: If you dismiss all right-wing women as morally or politically deviant, you never have to reconsider your assumption that liberalism is a female norm. By relying on personal accusations of disloyalty, you also avoid the intellectual challenge of arguing about legal and political ideas. You betray the progressive ideal of individualism by imputing political views to people on account of race, sex, or sexual orientation. Civil rights struggles are supposed to give people more freedom of thought, as well as behavior, not less.

Identity politics has atavistic appeal, I admit. I'm not above wondering why Jews vote Republican or give large sums of money to Harvard. I was always persuaded by the bumper sticker that proclaimed "If men got pregnant, abortion would be a sacrament." There is even some empirical evidence that people with common experiences of discrimination and common cultures do form political cliques, as voters or legislators. African Americans have tended to vote Democratic. Female legislators generally pay more attention to women's rights, health care, child care and other policy initiatives involving family life (according to ten-year-old studies by the Center for American Women and Politics at Rutgers University).

But even if the collective political preferences of racial minorities, women, or gay people can be discerned, the preferences of particular individuals are unpredictable. (Trends and averages obscure individual variations.) Collective preferences may also reflect simple political expedience: Perhaps female legislators pay more attention to child care and other "women's" issues because of biases that limit their credibility as experts on "men's" issues, like foreign relations. When sex, sexual orientation, ethnicity, and race no longer occasion discrimination, tribalism is likely to have diminished effect on political allegiances.

I'm not suggesting that people will cease forming associations based on personal experiences or social and religious affinities—associations that can nurture political advocacy. The history of the women's movement, dating back 150 years, exemplifies the evolution of private grievances into public demands: The nineteenth-century Women's Christian Temperance Union, for example, reflected the anxiety and anger of women who were abused by alcoholic husbands. But the marriage of personal and political concerns has hardly been unique to feminism or to other civil rights movements involving historically victimized groups. Parents concerned about their children's health initiate campaigns to clean up the environment. Others dissatisfied with the public schools lobby for educational reforms —smaller classrooms, higher education budgets, or the censorship of whatever they deem dangerous or offensive speech. The political power of the religious right today grew out of personal disgust with secular culture.

Voluntarism, the formation of political associations, can be divorced from identity politics. In fact, the tendency to group people according to their immutable identities, as women, homosexuals, or people of color, challenges the belief in self-invention that helped shape the associational tradition. Demographic identity groups are not exactly voluntary. As political theorist Nancy Rosenblum notes in her insightful book *Members and Morals,* identity groups compel association. They presume that the voice of the group into which you are born is or should be your voice, whether or not you acknowledge it. They condemn as traitors people who stray from the presumptively correct ideologies of their groups.

If your identity is unchangeable, it chooses you. But one tenet of American culture, reflected in the voluntary tradition, has been a belief that you can select or, at least, help shape your own identity. If you can't choose your sex, race, or genetic disposition toward disease, you can choose your group, or series of groups, your religious affiliation, your causes and ideals, remaking yourself (and perhaps society) in the process. Meanwhile, groups negotiate their own surprising developmental changes: At its inception in the late nineteenth century, the now quasi-libertarian NRA had close ties to the military and prospered with the aid of government handouts.

Identity need not be immutable, for individuals or groups; political orientation will not be predictable so long as freedom to associate—and disassociate—is respected. Affirmative action promises economic equality, not the ideological consistency of its beneficiaries. If immutable characteristics like race, sex, and sexual orientation can help locate an individual in a political community, they ought not to imprison her there.

GUN SHY

Gun sales are said to have increased dramatically after September II, to the bemusement of some who point out that guns won't protect us from terrorists armed with viruses or nuclear bombs. Still, it's long been clear that many Americans feel reassured by firearms, and if you fear the civil disorder that further attacks might bring, the desire for a gun is not entirely irrational.

So it's not surprising that people might assert their rights to own guns while they cede less controversial rights to privacy or speech by embracing electronic surveillance or supporting repression of dissent. It's debatable whether an increase in gun purchases will protect or endanger them. Armed with studies and statistics, advocates and academics on both sides of the gun debate argue about whether gun ownership deters and successfully interrupts violent crime or simply increases the chances of any assault becoming deadly, as well as overall levels of violence. People often choose sides in this debate reflexively (your views on gun control signal your position in the culture war), but questions about the practical effects of gun ownership aren't easily resolved. It's difficult to know how many people successfully use firearms in self-defense; estimates by dueling academics have varied. It's probably impossible to know how much crime is deterred by widespread gun ownership. How do you count crimes that never occurred or analyze their nonoccurrence? How do you compare them to the number of accidental shootings?

Questions about the cumulative effect of individual gun ownership are probably irrelevant anyway to someone who buys a firearm in order to feel more secure. I suspect that individual decisions about gun ownership are likely to be based on instinct, ideology, or experience, not statistics. If, for example, you feel capable of safeguarding your own gun, you're probably not going to be persuaded to relinquish it because some privately owned guns are liable to end up in the hands of criminals.

Empirical debates about the relationship between gun ownership and violent crime are also peripheral to debates about the fundamental right to "bear arms." The fact that rights are abused by some people is no excuse for denying them to all: My right to speak freely is not contingent on my neighbor's willingness to refrain from spreading malicious libels or issuing true threats of violence.

This piece appeared in The American Prospect, *January 28, 2002*

Constitutional scholars and historians right and left have been engaged in a lively debate about Second Amendment rights for some years. But outside the pages of law reviews, liberals tend to embrace gun control and scoff at the Second Amendment, asserting that it only ensures the power of the states or the collective right of the "people" to organize armed militias. The trouble is that the Bill of Rights was intended to empower individuals, not groups (and certainly not governments). It was intended to restrain organized majorities, not to arm them. Indeed, most liberal civil libertarians adamantly construe the First, Fourth, Fifth, Sixth, Seventh, and Eighth amendments as grants of individual rights. (They'd construe the Third Amendment similarly if the government ever tried forcing us to quarter troops.) Still they perversely single out the Second Amendment as a grant of collective rights, mostly because of a cultural aversion to guns. Liberals tend to disdain the right to own a gun the way conservatives disdain the right to read pornography.

I'm not advocating gun ownership or an end to gun controls. But considering my own fierce attachment to the First Amendment, which is often blamed for acts of violence, I have some sympathy for people fiercely attached to the Second Amendment, because they believe that individual autonomy depends on a right of self-defense. It's long past time for liberals to stop demonizing gun owners and fantasizing about virtually eliminating guns. We'd have to erase the Fourth Amendment (or what's left of it after the drug war) to rid American households of their firearms. We should, by now, have learned the lessons of Prohibition. The failures of efforts to ban alcohol, abortion, and various drugs have made clear the futility (and socioeconomic costs) of campaigns to criminalize behaviors in which millions of Americans indulge.

Consider the practical and political benefits of recognizing a basic right to own a gun. Liberals would be spared the embarrassment of passing foolish, largely symbolic laws like the 1994 ban on "assault" rifles, which arbitrarily applied to a small class of semiautomatic weapons (when most gun crimes involved handguns). Democrats would greatly enhance their electability in regions where support for gun ownership is high and NRA lobbying intense. And opposition to gun controls might decrease if gun owners did not fear that all restrictions on their rights were leading down a slippery slope toward prohibition.

There are, after all, compelling reasons to regulate guns, even if people have a basic constitutional right to own them, as a recent federal court decision suggests. In *United States v. Emerson*, the Fifth Circuit Court of Appeals held that the Second Amendment confers an individual right to own a gun, which may be subject to narrow, limited restrictions in particular cases. In this case, the court upheld a federal statute prohibiting possession of guns by people subject to restraining orders in domestic violence cases. Gun control advocates who have denounced this decision might someday find themselves indebted to it. To restrict gun rights effectively, we may first have to acknowledge they exist.

GUILT OF ASSOCIATION

Should evangelical Christian groups at colleges and universities be permitted to discriminate against gay and lesbian students? Do the Boy Scouts have a constitutional right to exclude openly gay males? The first question has been at the center of efforts by liberal colleges and universities to punish evangelical student groups for their illiberal views. The second question was decided by the Supreme Court in June 2000, in *Dale v. Boy Scouts of America.* Both controversies dramatize the challenge exclusionary private groups pose to laws and social norms that celebrate inclusion. How do we balance the free speech and associational rights of bigots with the drive for full equality?

I begin with the basic premise that individuals and their private associations have a fundamental moral and legal right to champion any prejudice or ideal that I don't share. ("Big of you," I imagine them saying.) Effective advocacy of ideas, or control of the message, requires some control of the messengers. So the same respect for individual autonomy and freedom of conscience, which mandates support for gay rights, also requires defending the rights of homophobes to band together exclusively and express their belief that homosexuality is sinful and deviant.

Public entities, however, have no First Amendment rights; instead they have an obligation not to discriminate. It follows that the right of any group to discriminate depends largely on whether or not the group is truly private. An organization that receives significant public support (other than a tax exemption generally extended to private groups) is a quasi-public entity that ought to abide by public norms prohibiting discrimination.

The New Jersey Supreme Court found that the Boy Scouts of America (BSA) was subject to state law against discrimination in public accommodations, partly because it greatly benefited from public support and services: Public schools assist in recruiting efforts and host various Scout meetings and activities; fire departments and law enforcement agencies sponsor Scout troops; military facilities are available to them; and New Jersey's Department of Environmental Protection is authorized to make sure that any body of water controlled by the Scouts is stocked with fish.

The view of the Boy Scouts as an essentially public group is also bolstered by its nonselective admission policies. As the New Jersey

This piece appeared in The American Prospect, *July 3, 2000*

court stressed, the Boy Scouts of America is hardly an exclusive club. It publicly solicits members and is essentially open to all interested boys. (Of course it does not accept girls, but New Jersey's antidiscrimination law exempts single-sex organizations.)

If the BSA is viewed as a de facto public organization (as I believe it may be viewed), we don't have to reach hard questions about the limits of private associational rights in considering the organization's right to expel homosexuals. But the Supreme Court did not focus on the public or private status of the Scouts; instead, the Court wrestled with the conflict between public antidiscrimination laws and rights of private association.

The Supreme Court has addressed this conflict clumsily in previous cases. In 1984, in *Roberts v. Jaycees,* it ruled that the Jaycees could be forced to admit women under Minnesota's public accommodation law. (The Court issued a similar ruling in 1987 requiring the Rotary Club to admit women under California law.) These cases offer a rather crabbed view of associational rights. The Court observed that freedom to associate qualifies as an "intrinsic element of personal liberty" primarily in the context of intimate associations, like familial relationships or selective, relatively small voluntary communities. In this view, freedom of association is not seriously impaired by government interference with large, nonselective civic or commercial organizations—unless government action substantially interferes with the group's freedom of expression.

In other words, the Court's analysis in the Jaycees case confers normative value upon intimate associations (they are intrinsic to liberty regardless of their purposes), while large voluntary organizations are given instrumental constitutional value, as vehicles for expressing ideas. This requires the Court to examine the organization's expressive purpose, or mission, and evaluate the government's impact upon it. The mission of the Jaycees, as stated in its bylaws, was "to foster the growth and development of young men's civic organizations." How this historic mission would be advanced by requiring the admission of women was not self-evident. Still, Justice Brennan's majority opinion held that the Jaycees' purpose (which Brennan didn't exactly define) would not be impaired by subjecting the organization to antidiscrimination law.

Maybe Brennan was right in this case (and maybe not); but his analysis ignored the inevitable effect of membership policies on organizational purpose. Isn't the voice of a group the collective voice of its members? It's worth noting that if Justice Brennan believed that there was a natural gender gap between men and women on political and social issues, he would have had to conclude that the Jaycees' mission, which in his view included staking out positions on controversial public issues, was bound to be affected significantly by admitting women.

Sometimes the destructive impact of discrimination laws on an association's purpose is clear: In a 1995 case, the Supreme Court unanimously (and correctly) held that organizers of Boston's St. Patrick's Day parade had a First Amendment right to exclude openly gay marchers because they promoted a message about gay rights that the organizers disdained. In a parade the marchers are the message, obviously. But the relationship between message and membership is often more subtle, which makes a judicial inquiry into it more troubling, entangling a court in the internal affairs of associations and imposing its values on them.

In *Dale v. Boy Scouts of America*, by a 5 to 4 vote, the Supreme Court rightly deferred to the BSA's assertion that accepting gay members would compromise the group's "expressive purpose," which includes, according to the BSA, promotion of a traditional moral code. Scouts are required to remain "morally straight" and "clean," according to the Scout oath and Scout law; the BSA has essentially argued that gay people are morally deviant and dirty, which disqualifies them as Scouts.

This is hardly an appealing or intelligent position (and it is belied by the successful twelve-year scouting career of plaintiff James Dale, an Eagle Scout who earned thirty merit badges before he was expelled from the Scouts for publicly acknowledging his homosexuality). But people have a right to their stupidities. It should not be the business of courts to decide the merits of a private association's vision of its own expressive purpose—just as it should not be the business of government to sponsor discrimination. By upholding the BSA's right to discriminate, the Court left the organization to choose between the right to indulge in its prejudices and the extensive public support it has traditionally enjoyed. In fact, the Court may have handed the Scouts a Pyrrhic victory; its insistence on excluding gay members has cost it prestige and sponsorship.

The question of governmental or quasi-governmental support for an exclusionary group at odds with prevailing public norms has also been raised by the treatment of conservative Christian groups on liberal campuses. At Grinnell College, Middlebury College, and Williams College, evangelical student groups have been penalized for their views on homosexuality. In a typical case, the Christian Fellowship at Tufts University was "de-recognized" by the student government in the spring of 2000, after it barred an openly gay member from a leadership post; de-recognition meant losing a $6,000 annual stipend, the use of classroom facilities, access to listing services, and use of "Tufts" in its name.

The Tufts case generated controversy off campus, and the Christian Fellowship's official status was quickly reinstated by the university after an internal appeal. Applying majoritarian notions of equality to student evangelical groups is particularly hard to justify, because it compromises religious freedom as well as associational rights. Many religious groups have exclusionary policies, which they regard as divinely ordained, and public antidiscrimination laws generally exempt religious organizations, in respect of their special status under the First Amendment. Private universities like Tufts are not subject to the First Amendment but they do generally claim to support religious freedom, as well as equality.

It's tempting to attribute these assaults on campus evangelical groups to political correctness, partly because it's hard to imagine liberal colleges punishing liberal groups that refused leadership roles to members who preached that homosexuals were sinners in need of reparative therapy. In any case, the punitive action against the evangelical students connotes a disdain for religious and ideological diversity. At relatively liberal campuses, conservative Christians tend to be more marginalized than gay rights activists.

Like most First Amendment rights, the right of association has particular value to beleaguered minorities. Private associations sometimes provide dissenters with refuge from the majority rule of their larger community, not to mention a valuable organizing base. Modern liberation movements have flourished precisely because women, gays, and racial minorities have enjoyed the freedom to associate with each other and disassociate, when need be, from their political enemies; they were free to form associations that voiced their collective demands for equality. At times they had to wrest their freedoms from actively hostile communities and governments, which means that they should know better than to deny the same freedoms to their opponents. It's sad to see the dream of equality become an excuse for repressing dissent.

9

ANTI-INDIVIDUALISM/RIGHT

WHEN CONGRESS PLAYS DOCTOR

When HMOs deny lifesaving care to their patients, members of Congress fulminate: In 1999, 275 of them, including 29 Republicans, voted for a patients' bill of rights. "Deny American citizens effective, lifesaving treatments or palliatives for pain?" I imagine them exclaiming indignantly to the HMOs. "That's our job."

At about the same time that the patients' bill of rights was considered, Congress and the Justice Department were busy malpracticing medicine, callously violating patients' rights. The Senate passed an antiabortion law prohibiting doctors from employing particular surgical techniques, even when they were necessary to preserve the woman's health. The Justice Department proceeded with the prosecution of two men stricken with cancer and AIDS, respectively, who used marijuana to alleviate nausea and pain. It relied on congressional declarations of the medical uselessness of marijuana. The House passed a bill effectively criminalizing physician-assisted suicide in Oregon, despite its endorsement in two statewide referendums. Congressional efforts to override the Oregon law failed, but the Bush Administration attempted to accomplish by executive fiat what Congress failed to accomplish legislatively. In November 2001 Attorney General Ashcroft issued a directive threatening doctors who prescribe lethal drugs under the state assisted suicide law with revocation of their registration under federal drug law. This directive, which relied on Ashcroft's reinterpretation of the federal controlled substances act, was struck down by a federal district court in April 2002.

Playing doctor (without regard for the Hippocratic oath), Congress and the administration make it easy even for liberal social engineers to hate the government. Sometimes they seem dedicated to increasing human suffering. Imagine yourself terminally ill and in unrelenting pain, desirous of ending your now unwanted life. Then imagine the federal government threatening your doctor with imprisonment or deprivation of the right to practice medicine if he or she prescribes a lethal dose of drugs at your request. All you can say is "how dare they," especially if you're a citizen in a state that has twice passed a Death with Dignity referendum. Shouldn't your wish to end your life prevail over the compulsion of a congressman (or attorney general) to prolong it?

A version of this piece appeared in The American Prospect, *January 3, 2000*

There is, after all, no evidence that Oregon's law has been abused by unscrupulous doctors, murderous families, or deranged patients. The Death with Dignity Act has safeguards aimed at ensuring that patients who choose death do so knowingly and willingly, and it applies only to terminally ill patients facing death within six months. Since 1997, when the law became effective, fewer than one hundred people have used it to end their lives with the aid of their doctors.

Still, Republican congressman Henry Hyde, who sponsored the aborted congressional override of Oregon's right to die law, charged that it turned doctors into "executioners." Not exactly a nuanced thinker, Hyde apparently didn't understand the difference between murdering people who wish to remain alive and facilitating the suicides of terminally ill people seeking more merciful deaths than their diseases will allow.

This heartless bill would also have deterred doctors from administering effective doses of pain medication, although it was deceptively entitled the Pain Relief Promotion Act. On its face, the bill prohibited the use of federally controlled substances intended to hasten death and included exceptions for drugs intended only to alleviate pain. (Doctors would have faced up to twenty years in prison for assisting suicides.) But who would determine the intent of a doctor in prescribing pain medication that facilitates the death of a terminally ill patient? As the bill's opponents pointed out, we probably don't want federal drug agents and prosecutors hovering over our death-beds, monitoring our doctors.

People who seek physician and patient autonomy from HMO bureaucrats may not welcome the medical interventions of politicians—unless they believe the politicians are acting at the behest of God, seeking a higher good. Opposition to right to die laws is fueled partly by the religious fervor of antiabortion activists. In their view, laws prohibiting assisted suicides or abortions aren't violations of individual liberty: They're restrictions on sinful individual license. Laws restricting or prohibiting abortions may even be framed by their supporters as patients' rights bill: To abortion opponents, the fetus is the primary patient; the pregnant woman deserves medical care only when it enhances fetal development, or, at least, poses the fetus no harm.

During the 1999 Senate debate on a bill purporting to limit late-term abortions, the bill's supporters cast themselves as patient advocates, intent on protecting the most vulnerable patients from unscrupulous doctors. Doctors who perform abortions are "executioners,"

Pennsylvania Republican Rick Santorum charged, echoing Henry Hyde. The apparently demented New Hampshire senator Bob Smith claimed that abortion clinics house "harvesters" in their back rooms who "take (the) baby, cut it into pieces, and sell it."

Is this the man you want making medical decisions for you or your family? Late-term abortion laws, which were adopted in some twenty-seven states, tended to be drafted vaguely so as to prohibit common procedures that may be used any time during a pregnancy. Because of their breadth and their interference with doctor/patient relationships, late-term abortion prohibitions have been enjoined or limited judicially in a majority of states in which they've been enacted. In June 2000, the Supreme Court struck down a prototypical late-term abortion prohibition passed by the state of Nebraska, but the battle over abortion procedures continues. In 2002, the Virginia legislature passed a "partial birth" abortion law that was vetoed by the governor.

Whether you view abortion prohibitions like this as malicious or benevolent government acts usually depends on whether or not you consider the fetus an equal to a human being who's actually been born. But even some who consider abortion sinful are bound to be troubled when women are killed or maimed by illegal abortions during periods of prohibition. People ambivalent about abortion may worry when women are deprived of the safest, most appropriate abortion techniques by legislative fiat. Whether or not abortions are cruel, when congressional controls disdain women's health, they are hardly kind.

Cruelty doesn't always come naturally to people. Federal prosecutors must be selected for their callousness, or perhaps they enter training programs designed to purge them of compassion. How else can we explain the prosecution of Peter McWilliams and Todd McCormick?

Both men were among a group of nine defendants charged with growing and distributing marijuana, after a federal raid uncovered more than 4,000 marijuana plants. McCormick explained that he smoked marijuana to alleviate pain from cancer treatments that fused several of his vertebrae. McWilliams said that marijuana successfully treated the nausea caused by the AIDS drugs that kept him alive. (His claim proved true. Prohibited from using marijuana while awaiting trial, McWilliams began vomiting frequently and not absorbing his AIDS medication; as a result, the *Los Angeles Times* reported, his virus raged out of control. In June 2000, he died, asphyxiated by his own vomit. It is not hyperbole to suggest that the federal prosecution killed him.)

This was one case in which the defendants' side of the story was compelling, so the prosecutors didn't want jurors to hear it. The government successfully moved to prohibit McCormick and McWilliams from raising a medical defense and telling their stories. The defendants were also prohibited from citing the federal government's own research into the medical uses of marijuana or explaining that their actions were permitted by state law: In 1996, California passed a referendum, Proposition 215, allowing for medical use of marijuana. Deprived of their ability to defend themselves in court, both McWilliams and McCormick pled guilty to conspiracy to manufacture and distribute marijuana. McWilliams died shortly before sentencing. McCormick began a five-year sentence in 2000.

According to prosecutors, their medical-necessity defenses were simply irrelevant. "It doesn't matter if they say, 'I'm doing this to save my life,' " a spokesman for the U.S. attorney explained. "It's illegal to manufacture or cultivate marijuana under federal law." (The Supreme Court subsequently agreed. In 2001, it held that federal law criminalizing marijuana allowed no defense of medical necessity.) But generally, in law and in fact, it matters a great deal if a defendant engages in otherwise criminal behavior in order to save his life, or the life of another. There's nothing novel about self-defense. The law allows you to kill someone who is poised to kill you. Surely, in defense of your life, the law should allow you to grow marijuana plants.

But the federal government's commitment to criminalizing the use of marijuana is unswerving. (In the fall of 2001, taking a break from its war on terrorism, the Bush Administration went to war on marijuana when the Drug Enforcement Agency began raiding medical marijuana clubs in California that were authorized by state law.) Washington's drug warriors seem to think Americans are better off dead than smoking dope. Federal law classifies marijuana as a class I substance, along with heroin and LSD, and prosecutors in the case against McWilliams and McCormick relied on congressional assertions that marijuana has no acceptable medical uses. District Court judge George King agreed that Congress knows best: The medical-necessity defense proposed by defendants would "explicitly contradict a congressional determination," he ruled. Judge King prohibited McCormick and McWilliams from telling their stories by invoking a doctrine of congressional infallibility.

Sometimes it's hard to know if the government is playing doctor

or God. Armed with faith in its own omniscience and absolute recti-
tude and assisted by federal law enforcement, the attorney general and
a majority in Congress have assumed the power to deprive people of
essential medical care in order to enforce a particular moral code. In
their view, marijuana use, abortion, and suicide are so evil that they
must be prohibited at any cost to individuals. Americans, it seems,
must be prepared to sacrifice themselves to this bureaucratic vision of
the greater good.

That is the logic of terrorists, demagogues, and other absolutists
who perceive no moral dilemmas: For them, the right path is always
clear. Fearful of falling into the pit of moral relativism, many members of Congress and the administration have cultivated a dangerous
sense of self-righteousness, unleavened by self-doubt. They need lessons in moral modesty. It is a great civilizer. People not troubled by
uncertainty are not hampered by compassion.

LAW AND MARRIAGE

These days I settle for small and subtle signs of progress. Take this report that appeared in the *Washington Post* February 14, 2001, on the demise of a proposal in the Virginia legislature that would have required public school students to recite the "Pledge of Allegiance." State Senator Warren E. Barry, sponsor of the legislation (which was passed by the state senate), blamed "libertarians and liberals" on a House Education Committee for softening his bill by exempting students who had a religious or philosophical objection to reciting the pledge. (The legislature subsequently passed a law requiring schools to allot time for students to say the pledge, presumably voluntarily.) Outraged by the defanging of his bill, Barry called the twenty-three members of the House committee "spineless pinkos," which, the *Post* felt compelled to explain, is "a Cold War reference to Communist sympathizers." Surely we've progressed a little if a phrase like "spineless pinkos" has passed out of the vernacular.

Still the culture of the fifties retains appeal for some. "It may be the twenty-first century out there but in this house, it's 1954," Tony Soprano reminded his daughter. It's not hard to imagine social conservatives nodding their heads in agreement (even if they consider the popularity of *The Sopranos* another sign of civilization's decline). If newly empowered social conservatives prevail, it may soon be 1954 in everybody's house.

What is perhaps most alluring to conservatives about the culture of the fifties is the marriage myth it helped perpetuate. My grade school readers were replete with pictures of contented suburban, two-parent families: They lived behind white picket fences and attended church on Sunday; the women wore dresses and high heels at home. *Just like my mother.* You can measure the divide between feminists and traditionalists by the way they react to this vision of bliss. Feminists tend to prefer a 50 percent divorce rate to the feminine mystique that accompanied prefeminist notions of marital stability. Traditionalists view divorce as a primary social ill, quite literally:

"Married people live longer and healthier lives," according to newspaper columnist Maggie Gallagher, coauthor with Linda J. Waite of *The Case for Marriage.* Gallagher, a spokeswoman for the right-wing marriage movement, imagines that marriage "wards off death" because it promotes healthier habits: Married people are "less likely to

This piece appeared in The American Prospect, *July 2, 2001*

hang out late at night in bars, get into fights, drink too much, or drive too fast. They save money and pay their bills responsibly, reducing financial stresses that undercut health." She doesn't add that married people are a lot more likely to commit adultery. Hasn't she ever been accosted by a drunken married man, hanging out late at night in a bar?

Or are philandering spouses mere anomalies? According to Gallagher, married people have less incentive to loiter late in bars because "to top it off, they even have better sex, more often, than couples who are not married." Maybe so, but it's not hard to imagine that the relative sexual satisfaction of married couples owes something to the high divorce rate.

But let's agree that people do derive many personal as well as economic benefits from amicable, stable marriages. If the drive to strengthen marriage were pragmatic, as Gallagher makes it seem, there'd be much less opposition to gay marriages. Surely gay people and their children would also benefit from wedded bliss, or at least wedded stability, and society would benefit in turn. But while many conservatives rally around calls for marriage education and laws severely restricting divorce, they rally against legislation that would give gay couples equal rights to wed (or work; they also oppose equal employment laws). "(H)omosexuality is a permanent, defining issue" for the Christian right, Frederick Clarkson observes in *The Public Eye* (the informative newsletter of Political Research Associates).

Moral fervor, not a pragmatic concern for health and welfare, drives the movement to promote heterosexual marriage. It exemplifies the anti-libertarianism of the right and the hypocrisy of its demands for smaller government and professed disdain for social engineering. The conservative Heritage Foundation proposed establishing a federal office to promote marriage. The Bush Administration has declined to create a federal marriage office, but, announcing his welfare plan in February 2002, the president did propose spending $300 million federal on programs to promote marriage among poor people and $135 million on abstinence programs.

This proposal was clearly intended to please the administration's right-wing base (and irritate liberals who condemned it as bureaucratic interference with private life). It was an implicit rebuke to proverbial liberal permissiveness—the reputed moral relativism of the 1960s—that conservatives generally blame for the increase in cohabitation and the decline of marriage. But disenchantment with marriage appears to be a complicated phenomenon; its causes are not so easily discerned. Divorce rates, for example, are particularly high in several Bible Belt states, including Arkansas and Oklahoma. It seems that secularism (another reputed legacy of the sixties) isn't entirely to blame for the decline of traditional families, among other frequently lamented social ills. Apparently, in at least a few states, the divorce rate correlates to an excess of piety, not the absence of it.

What do we make of this amusing correlation? I doubt that religiosity directly causes divorce, but in some cases it may cause marriage, by condemning premarital sex and cohabitation as sinful; and marriage, of course, is the one indisputable cause of divorce. Marry in haste; divorce when you come to your senses. "I had this vision that this is just what people do; get married, have kids, and Christ comes back," one Oklahoma divorcee told the *New York Times*. She remarried, but a great many Oklahomans apparently prefer living in sin. (Religion may not cause marriage after all.) The number of unmarried, cohabitating couples in Oklahoma increased 97 percent in the 1990s. It increased 125 percent in Arkansas and 123 percent in Tennessee. The average national increase in unmarried couples for the same period was 72 percent.

In responses to figures like these, several states have been experimenting with their own pro-marriage initiatives. (The Bush Administration will have little trouble finding ideologically compatible programs to fund.) Oklahoma has budgeted $10 million for marriage counseling and the hiring of "marriage ambassadors" to visit talk shows and schools. May 5, 2001, was "Save Your Marriage Before It Starts Day" for Oklahomans. Louisiana, Arkansas, and Arizona recognize covenant marriages—prenuptial agreements that greatly restrict the right to divorce. (Arkansas is in the midst of a "marital emergency," according to its governor, Mike Huckabee.) Florida requires high schools to offer classes in marriage and relationships, and numerous state legislatures are considering laws that would mandate counseling before marriage or divorce.

Conservative anxiety about marriage reflected by these measures has been heightened by 2000 census figures showing that less than 24 percent of American households consist of married couples with kids. Meanwhile, the percentage of families headed by single mothers has risen 25 percent in the past ten years. "We're losing; there isn't any question about it," virtuecrat William Bennett has warned.

Liberals routinely condemn covenant marriages, abstinence programs, and other efforts to reverse these trends and promote traditional heterosexual marriages as crusades to "legislate morality."

But the law and policy are naturally and often appropriately moralistic. The crusade for universal human rights is driven by moral convictions, not merely concerns about international economic and political stability. Equal employment laws are not simply pragmatic economic measures; they reflect a consensus about the immorality of discrimination—a consensus that liberals fought hard to create. Workplace regulations in general—minimum wage laws and health and safety regulations—are considered moral mandates by many on the left. Hate-crime legislation and campus speech codes all reflect the left wing's moralism; so do efforts to abolish the death penalty or end the deeply immoral war on drugs. So attacking right-wing moralism can be a bit misleading, if not downright hypocritical.

I don't quarrel categorically with all efforts to use law to promote morality. I do question the practical effects of some morally driven policies—like a preference for teaching horny teenagers everything about abstinence and nothing about contraception. The primary problem with abstinence programs is not their inherent moralism; it's the likelihood that they will increase the incidence of AIDS and teenage pregnancies. But my hostility to the right wing's social agenda is moral (or moralistic) as well as practical. It's based on my own rejection of the particular moral code that the right embraces. (I'm not always in agreement with left-wing moralists either, especially when they seek to limit speech.) The current conservative regime envisions an ideal world in which heterosexual couples can't divorce and gay couples can't marry; no one can get an abortion, and even contraception is scarce, especially for teens. Seriously ill people risk being imprisoned for using marijuana to relieve pain and nausea and maybe even prolong their lives. Poor people are imprisoned and killed by the state without ever receiving fair trials. Children will recite the "Pledge of Allegiance" (or else). It's not my moral vision of liberty, or justice, for all.

GAY RITES

While civil libertarians celebrated the 1999 decision by the Vermont Supreme Court recognizing the rights of gay couples to wed or enter domestic partnerships, Republican presidential candidate Gary Bauer suggested that gay marriages were more immoral than murder. "I think what the Vermont Supreme Court did last week was in some ways worse than terrorism," Bauer declared in the ignorant bliss that preceded 9/11.

Giving him the benefit of the doubt, I regarded this as political hyperbole. I assumed that, like most relatively sane people, even Gary Bauer would rather encounter two gay males holding hands than one terrorist. I assumed that he didn't really prefer the slaughter of innocents to the legalization of gay relationships, but perhaps this was wishful thinking.

Gay people have gained unprecedented rights and respect in recent decades, but homophobia continues to fuel moral reform movements on the right and exerts influence center court. Sometimes, our obsession with other people's sexual orientations seems second only to our obsession with race. It's baffling. I understand gossip and prurience, but not moral outrage or even concern about the sexual preferences of consenting adults. Homophobia can't simply be attributed to religion (there is considerable support for gay rights in some religious communities), although it is often cloaked in religious rhetoric. But fear and loathing of gay people does seem as visceral as love of God, and equally tenacious.

It is hardly a function of ignorance and infects elites as well as plebeians. Supreme Court justice Scalia has implicitly compared homosexuality to murder, suggesting that voters might be justified in passing laws that express their "animus" toward homosexuals. Scalia made these remarks in a vituperative dissent in *Romer v. Evans,* decided in 1996. In *Romer,* the Court struck down an amendment to the Colorado state constitution that prohibited cities and towns from enacting gay rights ordinances; the majority held that the Colorado amendment was a discriminatory expression of animus toward one group of citizens. "Of course, it is our moral heritage that one should not hate any human being or any class of human beings," Scalia conceded. "But I had thought that one could consider certain conduct reprehensible—murder, for example, or polygamy, or cruelty to animals—

A version of this piece appeared in The American Prospect, *February 28, 2000*

and could even exhibit 'animus' toward such conduct. Surely that is the only sort of 'animus' at issue here: moral disapproval of homosexual conduct . . ."

People opposed to gay rights typically characterize antigay laws as prohibitions on conduct, which obscures the frequent treatment of homosexuality as a sort of status crime: When people are fired or not hired because they are gay, they're being punished for who they are, not what they've done. While there is no bright line between identity and behavior (as the military's disastrous "Don't ask, Don't tell" policy showed), there is a blurry one, which homophobes consistently ignore.

Consider the ravings of syndicated radio host and pop psychologist Dr. Laura. She views homosexuality simply as "sexual deviancy" associated with pedophilia, bestiality, and sadomasochism (not to mention cross-dressing), which gay rights activists are conspiring to normalize, with the aid of big government: "Again, a conspiracy . . . I'm the *X-Files* queen at this point . . . When you're trying to establish a world order (in which) deviancy becomes the norm and everything is okay and there should be no judgment, the first thing you have to do is either remove kids from their homes to brainwash them, like if there were government day-care centers or mandatory preschools from the age of three."

Psychologists who claim that same-sex couples can raise healthy children are also part of the conspiracy that Dr. Laura perceives: The "stupid trash that comes out of the psychological community that says dad's not necessary (is) a plot for two women to have kids and justify it. If two lesbians can adopt children after the psychological community says that fathers are not relevant, then there's a lot of power, right? Believe me all the points connect to one place."

It's not that she lacks compassion, the good doctor stresses: "I don't want anybody hurt. I don't want anybody killed." It's just that, for her, gay rights are limited to the right to be cured of gayness: "I would like homosexuals to have the ability to get reparative therapy so they could live quote 'normal' lives and have the benefit of heterosexual relationships."

Dr. Laura is an easy target, I admit, and it's tempting to dismiss her as the lunatic fringe (except that she is a nationally known, best-selling author whose radio rants reach into the mainstream). A more sobering example of homophobia is mainstream and liberal opposition to gay marriage. The federal Defense of Marriage Act (DOMA), enacted in 1996, which greatly limited the effect of gay marriages legalized by any state, was approved by overwhelming majority in both houses. Supporters of this bill, originally championed by twice-divorced Georgia congressman Bob Barr, included such liberal stalwarts in the Senate as Paul Wellstone (D, Minn.), Barbara Mikulski (D, Md.), Pat Leahy (D, Vt.), and Frank Lautenberg (D, N.J.), as well as Bill Bradley, who went on to court gay voters in his 2000 presidential campaign.

It's worth noting that all of these senators supported a federal law to prohibit employment discrimination against gay men and women, which very nearly passed the Senate in 1996—an election year, the same year that the Defense of Marriage Act was passed. (The Employment Non-Discrimination Act, ENDA, was rejected by a 50 to 49 vote.) But ENDA did not involve sex, children, and the putatively sacred institution of marriage. It's hard to know how many votes in favor of the Defense of Marriage Act were cast merely for political expedience; but talking to legislators, you get the sense that opposition to gay marriage tends to be sincere, if inarticulate, even among supporters of equal employment laws for gays. Often, people can't quite explain why marriage should be limited to heterosexual couples; same-sex marriage just doesn't "feel right" to them.

How do you argue with a feeling? That's the challenge facing gay-rights activists. It's a challenge that has confronted all modern civil rights movements. For most of our history, traditional divisions of labor between men and women "felt right" to a great many Americans (and continue feeling right to some). Racial segregation was once the law of the land partly because it "felt right" to white majorities. You can't often defeat feelings like this with argument or logic. But as Martin Luther King demonstrated, you can successfully arouse competing feelings—passions for fairness, individual rights, and equal justice.

One of the legacies of the civil rights era has been the stigmatization of workplace discrimination; apparently it no longer "feels right" to a majority of Americans. According to a 1997 *Newsweek* poll, 84 percent of us profess to support equal employment rights for gay people. It is, however, difficult to gauge the depth of this reported opposition to discrimination, which has yet to be widely translated into law. In most states, you can be dismissed from your job because of your sexual orientation. Lacking civil rights under state law, you're not likely to find much protection in federal court either: In a 1997 case, *Shahar v. Bowers,* the federal appeals court for the Eleventh Circuit held that a lawyer in the Georgia attorney general's office could be fired because she was a lesbian.

The *Shahar* case is notable mostly for the hypocrisy it endorses.

Former Georgia attorney general Mike Bowers fired a female deputy, Robin Shahar, when he learned she was about to have a commitment ceremony with her partner. Bowers successfully argued that employing an openly lesbian attorney would compromise his ability to enforce anti-sodomy laws and address other "controversial" matters involving gay rights. (Even though the commitment ceremony was religious, the court found that Shahar's firing did not violate her First Amendment rights.) But a few days after the Eleventh Circuit's decision was announced Bowers (involved in an ultimately unsuccessful gubernatorial race) admitted that he had been cheating on his wife for years with an employee in the Department of Law. So much for defending marriage and the purity of the attorney general's office.

Shahar went back to the circuit court seeking a rehearing, pointing out that adultery, like sodomy, was prohibited by Georgia's penal law, but the court was unmoved by revelations about the attorney general's conduct. He didn't fire Shahar because of her sexual behavior, the court noted, pouncing on a questionable and highly irrelevant distinction; he fired her because she got married.

Over thirty years ago, in 1967, the Supreme Court struck down laws against interracial marrying, but only two years ago, it declined to review Robin Shahar's case. Fourteen years ago, in 1986, the Court upheld Georgia's anti-sodomy law in a notorious case that involved the arrest of a gay male engaged in consensual sex with another adult, in his own bedroom. In that case, *Bowers v. Hardwick*, the Court indicated that adult homosexuals could be arrested for sodomy, in their own homes, partly because they *weren't* married. The Court observed that previous Supreme Court decisions recognizing rights of sexual privacy all involved family, procreation—or marriage. In fact, Georgia attorney general Bowers (the same Mike Bowers) conceded that the anti-sodomy law could not be applied to married couples. (Presumably, it could have been applied to adulterers.) In 1998, the Georgia Supreme Court struck down the anti-sodomy law under the state constitution; but *Bowers v. Hardwick* has not been overruled, and anti-sodomy laws applying only to unmarried people are still permissible under the federal constitution.

What is the lesson of these cases for gay people? You can be fired if you get married and arrested if you don't. It would be hyperbole to denounce the denial of basic civil rights and liberties to gay people as legal terrorism. But it is another instance of gratuitous government cruelty. Whether or not it's unconstitutional, somehow it just doesn't feel right.

BAD VIBES IN ALABAMA

Advocates of censoring the Internet often argue that sexually explicit material today is "worse"—more graphic, more violent, more "deviant," and more available—than it was twenty-five or thirty years ago. If only we could return to the innocent days of the 1950s and '60s when *Playboy* was considered risqué, they imply: Then we wouldn't be confronted with a compelling need for censorship. This sense of urgency is probably sincere, just as it was 25, 50, and 150 years ago. Would-be censors and other authoritarians always exclaim that the "bad" speech or conduct they're targeting really is badder than any speech or conduct that has been targeted before.

But in fact obscenity and indecency laws are sometimes quaintly directed against the tamest, most familiar forms of sexual expression, like nude dancing. In 1991, the Supreme Court upheld a prohibition on nude dancing; to be precise, the Court held that a law against public nudity could be applied, constitutionally, to erotic dancing. The general ban on nudity was justified, the Court held, by the state's legitimate interest in preserving "order and morality." Like bestiality, sadomasochism, and cockfighting, public nudity was traditionally considered "immoral," Justice Scalia approvingly observed. Meanwhile, nontraditional attacks on nudity have emerged in the form of sexual harassment complaints. In a notorious case in the early 1990s, a reproduction of Goya's *The Naked Maja* was removed from the wall of an art history classroom at Penn State University after a professor complained that it made her students uncomfortable.

While some people are still putting fig leaves on statues (quite literally), others are outraged by sex toys. In 1998, Alabama criminalized the sale of vibrators and other "devices designed or marketed as useful primarily for the stimulation of human genital organs." Legislators in Alabama apparently consider masturbation immoral, although I doubt that they approach the issue with clean hands (1998, by the way, was the same year that Alabama's attorney general obtained an obscenity indictment against Barnes and Noble for selling books by respected photographers Jock Sturges and David Hamilton that included pictures of nude children).

As these cases make clear, the sexual revolution did not destroy the old regime. Puritanism (which H. L. Mencken described as fear that someone else might be having a good time) is tenacious; at least it

This piece appeared in The American Prospect, *December 4, 2000*

remains a respected tradition in the federal courts, as Justice Scalia's opinions suggest. In October 2000, in *Williams v. Pryor*, a federal appeals court actually upheld Alabama's ban on the sale of sexual devices, in an opinion that is either amusing or appalling, depending on your mood.

A lower federal court had struck down the ban by declaring it simply irrational. This was, as a matter of law, a highly unusual decision. The requirement that a law have a rational relationship to some legitimate governmental objective is the most permissive standard of judicial review; its use is usually a signal that a law is about to be upheld. It is only applied to statutes that courts do not consider infringements of constitutional rights (and the lower court in *Williams v. Pryor* declined to recognize a fundamental right to engage in the private use of sexual devices). The court did find that the state had a legitimate interest in banning "the commerce of sexual stimulation and auto-eroticism, for its own sake, unrelated to marriage, procreation, or familial relationships." (In other words, sexual pleasure, especially when it involves masturbation, may be banned unless it involves some greater good.) Still, the court held that the Alabama law was arbitrary and irrational, partly because it interfered with "sexual stimulation and eroticism" in the approved context of marital relationships (two of the plaintiffs in the Alabama case were married women).

The federal appeals court reversed this decision, not surprisingly, considering the lower court's reasoning. In applying the rational relationship test, judges are not supposed to substitute judicial for legislative judgment and invalidate laws that strike them as foolish. So, in deciding whether the Alabama law was rational, the appeals court was quite deferential to the state's power to regulate sexual morality. It did not laugh at the state of Alabama's argument that "a ban on the sale of sexual devices and related orgasm stimulating paraphernalia is rationally related to a legitimate interest in discouraging prurient interests in autonomous sex." Instead, with a straight face, the court quoted Alabama's brief approvingly: "(I)t is enough for a legislature to reasonably believe that commerce in the pursuit of orgasms by artificial means for their own sake is detrimental to the health and morality of the state."

Courts are, however, supposed to scrutinize public morals legislation that infringes on fundamental rights, and the Alabama law could and should have been struck down under a strict standard of judicial review, as a violation of a constitutional right to privacy. Constitutional arguments about vibrators are liable to verge on self-parody, I admit, but the principles of sexual privacy underlying the arguments aren't trivial. The right to read obscene material in the privacy of your own home, for example, prevents police from breaking into your house and arresting you because they don't like your reading habits. The denial of a right to engage privately in homosexual relations means that you can be prosecuted for what you do in your bedroom with another consenting adult (described in "Gay Rites").

Although the state sodomy law involved in Bowers was subsequently invalidated by Georgia's highest court, the decision in *Bowers v. Hardwick* still stands, as a denial of a federal constitutional right to sexual privacy. Indeed, it saved Alabama's vibrator sale ban. The appeals court in the Alabama case took the constitutional privacy questions seriously, but held that *Bowers* precluded it from ruling that the right to privacy includes a "broad fundamental right to all sexual autonomy, such as a privacy right to engage in any form of private consensual sexual behavior between adults." Pursuant to *Bowers*, the appeals court reasoned, Alabama's ban on the distribution of sexual devices was clearly constitutional as applied to homosexuals. (This suggests that the Alabama legislature could criminalize masturbation by homosexuals.)

Heterosexuals, however, have stronger privacy claims, since the Supreme Court has recognized sexual privacy rights in a line of cases involving the use of contraception and abortion. Alabama's law could yet be struck down as applied to heterosexuals. The appeals court directed the lower federal court to reconsider the privacy claims of four plaintiffs in *Williams v. Pryor*—two married women "who use sexual devices with their husbands" and two unmarried women "who began using sexual devices in marital intimacy but are now both single."

It's not at all clear if this case will eventually be appealed to the Supreme Court, which may be ready to reverse *Bowers v. Hardwick*. Alabama's ban on vibrator sales, and its underlying concern about the "pursuit of orgasms by artificial means," has been hard to take seriously (and attracted considerable mockery when it was passed). But the challenge to this silly law raises sobering questions about individual liberty and the morality of people who outlaw pleasure.

10

HOMELAND OFFENSE, PRE-9/11

AUTHOR'S NOTE

The essays that follow, "Taking Liberties" and "Games Prosecutors Play," were first published in 1999. I have revised them only slightly and left them in the present tense, in the hope that they'll convey the sense of urgency that civil libertarians felt before September 11. Attacks on liberty didn't commence on September 12, they intensified.

TAKING LIBERTIES

"Free speech is a bourgeois prejudice," Lenin explained to Emma Goldman in 1920. If only that were true. With the approval of the bourgeois press and public, Goldman had been deported to Russia in 1919, after serving two years in prison for criticizing the U.S. government during wartime. The American bourgeoisie, intolerant of free speech, strongly supported the prosecution, imprisonment, and exile of pacifists, anarchists, socialists, and other dissidents who opposed America's entry into World War I.

Goldman, like Eugene Debs, was imprisoned under the Espionage Act for opposing mandatory conscription. She was arrested, along with Alexander Berkman, shortly after delivering a speech at an antidraft demonstration, in which she attacked the right of the president "to tell the people that they shall take their sons and husbands and brothers and lovers and shall conscript them in order to ship them across the seas for the conquest of militarism and the support of wealth and power in the United States." Debs was convicted of delivering a speech about socialism in which he acknowledged that he abhorred war and told his listeners that they were "fit for something better than slavery and cannon fodder."

As these cases demonstrate, mere rhetorical exhortations and expressions of unpopular ideals were criminalized during the First World War. The Espionage Act, enacted in 1917, prohibited willful interference with recruitment, enlistment, or service in the military and was broadly construed to include political advocacy. It was amended by the Sedition Act, passed in 1919, which included a ban on the utterance or publication of "any disloyal, profane, scurrilous, or abusive language about the form of government of the United States, or the Constitution of the United States, or the military or naval forces of the United States."

The Supreme Court upheld these draconian restrictions on First Amendment freedoms, although a series of Espionage Act cases did help transform Justice Holmes into a free speech advocate, and, once converted, he helped shape the freedoms that antiwar protesters eventually enjoyed in the 1960s. Holmes authored the majority opinion upholding the conviction of Eugene Debs, but two years later, in *Abrams v. U.S.*, he wrote an eloquent landmark dissent, decrying the conviction of four immigrant anarchists for distributing leaflets pro-

This piece appeared in The American Prospect, *January 1999*

testing U.S. intervention in Russia. The defendants in the Abrams case had "as much right to publish" their leaflets "as the government has to publish the Constitution of the United States now vainly invoked by them," Holmes concluded.

Since the Abrams case was decided in 1919, the Supreme Court has greatly expanded rights of political advocacy and successfully invoked the Constitution to protect individuals against the government. Progress was hardly steady; leftists were prosecuted in the 1950s, under the Smith Act, for advocating or advising the overthrow of the government or merely associating with other rhetorical enemies of the state. The rights revolution that began in the 1920s proceeded sporadically; it did, however, proceed, as the Court began enforcing the Bill of Rights and applying it to exercises of state as well as federal power.

But while new guarantees of liberty emerged out of the repression of World War I, so did the modern American security state. J. Edgar Hoover got his start persecuting anarchists and other idealists like Emma Goldman. In 1919, the twenty-four-year-old Hoover was appointed head of the FBI's General Intelligence Division and quickly developed an alphabetical "radical index," consisting of files on left-wing individuals and organizations. As historian Richard Pollenberg reported in *Fighting Faiths,* a trenchant review of the Abrams case, Hoover bragged that his index covered "the activities of not only the extreme anarchists but also the more moderate radicals . . . At a moment's notice a card upon an individual, organization, or a general society existing in any part of the country can be obtained and a brief résumé on the card requested." We can only be grateful that Hoover predated computers.

For much of this century, descendants and defenders of World War I dissidents have been battling Hooverism, with some success. Members of racial, ethnic, and religious minorities and all women have gained unprecedented legal rights since midcentury; and, on balance, you are probably better off being arrested today than in 1960, before the Supreme Court extended the Bill of Rights to criminal suspects in state courts. So, looking back, we are better off today than we were fifty years ago. What's worrisome is looking ahead.

Left and right, freedom is falling out of fashion. Advocates of free markets will exclaim that freedom has been out of fashion for decades, and it's true that economic liberties have been sacrificed to the public interest in safe, humane, nondiscriminatory workplaces. Civil libertarians, who tend to be liberal, usually applaud the trade-off, since most are not sanguine about the virtues of economic liberty. Economic inequality, which unfettered liberty ensures, is a bar to the equal enjoyment of rights: That is the dilemma confronting liberal-rights advocates. So, the ACLU (of which I am an active member) does not go to court to protect the rights of employers to hire and fire whomever they choose. Instead, it tends to value civil rights and civil liberties equally, despite the fact that they sometimes conflict. (If you're seeking a consistent commitment to preserving all forms of liberty, join the CATO Institute.)

But if civil libertarians lack ideological purity, they started and helped sustain the expansion of individual liberty that has distinguished much of this century. By the 1990s, however, they constituted a small, ineffective minority. Eager to punish hate speech, prove their toughness on crime, or their horror of illegal drugs or Internet smut, relatively few liberals today can be trusted to defend the Bill of Rights. Some feminists, outraged by pornography or the extension of rights to suspected rapists, foolishly dismiss liberty as a tool of male oppression. Among liberal political theorists, communitarianism has become more fashionable than any commitment to individual rights. Liberal politicians have generally sped toward the center, following the lead of Bill Clinton, who has been uncharacteristically constant in his hostility toward civil liberty.

Meanwhile, conservatives choose the imposition of moral absolutes over autonomy and individual choice—except when they talk about guns or the freedom to discriminate. The National Rifle Association's respect for the liberty of gun owners has made it sensitive to Fourth Amendment violations. (The Fourth Amendment is a formidable bar to effective gun control.) But in its anxiety to appear tough on crime, since it is soft on guns, the NRA promotes a repressive criminal justice agenda; and it has always lacked a broad commitment to individual rights. NRA leaders seem to believe that once you insure the right to own a gun, all other rights will inevitably follow.

Many civil libertarians put similar faith in the First Amendment: They like to think that people imbued with rights of speech, association, and assembly will use those rights to demand others that secure liberty and justice for all. This belief in our collective commitment to fundamental American ideals is always tested. But if it seemed optimistic in the 1960s and '70s, by the 1990s, it was positively utopian. While guns proliferated, rights dwindled.

The political repression of the early 1900s might adumbrate our future as well as our past. The 1990s have been marked by renewed restrictions on civil liberties, notably free speech and privacy, and by assaults on the rights of criminal suspects, people convicted of crime, immigrants (including those guilty of nothing more than wishing to enter this country), and poor people. Many of the worst violations of liberty have been implemented by federal legislation, either championed or pointedly unopposed by the Clinton Administration. Many freedoms, particularly those secured by the Fourth Amendment, have been sacrificed to the war on drugs. But local legislation, like anti-gang laws, threaten basic liberties of movement and association; de facto police practices, like racial profiling on the highways, add to de jure abuses of power; and technology makes surveillance easy and practically commonplace. A comprehensive review of repressive or unduly intrusive laws and practices could spawn a small encyclopedia. (This article highlights a few.) We don't yet inhabit a police state, but it is not paranoia that imagines one taking shape.

Federal courts, which have been essential in expanding and preserving individual rights, have been stripped of their power to check actions by federal law enforcement agencies, state courts, and state prisons. [New federal limitations on judicial authority enacted after September 11 only accelerated a trend.] Court-stripping, regularly decried by civil libertarians, represents a wholesale assault on liberty and due process, not to mention the Constitutional system of checks and balances: If courts lose jurisdiction to hear cases involving constitutional violations, they lose the power to police Congress and enforce the Bill of Rights.

Congressional efforts to limit the power of the federal courts are not new. In the 1950s, the right wing tried unsuccessfully to strip the courts of power to review cases involving suspected Communists. The 1960s, '70s, and '80s saw efforts to strip the courts of jurisdiction in busing, abortion, and school prayer cases—all of which involve fundamental constitutional rights. All of these efforts failed. Barry Goldwater dismissed a proposal by Jesse Helms to disallow federal review of school prayer cases as the equivalent of "outlawing the Supreme Court." "Did you really write this bill," Goldwater reportedly asked Helms. "If I wrote it, I would be ashamed."

But Goldwater's conservativism is an anachronism today, and so is his sense of shame. In the past several years, Congress has eroded judicial authority by passing laws that eliminate or greatly limit judicial review and by refusing to confirm appointments to the federal bench (you don't have to deprive the courts of jurisdiction to hear cases if you simply deprive them of judges).

Some of the most grievous limitations on jurisdiction were contained in counter-terrorism and immigration reform laws enacted in 1996. These laws practically suspended the writ of habeas corpus in many criminal cases, depriving federal courts of considerable power to review state court convictions, especially in capital cases; and they gave federal officials virtually unchecked power to prosecute and deport legal residents and turn away people trying to enter the country.

Under the 1996 immigration law, the attorney general may exclude suspected terrorists without explaining his suspicions to a court. INS officials may summarily deport people seeking political asylum. INS decisions about asylum used to be subject to challenge in federal court. Now, individual border patrol agents have the power to make instant, unilateral, life-and-death decisions about whether someone seeking entry is likely to be subject to death, torture, or imprisonment on returning home. Human rights advocates have pointed out that the new law is particularly insensitive to torture victims, who are often too traumatized by their experiences to recount them readily to INS officials. (The INS has been summarily expelling an estimated 1,200 people each week at ports of entry.)

Immigration officials have also been rounding up legal residents convicted of relatively minor offenses. Immigrants convicted of serious, violent crimes have long been subject to deportation, but now offenses like drunk driving and shoplifting, committed years ago, may make a long-term resident with an American family deportable. In September 1998, in Texas, the INS swept up over 500 immigrants, mostly legal permanent residents, who have three or more drunken-driving convictions in their past. Agents did not distinguish between apparently incorrigible repeat offenders and people who are recovering alcoholics with steady jobs, strong ties to their communities, and families that depend upon them for support. The law that authorized their seizure gives immigration judges no discretion to consider factors like these that militate against deportation.

[In June 2001, the Supreme Court narrowly construed the court-stripping provisions in the 1996 immigration reform law: In *Calcano-Martinez v. INS*, the Court held that the federal courts retained jurisdiction to hear habeas corpus petitions by legal residents contesting deportation orders. This was a 5 to 4 decision; it's not hard to imagine that the Court would have ruled differently had this case been decided after September 11, when a willingness not to question the president and his law enforcement bureaucracy became a putative patriotic duty.]

Court stripping creates classes of dictatorial bureaucrats, accountable only to themselves—a hallmark of police states. The 1996 counter-terrorism bill also empowers the attorney general to try suspected terrorists, or people suspected of merely associating with terrorists, on the basis of classified evidence. In other words, federal officials can prosecute and deport people without telling them why exactly, and without giving them an opportunity to face their accusers and deny or counter the charges against them. They may have their day in court, but it is practically meaningless. Currently, over two dozen people are facing deportation or exclusion on the basis of secret evidence offered by secret accusers. Many of these people are accused only of associating with terrorists, and their alleged associations may consist of little more than attending rallies and lending financial support to Arab-American groups under suspicion. All of those accused are Arab American or Muslim. [Shortly before September 11, demands to repeal or reform this law were increasing and even enjoyed the support of presidential candidate George Bush.]

As these cases illustrate, the Clinton Administration has used its power under the 1996 immigration law to attack fundamental political rights of speech and association, in the name of protecting us from dangerous foreigners. Emma Goldman might feel depressingly at home in America today. Eighty years ago, however, ignoring the First Amendment was much easier: The Supreme Court had not yet given life to it. Today, the government must bypass the federal courts, which enforce the First Amendment, in order to have their way with it, and that is precisely what the Clinton Administration claimed the 1996 immigration law empowered it to do.

Consider the administration's action in the nearly ten-year-old case of *Reno v. American-Arab Anti-Discrimination Committee*. This case began in the late 1980s, when the Bush Administration tried to deport a group of seven Palestinians and one Kenyan, legally residing in California, for engaging in protected political advocacy on behalf of the Palestinians. (They were not accused of planning or engaging in any terrorist activities; they were simply charged with generally supporting the Popular Front for the Liberation of Palestine, which engages in some legal, humanitarian activities.) A series of federal court rulings enjoined the deportations, on First Amendment grounds. So, the government sought review in the Supreme Court, arguing that the 1996 immigration law deprived the federal courts of the power to hear the constitutional claims in this case and enforce the First

Amendment. [In February 1999, the Court ruled for the government.]

Where did Congress and the administration find the *chutzpah* to decide that the executive branch of government should not be held to account by the federal judiciary when it arguably violates fundamental constitutional rights? In part, they exploited public insensitivity to questions of checks and balances: The majority of voters probably haven't thought seriously about the relationship between the three branches of government since high school. In part, politicians, especially on the right, tap into deep popular resentment of "activist" federal judges, who enforce some unpopular rights, claimed by unpopular individuals (like criminal defendants). And, in part, court-stripping legislation was presented as a form of terrorism control.

New fears of terrorism combined with old-fashioned nativism lent public support to immigration and counter-terrorism laws, which were enacted in the wake of the Oklahoma City bombing. An Associated Press poll conducted shortly after the bombing found strong majority support for preemptive government action against suspected or "potential" terrorists. A majority of people surveyed agreed that the government should try to stop terrorists, even at the expense of some people's rights.

Of course, it's hard to imagine many people saying that the government should not try to stop terrorism, to the detriment of some unspecified rights. The majority's response to the AP poll presumes that counter-terrorism measures will succeed; it presumes the virtual infallibility of federal law enforcement agents. Only a minority of people surveyed (19 percent) said that government violations of rights were fruitless because officials could not stop determined terrorists (21 percent found violations of rights unacceptable). The results would probably have differed had pollsters asked people if they'd support the roundup of suspected terrorists if the government's suspicions were based on race or anonymous information that was difficult to confirm, or if government officials turned out to be wrong in a significant percentage of cases. The AP poll begs the question: How can the government successfully identify and prevent terrorist activity? Does public safety require the violation of "some people's" rights?

And, whose rights are they anyway? Usually when people support law enforcement measures that violate *some* people's rights, they mean other people's rights, not their own. What makes a civil libertarian is the capacity to imagine yourself as the accused, not the accuser. (All civil libertarianism requires, at heart, is embrace of the golden rule.)

It's no coincidence that repressive law enforcement measures often begin by targeting unpopular groups in society, groups with which majorities of voters are least likely to identify and most likely to consider "other people." If the majority of voters feared being arrested more than they feared being victimized by crime, the rights of criminal suspects and prison inmates would be secure.

But the majority of voters, it seems, do not expect that they or their family members will ever be subject to abusive arrests and prosecutions and wrongly convicted of crimes. Instead, fear of being victimized and fury over violent crime prevails. The belief that we should treat people accused or convicted of crimes the way we would like to be treated in similar circumstances is easily defeated by the contrary impulse to treat violent criminals the way they have treated their victims. So there is strong majority support for the death penalty (although it weakens when people are presented with the alternative of life without parole) and a drive to expedite executions. Congress and the president seemed in tune with popular opinion when they enacted the Effective Death Penalty Act of 1996, which eviscerated the writ of habeas corpus and the power of federal courts to review the constitutionality of convictions by the state, especially in capital cases. Included in the 1996 Counter-terrorism Act, it is sure to have virtually no ameliorative effect on terrorism: Most death penalty cases involve indigent defendants convicted of decidedly nonpolitical, often impulsive, random homicides. [By 2001, support for the death penalty had decreased, partly in response to revelations about mistakes and injustices that plague capital cases.]

The restrictions on habeas affect the rights of all inmates to challenge their convictions and imprisonment in federal court, but they were aimed mainly at people condemned to die. The purpose of the legislation was to deprive death row inmates of appeals. It prohibits the filing of more than one habeas petition in most cases and imposes an unprecedented statute of limitations on habeas petitions; they must be filed within one year of the time the conviction becomes final. In practice, these limitations of review by the lower federal courts are likely to result in the executions of people wrongly convicted of murder: New evidence of innocence or egregious misconduct by the prosecution in capital cases has sometimes been uncovered only after several years and successive habeas petitions. The appalling frequency with which poor people charged with capital crimes are denied competent trial counsel exacerbates the injustices of allowing only one habeas petition, subject to a stringent filing deadline.

Congress has also tried to make it more unlikely that any habeas petition will succeed. The 1996 law requires federal courts to let stand state court rulings on questions of constitutional law, even if the state court decisions are wrong. For a federal court to grant relief, the state court must be unreasonably wrong in its application of "clearly established federal law," or it must have erred in its initial statement of the law. (Most cases involve questions of applying the law, not questions of stating it. You will rarely find, for example, a state court decision denying that a defendant had a right to effective counsel, but you will find many questionable notions of what effective counsel entails.)

State courts have thus been granted considerable leeway to make mistakes and wrongly interpret federal law. This effectively transfers the power to interpret and apply the U.S. Constitution from federal to state court judges, (which means that constitutional rights of people accused and convicted of crimes may vary from state to state, depending on the local judiciary).

Attorneys, judges, and legal scholars are still arguing over how precisely to interpret the Effective Death Penalty Act itself. The Supreme Court had already imposed limitations on habeas petitions, in several rulings handed down over the last ten years, including limits on successive petitions. Some argue that, in 1996, Congress merely codified previous Court rulings. Others claim that Congress authorized even more restrictions on habeas than those previously issued by the Court. In any case, state courts and, by extension state police and prosecutors in death penalty cases, run little risk of being held accountable for their actions in federal court.

State prison officials have also been relieved of considerable federal oversight. The Prison Litigation Reform Act (PLRA), enacted in 1995, ensured that in cases involving prisoner's rights the federal courts would no longer be able to use consent decrees—the most common and effective vehicles for correcting unconstitutionally brutal conditions in state prisons. Prior to passage of the PLRA, prison lawsuits were settled when state officials consented to remedy substandard conditions, before proceeding to trial and without admitting any guilt. Federal judges then monitored their progress and compliance with the law. Now, consent decrees are limited to two years and are only available to cases in which officials are willing to acknowledge that they've violated the Constitution (making themselves personally liable). As a result, lengthy, costly trials will be required to obtain any relief.

Like most court-stripping measures, the PLRA does not deprive people of their constitutional rights in theory; it simply deprives them of their remedies when rights are violated. The stated purpose of this law was to curb frivolous suits by prisoners; its primary effect will be to facilitate their brutalization—the rape and near deadly assault of prisoners by guards, the maintenance of virtual dungeons (overcrowded, unsanitary rat-infested cells), and the violence inmates are permitted to visit upon each other.

Still, the PLRA was a popular law, perhaps because many people believe that prisons are like motels with good gym facilities and color TV, or because prisoners are not generally considered deserving of human rights. This tendency to dismiss any group of people as less than human, can eventually threaten everyone's freedom: Repressive regimes depend on the belief that people have to deserve or earn their rights. Americans are supposed to believe that rights are inalienable. Of course, people sentenced to prison are necessarily deprived of some very basic freedoms and rights, but they should surely retain the rights to be treated humanely.

You don't have to be imprisoned, however, to lose many fundamental rights. You could simply lose all your money. It's not only a free press that belongs to those who own one, as A. J. Liebling famously remarked. Abortion rights and the rights to a fair trial, for example, are also much more readily available to rich people than poor. Thanks to recent congressional efforts to defund and defang the Legal Services Corporation, poor people have even fewer enforceable constitutional rights against the government. Funding restrictions bar legal services programs that receive any federal aid from challenging the constitutionality of welfare reform legislation, even if the challenges themselves are privately funded. (In February 2001, the Court struck down this restriction on Legal Services lawyers in *Legal Services Corporation v. Velasquez.*)

This effort to prevent lawyers for the indigent from raising constitutional claims was not exactly court stripping but it did have a similar effect: It decreased the accountability of executive and legislative actions. Instead of stripping the courts of power to hear cases involving the constitutional rights of poor people, Congress simply stripped advocates for the poor of the power to bring constitutional claims. You don't have to regard the restrictions on legal services lawyers as a form of political repression in order to recognize it as another way of immunizing elected officials and bureaucrats from constitutional limitations on their behavior.

The fight to maintain liberty is, from one perspective, a fight to prevent agents of the state from exercising arbitrary, unaccountable power. Unlike the cops, say, of *NYPD Blue,* real-life law enforcement agents do not have an unerring instinct for only abusing the rights of guys who turn out to be guilty.

In Maryland, on Interstate 95, for example, state troopers have targeted innocent African-American motorists for "random" searches, in the war against drugs and the de facto offense of driving while black. The searches are not mere inconveniences: People are pulled over and asked, with varying degrees of belligerency, to "consent" to thorough searches of their cars, and everything in them. If they decline, they are not free to leave; they are forced to wait on the side of the road for the arrival of drug dogs, who sniff and paw through their belongings and sometimes urinate in their cars.

Because it affects so many innocent people, and because it is clearly discriminatory, racial profiling is difficult to defend. So, police are apt to deny that they engage in it when threatened with legal action. Courts do maintain their power to enforce the Fourth and Fourteenth Amendments in cases like these, after all. In 1993, without acknowledging guilt, the Maryland State Police settled a lawsuit brought by the ACLU of Maryland on behalf of an African-American attorney, Roger Wilkins, who was stopped and searched while driving on I-95 with his family. In 1996, the ACLU went back to court, charging the Maryland State Police with continued discriminatory enforcement: Relying on the state's own computerized records (now maintained under court order), the ACLU found that 75 percent of motorists searched by police were black, while 20 percent of motorists searched were white; but 75 percent of traffic violators on I-95 were white and only 17.5 percent were black. The great majority of these searches did not uncover evidence of crime, and statewide in Maryland, equal percentages of black and white motorists (about 28 percent) are caught with illegal drugs.

Imagine the outcry if middle-class white motorists were routinely subjected to degrading, highly intimidating, intrusive, and fruitless random drug searches like those conducted by the Maryland State Police. Many of them would not consider charges of "Gestapo" tactics mere hyperbole. The Maryland case is not only about racism; it is about police practices that violate the basic freedom to venture out in public and travel without risking arrest.

The right to stand still in public is also under attack. Antiloiter-ing laws are being extolled by cities across the country as effective anti-gang measures. Should the freedom to engage in conversation on a public street be sacrificed to a war against gangs? That's the question raised by a challenge to a Chicago ordinance providing that "when-ever a police officer observes a person whom he reasonably believes to be a criminal street-gang member loitering in any public place with one or more persons, he shall order all persons to disperse and re-move themselves from the area." People who disobey the order are subject to arrest.

In *Chicago v. Morales,* the Illinois Supreme Court held that the or-dinance was impermissibly vague on its face: It did not adequately de-fine loitering so as to provide people with notice that their activities (or inactivities) were prohibited. Under the Chicago law, loitering meant whatever a police officer said it meant. The Illinois Court also held that the ordinance constituted an unreasonable and arbitrary interference with civil liberty. It abridged First Amendment rights of speech and association as well as Fourth Amendment rights not to be arrested without reason. The Appellate Court of Illinois described the ordinance as "a transparent attempt to avoid the probable cause requirement," and, indeed, ordinances like these are aimed at em-powering police to arrest people who do not appear to be engaged in any illegal activities. As the city of Chicago acknowledged, the ordi-nance is supposed to "stop crime before it occurs."

It should hardly need to be stressed that in a free society, the po-lice enjoy the power to arrest you after you have committed a crime, not before. Police should and often do endeavor to prevent crime, but these efforts generally involve improving relations and establish-ing programs in cooperation with local communities (which is why community policing has occasionally been derided as social work). The street sweeps envisioned by antiloitering statutes are not permis-sible crime-prevention measures.

Of course, the antiloitering laws are not intended to rid the streets of all citizens; they only target those citizens merely suspected by police of belonging to gangs, and their conversants. The Chicago law allowed police to disperse and arrest people who talk to suspected gang members. While the antiloitering law was in effect in Chicago, police arrested nearly 45,000 people. Most were African American and Hispanic; many did not belong to gangs.

Laws like the one at issue in the Morales case do not just invite discriminatory enforcement; they endorse it, encouraging police to rely on their own biases (or suspicions) when applying the law. It's worth noting that the Supreme Court struck down broad-ranging antiloitering laws during the civil rights movement, when police used them to disperse people protesting segregation. Three decades later, it's sad and sobering to see similar laws used primarily against Black and Hispanic youth.

The Supreme Court's previous decisions on antiloitering and vagrancy laws are no less compelling today. In the 1965 case of *Shuttlesworth v. City of Birmingham,* the Court invalidated the arrest of a civil rights activist, Fred Shuttlesworth, for standing outside an all-white department store in a small group of people. Shuttlesworth had failed to move on promptly when ordered to clear the sidewalk and was arrested under a law that prohibited standing on a street or sidewalk "after having been requested by any police officer to move on." Taken literally, Justice Stewart observed, this meant "a person may stand on a public sidewalk in Birmingham only at the whim of any police officer of that city. The constitutional vice of so broad a provision needs no demonstration . . . that kind of law bears the hallmark of a police state."

Shuttlesworth's arrest was invalidated, but the statute at issue in his case was saved by the narrow construction of it offered by the Alabama courts. A few years later, however, the Court struck down Jacksonville, Florida's antiloitering and vagrancy laws, ending an era in policing that anti-gang ordinances threaten to revive. In the 1972 Florida case, *Papachristou v. City of Jacksonville,* the Court warned that, because they encompassed innocent pastimes (like talking to your friends), these laws invested police with unfettered discretion. "Where the list of crime is so all-inclusive and generalized . . . those convicted may be punished for no more than vindicating affronts to police authority," Justice Douglas wrote for the majority.

Florida had rationalized its vagrancy ordinance as a crime prevention measure (as the city of Chicago rationalized its antiloitering law). But Douglas pointed out that in America, people are not supposed to be arrested because a police officer suspects they may commit crimes in the future. Such laws, "long common in Russia are not compatible with our constitutional system . . . A direction to a legislature to the police to arrest all 'suspicious persons' would not pass constitutional muster."

The Chicago ordinance would not survive Justice Douglas's vision of civil liberty. [And it did not survive in the Supreme Court; in 1999, the Court struck down Chicago's antiloitering ordinance.]

The rights at stake in disputes over antiloitering laws are not marginal. They define citizenship in a free society. Or, as Douglas remarked, they are "historically part of the amenities of life as we have known them . . . they have dignified the right of dissent and have honored the right to be nonconformists and the right to defy submissiveness. They have encouraged lives of high spirits rather than hushed, suffocating silence."

The trouble is that many people are becoming accustomed to submitting to authority, in the hope of remaining safe. Most of us trudge sheeplike through the airports, readily complying with all the demands of low-level security personnel. Some putative security measures we see, and some we don't.

Passenger profiling is now used by most domestic airlines for most domestic and some international flights. The adoption of Computer-Assisted Passenger Screening (CAPS) followed the crash of TWA flight 800. (It was mandated by the Federal Aviation Commission, following the recommendation of the White House Commission on Aviation Safety and Security.) CAPS identifies certain passengers as security risks, which makes them likely to be detained, questioned, and subjected to thorough searches of their belongings, often rudely and in front of other passengers. On occasion, they may be stripped and subjected to full body searches.

What characteristics might make you the target of "security measures" like this? Most criteria for selection as a security risk are secret, of course. But it would be naive to assume that they do not include race or ethnicity, and preliminary reports from passengers subject to searches (collected by the ACLU) provide anecdotal evidence of discrimination. If you have an Anglo-Saxon name and look like Grace Kelly you are probably less likely to be stopped and searched than someone with a Middle Eastern name who looks more like Yasser Arafat. Other profiling criteria are more innocent but rather intrusive; they include information about passengers like address, credit card numbers, departure date, origin and destination of flight, date of ticket purchase, car rental plans, the identity of traveling companions, and other information in the frequent flyer database.

Do these intrusions on everyone's privacy, coupled with the detentions and searches of the unlucky few selected by the airline's computer make us more safe? Not likely. Efforts to stop hijacking in the 1970s demonstrated that putting all carry-ons through X-ray machines was more effective than profiling. Very little of the luggage loaded on planes is thoroughly scanned as a result of profiling, and terrorists who are smart enough to plan their attacks may be smart enough to avoid looking like stereotypical terrorists when they board airplanes. They may even be smart enough to use false passports and travel under false names, which makes the requirement that passengers display photo IDs before boarding particularly idiotic as a security measure. It is, however, an effective revenue enhancer that enables the airlines to catch passengers using other people's discount tickets.

Unnecessarily intrusive, faux-security measures at the nation's airports are the products of a disturbing partnership between government and private industry. Already, large corporations sometimes exert de facto governmental power over individuals: Media conglomerates control the flow of information, analysis, and ideas, and many people feel more repressed by their employers than their senators. But the government regulates some abuses of private power, through antidiscrimination or workplace safety laws, for example, in order to protect individuals. If the government is formally allied with a corporation, then individually and collectively, people lose a powerful, potential advocate.

Privatization, therefore, doesn't only involve the subordination of public interests—in good schools or safe air travel—to private profits; it deprives individuals of a primary means of holding the private sector to account. When an airline passenger is wrongly detained and subject to a humiliating, intrusive search because he was singled out by a profiling system, or when he is required to display his official government-issued picture ID, he is being victimized by the government acting in collusion with the airlines, and by airlines sharing in the power of government. To whom can he turn?

Perhaps to the courts, in some cases. If the Supreme Court ultimately invalidates court-stripping efforts, the federal courts will retain the power to preserve individual liberty (although there is no telling how they'll exercise it). But the court system itself cannot withstand a concerted legislative attack on its power. In the end, Congress can bypass the courts by amending the Constitution, as it has lately been endeavoring to do. The federal judiciary has been demonized by the far right, which blames it for the legalization of abortion, the recognition of gay rights, the abolition of involuntary school prayer, and other liberties generally associated by the right with the decline of Western civilization.

In interpreting and enforcing the Bill of Rights, the courts have usurped the political power of majorities, former Nixon aide Charles Colson has written, with some accuracy. The courts have indeed denied majorities the power to repress minority rights. In my view, the federal courts have kept faith with the Constitution. In Colson's view, they have broken a covenant with God: Their usurpation of political power "compels evangelical Christians and, indeed, all believers to ask sobering questions of the current political order and our allegiance to it."

Colson seriously considered the legitimacy of an "open rebellion" against the government, and a war against the courts and the Constitution is already underway. Stymied by the Supreme Court's approach to religious liberty, the religious right has lobbied hard for a constitutional amendment allowing official school prayer. (A prayer amendment was defeated in the House last spring.) Chafing at the rights afforded criminal suspects, Congress has proposed a Victim's Rights Amendment to the Constitution, to qualify the rights of the accused and undermine the fundamental purpose of the Bill of Rights—preventing abuses of government power by imbuing people prosecuted by the government with enumerated rights. Unhappy with a recent Supreme Court decision upholding the First Amendment right to burn a flag as form of political protest, Congress nearly passed a constitutional amendment qualifying the First Amendment and criminalizing flag desecration. The flag desecration amendment passed the House twice but was narrowly defeated in the Senate. It is sure to come before the Senate again next session and is likely to pass. [It was narrowly defeated again, but may eventually pass in the wake of 9/11.]

The flag desecration amendment is the equivalent of the World War I Sedition Act, which criminalized "scurrilous" speech against the government (except that unlike a censorious law, a censorious constitutional amendment is quite unlikely to be repealed). Burning a flag is political dissent, as the Supreme Court has recognized. It is an expression of contempt for the government or anger at its policies, which many Americans find deeply offensive, "scurrilous," or "abusive." That, of course, is precisely why the right to burn a flag must be protected. We don't need the First Amendment to protect popular speech, or relatively inoffensive speech to which the majority does not object.

The prohibition of flag desecration is often extolled by its advocates as a means of establishing and preserving community. They even characterize it as an effort to instill tolerance for community values, as some Muslim fundamentalists characterized the Fatwa against Salman Rushdie as an effort to achieve religious tolerance. Kill or imprison all "abusive" speakers, and you may eliminate or deter abusive speech, but the involuntary silence of dissenters is hardly a sign of tolerance. Passage of the flag desecration amendment would be a tribute to mob rule, not community.

"National unity" can only be achieved through persuasion, not coercion, Supreme Court Justice Robert Jackson stressed in a 1943 case, upholding the right of Jehovah's Witnesses not to salute the flag. Writing during World War II, when the consequences of coercive nationalism were horrifyingly clear, Jackson (later the Nuremberg prosecutor) observed "those who begin coercive elimination of dissent soon find themselves exterminating dissenters. Compulsory unification of opinion achieves only the unanimity of the graveyard."

At the risk of seeming trite, Jackson added, it seemed necessary to say that the First Amendment "was designed to avoid these ends by avoiding these beginnings." The flag desecration amendment takes us back to the beginning of this century, when dissent was punishable by imprisonment. Its popularity signals our rejection of fundamental liberties that have been forged since the 1920s, when the rights revolution began. The message of a flag desecration amendment is that the majority always rules: It needn't tolerate the expression of offensive minority speech; it can simply imprison the speaker.

The flag amendment, which has been championed by the right, also testifies to the corruption of contemporary conservativism, which is supposed to respect individual liberty. Indeed, when opposing affirmative action and other civil rights initiatives, conservatives like to point out that the Constitution protects individual rights, not group rights. Yet criminalizing flag desecration will enshrine group rights, at the expense of individual protest: The community's right not to be offended by a flag burning is said to trump the individual's right to engage in offensive political speech, however peaceful. That, of course, is the philosophy of political correctness, usually advanced by the left.

Abandoned by liberals and conservatives alike, liberty languishes. Outside the ACLU or the CATO Institute (or the militia movement), few people even talk about liberty anymore. When did you last hear a mainstream political candidate promise to make the preservation of freedom a priority?

"The average man doesn't want to be free," H. L. Mencken asserted. "He simply wants to be safe." Mencken was exaggerating: The average man (whoever he may be) probably wants both safety and freedom but can be persuaded to sacrifice the latter to the former. Individual rights are routinely characterized as threats to our collective security, which is why restricting the rights of criminal suspects, pornographers, flag burners, immigrants, and even millions of air travelers enjoys public support.

But the public has been conned: Most repressive laws and practices recently thrust upon us make us less free without making us more safe. Racial profiling on the highway will not decrease the violent trafficking in illegal drugs or problematic drug use (although decriminalization might). Searches of selected air travelers with Middle Eastern names will not prevent terrorist attacks on airplanes [and would not have prevented the attacks on September 11]. Luggage matching, ensuring that no checked luggage gets on a plane without the passenger who checked it, would be less intrusive and more effective. Some repressive police practices may prevent crime, of course: You can decrease street crime if you eliminate the right to venture out in the street. But if some criminals are easily controlled in police states, others, like abusive law enforcement agents, are unleashed.

Recent restrictions on individual liberty are not, however, simply aimed at making us more secure; they're supposed to make us more pure. What's striking about repression in America today is the moralism that drives it. On the left, champions of political correctness at war with the First Amendment aim to rid individuals of bad attitudes toward select, historically victimized groups. On the right, aspiring theocrats want us to be ruled not by our own consciences or individual proclivities but by their understanding of scripture. The underlying assault on the federal courts is a jihad (as Charles Colson's rhetoric makes clear).

For much of this century, we progressed toward freedom, however erratically. Now freedom is condemned as a rejection of God. (Satan sought freedom we're told.) The message is familiar. Moralism, combined with an intolerant religiosity, is an American perennial, as H. L. Mencken gleefully observed. But if the current wave of repression is not unprecedented, it is, at the very least, depressing. You need the passion of Emma Goldman, or the misanthropy of Mencken, to feel inspired by it.

GAMES PROSECUTORS PLAY

It is probably true that the majority of prosecutors, police officers, and federal law enforcement agents are fair, ethical, and maybe even compassionate public servants; but arrogance, self-righteousness, and a tendency to push people around are occupational hazards for individuals invested with authority to enforce the law. Am I being too harsh? Consider what Americans have learned about law enforcement in the past year:

Racial profiling on the nation's highways, streets, and in airports is common; state troopers and local police routinely harass and occasionally assault black and Latino drivers and male residents of inner city neighborhoods, while U.S. customs officials single out racial minorities for degrading strip searches. Innocent people languish for years on death row because of police or prosecutorial misconduct. People guilty of minor, nonviolent offenses, or no offenses at all, are imprisoned for years by federal prosecutors who seek convictions at all costs, misleading grand juries, intimidating witnesses, encouraging perjury by informants, and suppressing exculpatory evidence.

You don't have to read ACLU newsletters or low-circulation progressive magazines to be aware of these abuses: The mainstream press has covered them. In the past year, NBC's *Dateline* ran a story about the targeting of black females by customs officials at Chicago's O'Hare airport, while the *New York Times* has reported on racial profiling and the periodic exonerations of inmates on death row. Regional newspapers have also highlighted abuses by state and local prosecutors: A series of reports by the *Chicago Tribune* uncovered hundreds of state homicide cases involving serious misconduct by prosecutors nationwide. (The release of twelve people from Illinois' death row in the past twelve years, through the extraordinary efforts of activists and defense attorneys, and no thanks to the state, has been widely reported.) *Time* has expounded upon the failures and gross injustices of mandatory minimum sentences. *Frontline* has dramatically exposed the corrupting influence of informant testimony, routinely used in federal cases. And, in the wake of Kenneth Starr's investigation of Bill Clinton's sex life, news stories, editorials, and op-ed pieces about prosecutorial misconduct, especially at the federal level, appeared in national and local papers ranging from the *Wall Street Journal* to the *Pittsburgh Post-Gazette*. If Americans have less reason to fear each other, now that vio-

This piece appeared in The American Prospect, *September 1, 1999*

lent crime has declined, they have more reason to fear the law enforcement bureaucracy.

This is, however, a bureaucracy that the public demanded and helped shape by electing political demagogues who promised to be tough on crime. In the 1980s and '90s, with apparent public approval, Congress enacted laws greatly expanding federal criminal jurisdiction, restricting appeals of convictions, imposing harsh mandatory sentences on nonviolent offenders, and encouraging the states to pass their own mindless "three-strike" laws, which have resulted in life imprisonment for three-time felony offenders, regardless of the seriousness of their crimes: In a notorious California case, a twenty-seven-year-old man was sentenced to twenty-five years to life for swiping a slice of pizza. [In April 2002, the Supreme Court agreed to review the constitutionality of these laws.]

Some attribute the recent decrease in violent crime to an increase in the prison population occasioned by such laws. But violent crime is affected by numerous factors, including demographic trends and police practices, and the effect of long-term imprisonment on the crime rate is debatable: Prison terms increased dramatically during the 1980s, but while violent crime decreased in the early '80s, it rose in the latter half of the decade. In a 1993 report, the National Research Council concluded that increased sentences in the 1980s had little effect on crime, adding that "a 50 percent increase in the *probability of incarceration* would prevent twice as much violent crime as a 50 percent increase in the average term of incarceration."

But criminal justice policy has not reflected much rational analysis and is not simply focused on crime control. It is also an anti-vice crusade. Repressive criminal laws and practices initiated in recent years are weapons in an ongoing, consistently ineffective government war against drugs—a war against some drugs, that is, like crack cocaine and marijuana. Racial profiling was designed to catch drug offenders, and mandatory minimums were designed to punish them. The government war against drugs quickly turned into a government war against its citizens—a war against some citizens, that is, notably (but not exclusively) racial minorities. Twelve percent of our general population and over 50 percent of our prison population is African American. As David Coles observes in his incisive 1999 book *No Equal Justice*, while African Americans make up an estimated 14 percent of drug offenders, they are subject to 55 percent of all drug convictions and 74 percent of all sentences for drug offenses.

Progressives have long held that if these figures were reversed—if middle-class whites were targeted by police and prosecutors and incarcerated in such grossly disproportionate numbers—the public would revolt. In fact, the revolt would start long before the imprisonment of so many whites. The attention paid to misconduct by federal prosecutors during the Starr investigation was prompted partly by the spectacle of white women—Susan McDougal, Julie Hiatt Steele, Monica Lewinsky and her mother Marcia Lewis—being prosecuted or coerced by Kenneth Starr. Concern about federal prosecutorial abuses may also reflect an increase in federal prosecutions of technical, white-collar crime. One criminal defense attorney reports that there are growing numbers of businessmen being indicted for what might have once been considered "sharp" (but legal) business practices. The government's antitrust case against Microsoft could easily have been criminalized, he observes.

I'm not suggesting a majority of voters will knowingly tolerate injustice so long as it does not appear to threaten them. I suspect, instead, that many people simply don't recognize injustice unless they can identify with its victims. Ignorance, or insensitivity, helps reconcile public mistrust of government with public support for the criminal justice bureaucracy. Fear of crime and prejudice about the use of drugs associated with the counterculture or the African-American community are stronger than logic and political consistency; and people blessed with no firsthand knowledge of the justice system have probably been unaware of its abuses. Many seemed genuinely shocked by the conduct of the Starr investigation, which as defense attorneys quickly observed was typical of many federal prosecutions and considerably less abusive than some.

Prosecutorial misconduct is endemic. According to Arnold Burns, deputy attorney general in the Reagan Administration, prosecutors have lost their "sense of proportion" and aggressively use their "full artillery" against minor offenders. A chilling 1998 series in the *Pittsburgh Post-Gazette* by investigative reporter Bill Moushey documented the resultant abuses. Moushey spent two years reviewing 1,500 allegations of prosecutorial misconduct; he uncovered dozens of cases in which government stings "trapped the innocent or exaggerated the misconduct of suspects," hundreds of instances in which prosecutors violated the law by failing to provide the defense with exculpatory evidence, and hundreds of cases in which they "tolerated or encouraged perjury."

Often the concealment of exculpatory evidence and reliance on perjured testimony are related: Prosecutors sometimes fail to disclose incentives for their witnesses to lie or evidence that witnesses have lied on the stand. In one case examined by Moushey, prosecutors concealed the fact that their star witness was testifying under a false name and had a prior perjury conviction. In another, they did not disclose that their witness, an imprisoned cocaine dealer seeking a reduction in sentence, had bragged to fellow inmates about providing false testimony. The violations involved in cases like these are not mere legal technicalities: They bear directly on factual questions of guilt and innocence.

That these are old stories to people familiar with the system underscores the pervasive corruption they represent. "The entire criminal justice system knows that perjury is the coin of the realm," Eric Sterling, president of the Criminal Justice Foundation, remarks. Perjury drives the prosecutions of federal cases, Moushey's investigation confirmed: "People's homes are invaded because of lies. People go to prison because of lies. People stay in prison because of lies, and sometimes bad guys go free because of lies." Federal prison inmates "routinely buy, sell, steal, and concoct testimony, then share their perjury with federal authorities in exchange for a reduction of their sentences." In addition, as Ken Starr's pursuit of Susan McDougal suggested, prosecutors often invite perjury by threatening witnesses whose grand jury testimony does not support the government's case. Some defense attorneys, like Boston-based Harvey Silverglate and Andrew Good, will not represent informants or even people inclined to plead guilty, because of the likelihood that they're trading perjured testimony. In these cases, Silverglate says, "You have to teach clients not just to sing but to compose."

This is how low-level offenders, minor players in a criminal enterprise, sometimes incur long mandatory sentences; they have no information to trade, decline to lie, and are the last people standing when the music stops. A 1999 edition of *Frontline* told the awful story of Clarence Aaron, a twenty-three-year-old black male college student with no criminal record, sentenced to three concurrent life sentences without the possibility of parole, for conspiracy to distribute crack cocaine: No drugs were introduced into evidence in Aaron's case, even though the actual amount of drugs allegedly involved in an offense determines the sentence. Aaron's conviction was based on the testimony of his alleged coconspirators—childhood friends, including a first cousin. Apprehended dealing drugs, they all turned on Aaron, whose role in the "conspiracy" was chauffeur. All of the coconspirators had prior convictions; one, the self-proclaimed "kingpin," is serving a twelve-year sentence, two received sentences of less than five years, one escaped with no jail time.

It's worth stressing that this was not necessarily the jury's notion of justice. Jurors are not informed of the sentences dictated by their guilty verdicts, and one of the jurors in Clarence Aaron's case told *Frontline* that he expected Aaron to receive a relatively short sentence, perhaps three to five years. "He seemed a pretty promising boy," the juror recalled.

U.S. Attorney J. Don Foster, who presided over Aaron's case, disagrees. Interviewed by *Frontline*, he seemed satisfied with the outcome and unconcerned that his witnesses had enormous incentive to lie. Although they were perhaps "guiltier or more culpable" than Aaron, "they helped solve the case," Foster remarked. "We try to go up the ladder, if we can, starting with the little fish and going up the ladder to the big fish. But sometimes you've got the big fish and you need to come down the ladder." It is a perverse system of justice that condemns "little fish" to serving life without parole, while the big fish swim free. But in Foster's view Aaron was appropriately punished for refusing to cooperate and demanding a trial: He suffered the consequences of his own "arrogance." From this perspective, innocence, or negligible guilt, is hardly relevant. What matters is not offending the prosecutor.

How did prosecutors attain such fearsome power? It has been building for at least thirty years. Since 1970, Congress has steadily increased federal jurisdiction over crimes that used to be the province of the states, while the number of federal prosecutors has increased from 3,000 to 8,000. According to a 1999 American Bar Association report, 40 percent of all federal criminal laws enacted since the Civil War date back only to 1970.

This dramatic expansion of prosecutorial power was not accompanied by checks on its exercise. The law generally immunizes prosecutors from civil liability for bringing frivolous cases or for their misconduct at trial; so people who have been wrongly tried or convicted generally have no civil remedies if misconduct in their cases is uncovered. This increases the need for judicial monitoring of prosecutorial practices, but the Supreme Court has deferred to prosecutors, encouraging lower courts to uphold convictions in cases involving substantial violations of defendants' rights. The Court has also held that constitutional rights enjoyed by defendants at trial (at least theoretically) do not apply in grand jury proceedings. Witnesses and potential targets of investigations are not even allowed to bring their lawyers into the grand jury room when they testify. As a result, grand juries, designed to protect citizens from prosecutorial abuse, now function as arms of the prosecutors: Virtually all defendants called before federal grand juries are indicted.

While the Court declined to police prosecutors effectively, Congress enacted sentencing laws that made prosecutorial misconduct practically inevitable and perjury "the coin of the realm." Mandatory minimum sentences for drug offenses, feverishly passed by Congress in the 1980s, greatly increased the power of U.S. attorneys (by eliminating the sentencing role of judges) and encouraged the use of informant testimony. Mandatories were enacted largely for their symbolic value in demonstrating a congressional commitment to eradicating drugs. The public was given virtually no information about their consequences; but it's likely that lawmakers had little information to share and little understanding of the effects of legislation enacted with no deliberation. Eric Sterling, counsel to a House subcommittee on crime in the 1980s, reports that mandatories were passed in haste, with "no hearings, no consideration by the federal judges, no input from the Bureau of Prisons . . . even DEA didn't testify . . . the whole thing was cobbled together with chewing gum and baling wire. Numbers were picked out of the air." (Sterling characterizes his own involvement in the formulation of these laws as "the greatest tragedy of my professional life.")

This too is an old story; mandatories have been the subject of harsh but devastatingly accurate critiques since their enactment, by judges, attorneys, criminologists, and relatives of the laws' victims. Privately, many lawmakers are likely to acknowledge their disastrous effects. Yet the sentences are still in place, so the story still needs to be told.

Mandatory minimums were supposed to eliminate discretion in sentencing, which was a focus of liberal concern in the 1970s, because it was associated with discrimination. But in the 1980s, when Congress began passing the mandatory sentences that are inflicted upon people today, sentencing discretion was already quite limited by federal guidelines enacted in 1984. Sentencing guidelines were originally conceived in the seventies as a liberal reform, championed by Senator Kennedy, but they were implemented a decade later, at about the same time that mandatory minimums came into fashion, when liberals were growing anxious to enlist in the war against drugs and prove their toughness on crime. (Sterling recalls that late House Majority Leader Tip O'Neill initiated a rash of new mandatories in

1986, in response to the highly publicized drug-related death of Boston Celtic draftee Len Bias.)

Federal-sentence guidelines are inflexible and provide for long sentences. Mandatory minimums are written in stone, but even they don't eliminate discretion in sentencing: They transfer discretion from judges to prosecutors. Traditionally, judges fixed sentences, weighing recommendations from prosecutors, defense attorneys, or probation officers. Now in cases controlled by 1984 federal guidelines, they consult a complicated sentencing grid, which gives them very little discretion. In cases controlled by mandatory minimums, judges have no sentencing discretion at all. They are required by law to impose long prison terms, even in cases involving first-time, nonviolent, low-level offenders that call for probation. Thus, the prosecutor chooses the sentence when he chooses the charge. Prosecutors traditionally enjoy virtually unfettered discretion in deciding whether or how to charge, thus mandatory minimums give them unfettered discretion to sentence.

Their power to sentence enables prosecutors to win convictions routinely by targeting people for prosecution and offering them reduced sentences—in exchange for testimony. Defense attorneys have pointed out this practice is the equivalent of bribery, noting that if they engage in similar behavior—offering to compensate witnesses for testimony—they violate federal bribery law. In 1998 this argument briefly prevailed in federal court. In *U.S. v. Singleton,* a three-judge panel of the Tenth Circuit Court of Appeals reversed the conviction of Sonya Singleton for money laundering and conspiracy to distribute cocaine, ruling that the prosecutor's promise of leniency to the alleged co-conspirator who testified against her was prohibited by the federal penal code.

The law is clear: "Whoever . . . directly or indirectly, gives, offers, or promises anything of value to any person, for or because of the testimony under oath or affirmation given or to be given by such person as a witness upon a trial . . . before any court . . . shall be fined under this title or imprisoned for not more than two years, or both." The three-judge panel sensibly concluded that the plain language of this statute extends its bribery prohibition to U.S. attorneys, who are clearly included in the pronoun "whoever." More importantly, the court held that the purpose of the statute—the prevention of wrongful convictions based on false testimony—required its application to federal prosecutors. A reduced prison sentence is surely something "of value" to a witness, providing strong incentive to lie.

"It is difficult to imagine anything more valuable than personal physical freedom," the court observed, adding that "Decency, security,
and liberty alike demand that government officials shall be subjected
to the same rules of conduct that are commands to the citizen."

That people who enforce the law should obey the law seems uncontroversial, but it's not surprising that this decision evoked howls
of protest from prosecutors, lawmakers, and some editorial writers.
It threatened thousands of convictions based on informant testimony. It outlawed routine practices deeply embedded in the system.
So, some six months after its initial ruling in *Singleton,* the Tenth Circuit issued a "never mind." The court reheard the case, en banc, and,
in a 9 to 3 decision, held that federal bribery laws do not bind U.S.
attorneys. "We simply believe this particular statute does not exist
for the government," the majority declared, stressing that grants of
reduced sentences in exchange for testimony were "long-standing
practices . . . deeply ingrained in our criminal justice system." In
fact, the court added, the use of accomplice testimony procured by
promises of leniency was so ingrained that it "has created a vested sov-
ereign prerogative in the government . . . it has acquired a practice
akin to the special privileges of kings."

Once deference to the rights of kings inspired revolution. Today
this defense of the Justice Department's monarchical power is more
likely to be dismissed as merely tactless; it clumsily expresses a common impulse to respect the status quo. The more prevalent a prosecutorial practice, the more likely it is to be respected by the courts, regardless of its fairness or potential for abuse. Perhaps the grossest
example of this judicial passivity was the 1986 case of *McClesky v. Kemp,*
in which the Supreme Court declined to invalidate the death penalty
despite strong statistical evidence of race discrimination in its application. The Court observed that if it recognized evidence of discrimination in capital cases, it would have to recognize it in noncapital
cases as well, and the system would be severely disrupted. As dissenting Justice Brennan observed, the Court harbored "a fear of too
much justice."

Judicial fear of disrupting the criminal justice system has been
partly responsible for growing misconduct by prosecutors. While
judges have lost sentencing authority in many cases, they retain the
power to reverse convictions when prosecutors break the law and
abuse defendant's rights. But they invoke that power rarely.

This abdication of authority by courts designed to defend due
process and protect individuals against government excesses is ratio-

nalized by a "harmless error" rule, enunciated by the Supreme
Court. In a series of cases, the court has held that even gross violations
of a defendant's constitutional rights do not require a reversal of conviction if the violation (or "error" by the prosecutor) was harmless—
if, considering other evidence, the appellate court decides it did not
affect the verdict. In other words, defendants essentially have to show
that but for the "error," they would have been acquitted.

Initially the harmless-error rule applied only to relatively minor
prosecutorial lapses that did not involve fundamental constitutional
rights. But in 1967 the Court held that constitutional violations could
also be considered harmless; since then it has ruled that even the admission of a coerced confession obtained in violation of the Fourth
Amendment could qualify as harmless. Indeed, according to Chief
Justice Rehnquist, in the context of a criminal prosecution, "most
constitutional errors can be harmless."

That is a remarkable statement from someone sworn to defend
the Constitution. It implies that the Bill of Rights is merely hortatory
and needn't actually be enforced. It suggests that constitutional rights
have only instrumental value, that there is no inherent, normative
value in, say, the right to prevent police officers from invading your
home for no good reason or beating you up to obtain a confession.

But even if you accept the notion that in a criminal trial constitutional rights are merely instrumental, you'd be hard-pressed to uphold a conviction based partly on a coerced confession. A confession
obtained at the point of a gun (metaphorically speaking) is not terribly reliable; it isn't likely to lead us to truth. Yet jurors are apt to find
any confession persuasive, especially if they're not fully informed of
its circumstances. How can an appellate court ever hold, beyond a
reasonable doubt, that the admission of an involuntary confession
did not affect the verdict and raise the strong possibility of an unjust
conviction? And what is an appellate court doing reviewing evidence
of guilt anyway? First-year law students learn what Supreme Court
justices sometimes forget: As a general rule, findings of fact are the
province of trial courts; appellate courts are supposed to determine
questions of law.

The law provides that prosecutors have an obligation not to rely
on illegally obtained evidence and not to encourage police violations
of our Fourth Amendment rights. The law provides that prosecutors
must reveal all evidence exculpating the people they seek to convict.
The law provides that we, the people, have rights against self-
incrimination that can only be waived voluntarily. The law provides

that we have a right to confront witnesses testifying against us. The judiciary's job is to uphold these laws, not condone their persistent violations. Judges are obliged to punish prosecutors for breaking the law, to ensure that trials are reliable and fair and that law enforcement officials investigating and prosecuting crime don't oppress the citizens they're supposed to protect.

The harmless-error rule formulated by the Supreme Court reveals the Court's priorities: It is less concerned with upholding the law than upholding convictions, saving the states the time and money of retrying people whose convictions were wrongly obtained. The rule, after all, is not an attempt to free prosecutors from exacting compliance with mere technicalities. It frees them from respecting fundamental rights designed to prevent wrongful convictions. In fact, the Court has clung to legal technicalities when they bolstered convictions. In a 1993 death penalty case, *Herrera v. Collins,* the Court dismissed an appeal based on a strong claim of innocence, noting that "A claim of actual innocence is not itself a constitutional claim," suggesting that states might execute innocent people, so long as they observed the technicalities. As the late Justice Blackmun observed in his dissent, the majority's ruling in this case was "perilously close to murder."

If the Supreme Court helps establish the climate in which federal prosecutors operate, it's hardly surprising that many now seem to feel liberated from constitutional constraints or even common notions of morality. The Justice Department, as well, encourages and protects their arrogance. According to its critics, the department's internal watchdog, the Office of Professional Conduct, has been negligent in monitoring prosecutors and excessively lenient in punishing misconduct. A notorious Justice Department policy, implemented by former attorney general Richard Thornburgh, exempted U.S. attorneys from state ethics rules applying to everyone else, including, most notably, the rule requiring prosecutors not to deal directly with people represented by counsel. This policy was nullified by federal legislation, the 1998 Citizens Protection Act, which the Justice Department vigorously and angrily opposed. One congressional aide remarked that U.S. attorneys "get hysterical about being subjected to external ethical standards . . . they don't want to have to live by rules."

It is past time for them to learn that in a relatively civilized society, prosecutors as well as citizens respect the rule of law, democratically imposed. And, given the scandal of the Starr investigation, Congress seems poised to consider curbs on prosecutorial excesses, like grand jury reforms and repeals of some mandatory minimum sentences. Proposals for repeal might find considerable congressional support, if members dared to express their private opinions about mandatory minimums in public. But following the lead of the Clinton Administration, many Democrats spent the 1990s marketing a repressive law-and-order agenda, proving that they can trample individual rights with the resolution of right-wing Republicans.

Still strange alliances could form [and most likely would have before 9/11]. Conservatives who are wary of federal bureaucracies could turn their ire against the apparatus of federal law enforcement, as they have turned it against the IRS. Liberal reformers could appeal to our patriotism. Expose gross prosecutorial abuse, and many people recoil, as the Starr investigation showed. It is simply un-American. People who resist imbuing presidents with kingly prerogatives may hesitate to confer them on prosecutors.

ACKNOWLEDGMENTS

Thanks to Helene Atwan at Beacon Press for her interest in my work and her kindness in accommodating the demands of my personal life; to Scott Stossel, formerly my excellent laissez-faire editor at *The American Prospect;* and to my husband, Woody, although he finds my essays insufficiently polemical.

Also by
WENDY KAMINER

Sleeping with Extra-Terrestrials

True Love Waits

It's All the Rage

I'm Dysfunctional, You're Dysfunctional

A Fearful Freedom

Women Volunteering